ARCHAEOLOGY OF ENTANGLEMENT

ARCHAEOLOGY OF ENTANGLEMENT

Edited by
Lindsay Der and Francesca Fernandini

Routledge
Taylor & Francis Group
LONDON AND NEW YORK

First published 2016 by Left Coast Press, Inc.

Published 2016 by Routledge
2 Park Square, Milton Park, Abingdon, Oxon OX14 4RN
711 Third Avenue, New York, NY 10017, USA

Routledge is an imprint of the Taylor & Francis Group, an informa business

Library of Congress Cataloging-in-Publication Data:

Names: Der, Lindsay, 1984- | Fernandini, Francesca.
Title: Archaeology of entanglement / Lindsay Der and Francesca Fernandini, editors.
Description: Walnut Creek, California : Left Coast Press, Inc., 2016. | Includes bibliographical references and index.
Identifiers: LCCN 2015032583 | ISBN 9781629583761 (hardback : alkaline paper) | ISBN 9781629583785 (institutional eBook) | ISBN 9781629583792 (consumer eBook)
Subjects: LCSH: Social archaeology. | Archaeology—Philosophy. | Archaeology and history. | Material culture—Social aspects—History. | Material culture—Psychological aspects—History. | Antiquities—Social aspects—History. | Antiquities—Psychological aspects—History. | Social ecology—History. | Social interaction—History. | Dependency (Psychology)—Social aspects—History. | BISAC: SOCIAL SCIENCE / Archaeology.
Classification: LCC CC72.4.A7353 2016 | DDC 930.1—dc23
LC record available at http://lccn.loc.gov/2015032583

ISBN 978-1-62958-376-1 hardback

Contents

Rethinking Dependences and Dependencies: Contemporary Perspectives on Entanglement in Archaeology

Illustrations

Figures

Tables

Acknowledgments

This book would not have been possible without the guidance and support of many individuals to whom we owe our gratitude.

First and foremost, we would like to thank Ian Hodder for providing indispensable advice and innumerous words of encouragement, putting up with our countless questions and emails, and his helpful comments and suggestions on draft copies. It was his "Things" seminar that served as the inspiration for this volume; for this we are forever indebted to him.

Stanford University, Koç University's Research Center for Anatolian Civilizations, and Pontificia Universidad Católica del Perú provided financial support to the editors during this project. We thank the Stanford Archaeology Center in particular for its sponsorship of the Entanglement in Archaeology conference as well as the Entanglement Theory Group at Stanford University, both of which generated discussion that would later be influential to this volume. We thank our "Things" colleagues Tiffany Cain, Noa Corcoran-Tadd, Pedro Gonzales, Andrea Milly, Guido Pezzarossi, and Leonardo Wilson for intellectual stimulation.

We are grateful for the guidance and support given by Lynn Meskell, John Rick, and our family; our friends also furnished much-needed moral support. We thank the two anonymous reviewers who commented on an earlier draft of this manuscript. Last, but certainly not least, we thank all the individual contributors of this volume for their tireless patience and hard work.

Lindsay Der and Francesca Fernandini
Istanbul and Lima, September 2014

Introduction

Lindsay Der and Francesca Fernandini

The idea for this book first emerged from Ian Hodder's "Things" seminar at Stanford University. The course was a welcome forum to discuss how people and things interact and the repercussions of this interaction. One particularly intriguing perspective is the human and nonhuman interactions that entangle and are entangled within these relationships, and how they are understood in regards to the inevitable and often unexpected dependencies that derive from them, not simply from the links which connect people and things. Despite the potential utility of such a perspective, archaeologically focused literature on the subject is somewhat limited, strangely so considering the increasing number of entanglement-themed conference sessions in recent years. For example, most publications on entanglement are related to colonial contexts; until now, there has been no comprehensive, multiauthored volume showcasing the utility of entanglement as a conceptual tool that provides scholars with a common language that goes beyond region or scale, reducing the breach between more limited-area or topic-based approaches (see also Hegmon et al. in chapter 7 and Mrozowski in chapter 8 for more on the need to increase the breadth of entanglement publications). Thus, as the seminar drew to a close, we sought to compile a volume of a variety of archaeological case studies that use an entanglement approach to highlight the subtle and unacknowledged paths that configure historical circumstances and bind human intentionality. *Entanglement,* in this volume, is a metaphor for the complexities and feedback loops elicited from relations between people and things, and between things and other things. It is a useful way to think about how people and things create relationships and become ensnared in these relationships. Rather than focusing on the networks formed by these relationships, entanglement as a metaphor emphasizes the repercussions of these connections, their manifestations, and their ability to create new relationships, entanglements, and entrapments.

The essays presented here were specifically written for this collection and are intentionally diverse to present the broad and encompassing nature of entanglement as a useful metaphor in archaeology. This use of entanglement in archaeology incorporates the underlying mechanisms of actual past interactions in addition to how scholars think about the past. The authors examine constructions of personhood, the rigidity of path dependencies, the unpredictable connections between humans and things and, in general, the intricate paths of past events in varied geographic and historical contexts that channel and sometimes precipitate future actions. This broad focus is diachronic, inclusive of early complex developments in Asia and Europe, imperial and state strategies in the Andes and Mesoamerica, continuities of post colonialism in North America, and the unforeseen and complex consequences that derive from archaeological practices. Readers will recognize work from established and well-known researchers as well as a few newcomers who we think will further showcase the spectrum of entanglement as a metaphor in the discipline. Yet, the consistent thread that binds these archaeological case studies together is the notion of entanglement as more than simply just the relations of people and things; the focus is on the multidirectional and multiscalar entrapments that emerge from these interactions.

In this introduction, we first provide a brief historical outline that charts the emergence of entanglement as a useful lens for the study of human phenomena, culture, practice, and behavior in the humanities and social sciences. The roots of entanglement as a conceptual point of reference in archaeology can be traced largely to discussions about interactions between people and things in the disciplines of sociology, philosophy, and anthropology. Although space restrictions preclude us from undertaking an extensive literature review of entanglement iterations and predecessors in contemporary scholarship, we highlight here those we find most pertinent to and which have collectively influenced the chapters in this book. In no way does this volume claim to be the only inflection of entanglement; it simply provides an understanding of entanglement as a metaphor that we—as well as the chapter authors—have found particularly useful in our own research and that we suggest is a fruitful path for others in archaeology. We acknowledge that other theorizations of culture, including practice theory (Bourdieu 1977; Ortner 1984, 2006), distributed models of culture (Latour 1987, 2005; Strathern 1988), and "communities of practice" perspectives (Dietler 1998, 2010; Stahl 2009) have contributed notions of identity, agency, and power that can also arguably invoke processes of entanglement. However, the authors in this text are more concerned with the way interactions between people and things, in whichever form they manifest, inevitably create dependent relations that entrap them in certain paths rather than giving primacy to the interactions themselves as a means of satisfying social, political, and economic needs. We also consider this volume's application of entanglement as a metaphor for the past, with particular focus on its ability to penetrate multiscalar trajectories of time and space within the framework of a relational approach. Finally, we end with a look at the chapters in this volume and their engagement with entanglement through specific contexts and research questions. These chapters arise from three key themes or types of entanglement: 1) between different groups or cultures, 2) between people and the environment, and 3) between people and things. Although entanglements may and do take an array of forms, arising from varied causalities, the ensnarement of relationships, practices, and meanings provides the commonality that the entanglement metaphor so succinctly describes and that we argue lends to more nuanced interpretations of the past.

Inflections of Entanglement

Various authors have approached the concept of entanglement from a series of angles that describe the networks, mixes, meshworks, and engagements that result from the interactions between humans and things and the possible combinations among them. Heidegger (2002, 2008) proposes a phenomenological approach to human perception that rested on the notion of our relatedness to the world as entangled beings fundamentally involved in networks of human and nonhuman relations. Heidegger's analysis of things and their relation with beings sets the pace for further research. He proposes that there are three sorts of *things*: 1) the objects around us, 2) our human attitudes and actions, and 3) the totality of these two in interdependence together (2008). It is the third "thing" that Heidegger uses to introduce the concept of *Dasein,* or "being-in-the-world," which assumes the "being" as unfolding through the course of human interactions and entails *situatedness* within this world (2002). Heidegger explores this unfolding, or unconsciousness of ourselves and our existence, by examining how people understand things through equipment totalities. In other words, it is the connections of a thing with other things, or equipment totalities, that give a thing its essence, rather than the "present-at-hand" material properties that merely denote objects. Things are tools, and tools cannot exist on their own but only in a network of other things that afford them their ability to perform actions or to be useful in a "ready-to-hand" state. Objects, in contrast, possess a "present-at-hand" state. They are not considered in the context of their relations, but instead as they simply exist when viewed closely. Heidegger introduces the concept of "thingness" through the example of a ceramic jug. The jug's thingness is not found in the material from which it is made, nor is it in its form or its use; rather, it is the void inside it. The jug shapes the void, which in turn shapes the jug, so that "the empty space, this nothing of the jug, is what the jug is as a holding vessel" (Heidegger 2002:167). Thus, it is the series of connections that exist between the ceramicist who shaped the clay, the walls and floor of the jug, and the action of pouring liquid that afford the jug's void its ability to hold and which in turn is the essence of the jug's thingness. What makes the jug a *thing* and not an *object* is that it gathers, it embeds within it all the relations that give it its essence, its usefulness. For Heidegger, this gathering is ultimately what he considers to be the unification of the "four-fold" (the earth, sky, divinities, and mortals) because this unification can only happen in the places (or dwellings) created by things constituting themselves in the world. In this sense,

Heidegger's treatise on things is an important building block for the metaphor of entanglement in that it emphasizes a relational approach rather than an object-focused one.

This more phenomenological view of the relationships between people and things has also been taken up by archaeologists such as Chris Gosden (1994), Julian Thomas (1999), Chris Tilley (1994), Nicole Boivin (2008), and Bjørnar Olsen (2010), where the materiality of constructions, landscapes, tools, and particularly the processes behind their constant production, maintenance, reuse, and discard are emphasized. Within these standpoints there is an inextricable relation between things and the material practices in which they become ingrained. There is a strong focus on the ways in which humans perceive things as having agency, and increasing concern with the different ways in which matter is construed and understood (and manipulated) for social ends in different cultural contexts.

From a different standpoint, Latour (2005) introduces the concept of actor-network theory (ANT), in which he breaks away from Cartesian subject-object dualism—which he argues was initiated by modernity—and proposes to understand the relationality of materials and humans. Latour discusses the idea of heterogeneous assemblages of humans and nonhumans and the generative potential of each of these actors "to make other actors do unexpected things" (Latour 2005:129). In his view there exists a generalized symmetry between humans and nonhumans, and he sees agency as diffused within networks. Key to understanding this diffusion of agency is the idea that objects act as delegates. For instance, Latour presents the example of a speed bump, or sleeping policeman, used to make cars slow down to present how nonhuman delegates exercise agency within a network. The speed bump does this by "standing in for human actors" (Latour 1999:189) and quite literally acting as a delegate for a real policeman. His approach focuses on the infrastructure of actor-networks, how they form and are held together, rather than on explaining why networks exist.

For Latour, understanding the interaction between humans and technology is crucial for the development of these networks. He argues that the integration of these two "ghosts," society and technology, does not create a singular composite object, but rather a "sui generis object: the collective thing" (Latour 1992:175). This collective thing presents us with a world where humans increasingly delegate their competences to nonhumans, establishing an ever-growing inextricable relation between humans and nonhumans. In this sense, Latour argues that society and technology are interconnected and interdependent, rendering the study of social relations without nonhumans impossible (Johnson 1988).

While this necessity to understand the social through its tangled relations between humans and nonhumans—particularly the emphasis on how humans competences are delegated on objects, resembles entanglement's notion of dependence—we believe ANT fails to account for temporality in the sense that networks are made up of chains or operational sequences; one thing has to be done before another is possible, as in the archaeological concepts of behavioral chain and *châine operatoire*. In addition, the lives of humans and different material things vary, and entanglement is often affected by the clash between these different durations. Moreover, we find it more fruitful to move beyond the diffusion of agency to objects, focusing instead on the entrapments created by these relations; this is one of the core strengths of an entanglement approach (Hodder 2012). Unlike ANT, which stops at the assembly of associations (Latour 2005), entanglement extricates the paths of dependencies between things and the historically contingent intersections that create them (Gosden 2005; Hegmon et al. 2008; Mahoney 2000; Pierson 2000).

Building upon Latour's ANT, Olsen advocates a return to things, and seeks to build an archaeology that ascribes agency to nonhuman actors (2003, 2007). Calling for a symmetrical archaeology, Olsen maintains that the more recent wave of theories of materiality fall short in that they still relegate things to a secondary position behind the social or humanistic, a position where things only exist as an outcome of human intention and action. As a result, material culture studies draw heavily on the philosophy of Kant in that things are not part of the lived experience, but are subjugated to the ways in which humans create them. In this way, there is a lack of recognition of the actual materials of things as viable objects of study on their own instead of a means to reference culture and society. Slamming materiality as a throwback to fetishism and antiquarianism, Olsen cites the subject-object divide as the ontological reason for things simply being considered background players as opposed to leading actors in social analyses. One example given by Olsen is the way that things are said to embody social relations. Embodiment intrinsically implies the binaries of mind-matter and subject-object, binaries for which humans are the dominant force and thus have the power to attribute symbolic qualities to things. This ontology is wrong, according to Olsen, as things mediate the world and exert just as much influence as humans, participating in the formation of collectives and constructing subjects. The staunchness of this ontology gives insufficient attention to material culture, placing things into a limbo where they are neither fully culture nor nature. However, there is the simple fact that things themselves bring their own affordances to the table, and that these are activated upon intermingling with humans in the lived world. The entwinement of humans and nonhumans is historically inescapable; if anything, it has only increased through time with an amplified reliance of people on things. Furthermore, all cultural change has precipitated from the upward interfacing between the two. These last two points of Olsen's symmetrical archaeology resonate most with the metaphor of entanglement. The idea of trajectories in which there are multiplying and continuously transforming entrapments emerging from interactions between humans and nonhumans is one of the key tenets of entanglement in this volume, though we contend that things also rely on people rather than suggesting a more unidirectionally dependent relationship.

Also questioning the reinvigoration of material culture studies, Ingold introduces the notion of a *meshwork*, in which the organisms of life are considered bundles of interwoven lines of growth and movement, constituted in fluid space (2010). Ingold denies the value of a distinction between things and their relations, arguing that humans and things co-constitute each other, thereby bringing themselves into existence. This co-constitution is explained through the metaphor of weaving as a process that reflects how the temporal rhythms of life gradually build the structural properties of things. In the words of Ingold, the "world of our experience is, indeed, continually and endlessly coming into being around us as we weave [so that] culture lies in the very texture and pattern of the weave itself" (2000:361). Thus, Ingold is not concerned with relationally focused networks but instead with meshworks that center on the flow, mix, and transformation of materials, which then produces and dissolves people and things. The flux of things in these meshworks is what makes them active, not agency.

This standpoint emerges from Ingold's pushback against material culture studies, which he maintains separate interpretation and theory from observation. Materiality is not universal nor is it intrinsic to all things, but is an intangible abstract concept set aside from reality. According to Ingold, material culture studies ignore the production of things, neglecting the actual physical material substance from which things are derived and which spans the life of the things, replacing these instead with a concentration on representation and signification. Although divergent from Heidegger's phenomenological stream of thought, Ingold too sees things as constituting themselves in the world with life histories embedded within a material's properties as they transform and circulate in the world. Although our focus on entanglement also emphasizes dynamism and multidirectionality, for Ingold, the constitution of this mesh lies in the entanglement of the lines rather than in the connecting points. He is interested in how "every thing is itself an entanglement" as opposed to the entanglements between people and things, things and things, or people and people. Moreover, he seems to designate the material as the locus or originator of relations between people and things; we do not necessarily agree that materials can be said to be the only instigators of interactions.

Using a cognitive approach to archaeology, Renfrew argues for his concept of "material engagement," in which things are given agency by their involvement in a social network (Renfrew 2004; see also Malafouris and Renfrew 2010). More specifically, he is concerned with the use and status of material objects that mediate interactions between people and between people and the environment. Renfrew is primarily interested in cultural change: he sees the physical and conceptual (or matter and mind) as emergent in a unitary relationship, a relationship that underlies all dualisms. A theory of material engagement is therefore similar to phenomenology in that it stresses the individual's experience in the world as constitutive, yet at the same time differs in its consideration of space and time as well as recognizing how social processes impart knowledge to the individual through enculturation. In his view, entanglements originate in the constitution of social facts: the manner in which concepts of value emerge in different societies and the role they play in cultural change (Renfrew et al. 2008). One example Renfrew highlights is gift giving and the way that material objects that are exchanged are inherently embedded with notions of property and ownership. In addition, when materials act as mnemonic devices, evoking communal and personal histories, such as the sand paintings of the Navajo, they perpetuate material engagement via the continuous power of memories carried by the object. For us, material engagement is relevant to entanglement not least for its acknowledgement of context, but also because it allows for the creation of new relationships, expected or unexpected, to emerge from the interactions that occur between humans and nonhumans. Although we see these parallels, Renfrew's approach ultimately focuses on the action, the material engagement, whereas entanglement emphasizes the dependencies, good or bad, that arise from interactions.

Also in the cognitive theory stream, Knappett argues that the meaning of material culture arises from distributed cognition, in which objects sit at the nexus of the mind, material, and agency (2005). Distributed cognition maintains that people are agents, have intentionality, and actively interact with the environment so that the mind adapts to solve everyday problems. Here, as in Renfrew's material engagement theory, action takes primacy and dualisms collapse in a model of codependency in which objects mediate mind and matter. Knappett advocates for a fluid cognitive approach in which meaning is distributed between ideas and the physical object, situated, and embodied. Knappett uses Gibson's concept of *affordances* (Knappett 2005:62) to track the possible actions an object can afford and at the same time stresses an object's *associations* or the interaction of these *affordances* in context. Thus, perception of an object's function is both direct (affordances) and indirect (categorization). While we appreciate Knappett's inclusion of culture as key to any relational approach, we again find that this framework stresses action and networks of association, which is more akin to Renfrew's approach than to entanglement as a metaphor.

In *Entangled Objects*, Thomas (1991) explores the multiplicity of indigenous responses to colonialism by reevaluating the role of objects in the creation of alterity. Thomas finds the singularity of the process of colonial contact lies in the "local situation" rather than in the colonizer-colonized power balance. He argues for a "creative recontextualization" (1991:5) that aims to situate the uses of material objects within their own historical and cultural scenarios. For Thomas, material objects, whether foreign or local, become embedded in relations of power and politics, introducing new opportunities for negotiation and improvement within their local contexts. This internal ascription of significance recognizes the appropriation of objects through a symmetrical lens in which local people introduce foreign elements into their own political, economic, and social spheres, divorced from the values these objects might have had in western contexts from which they originated. Furthermore, Thomas observes that both sides, European and indigenous, change the purpose of "abducted treasures" by imagining a narrative of contact that is "objectified in artifacts of alterity and artifacts of history" (Thomas 1991:184), thus representing the other under their own terms and categories. This perspective advocates for a proportional appropriation of objects for both locals and nonlocals, and considers the entanglement of objects within the contexts they were inserted instead of through the colonized-colonizer power dyad. Thomas argues that objects become entangled because, despite their material stability, objects are inherently mutable, allowing them to become entangled within the combination of both old and new relations emergent from their appropriation.

The concept of entanglement advocated through this book builds upon Thomas's historically and culturally contingent reanalysis of the colonial encounter, with particular regard for his metaphoric use of the unintended and mutable role of objects. In this way, Thomas has led the way to a series of archaeological studies (Dietler 1998, 2010; Gosden 2004; Orser 1996; Stein 2005) focusing on a historically accurate consideration of "the complexities of the colonial encounter" (Martindale 2009:61). As Silliman points out in chapter 2 in chronicling the utility of an entanglement approach in colonial contexts, one of the greatest potentialities of entanglement is its ability to interrogate assumptions of identity and to elucidate cultural persistence for marginalized groups.

Entanglement as a Flexible Framework

More recently, Hodder (2012) has defined the term *entanglement* and its relation with things as the "double bind" in which humans get caught by "depending on things that depend on humans" (Hodder 2012:88). In this sense, Hodder argues for a "dialectic relationship between dependence, often productive and enabling, and dependency, often constraining and limiting" (2012:88). These dependences and dependencies entangle humans and things, inevitably generating further investments and entrapments in an inescapable way. As such, Hodder proposes that the webs in which people live are as much symbolic, meaningful, spiritual, religious, and conceptual as they are practical and technical, economic and social. In this sense, the interactions between humans and things are a web of sticky entrapments in which everyday life and power become embedded within the irreducible nature of life (Hodder 2011), instead of a network of delegate agency (Latour 2005) or a fluid meshwork (Ingold 2010). The notion of entanglement thus permits a flexible framework for archaeological inquiry that focuses on the relations, affordances, and dependences that bind human-thing interactions through a multidirectional focus on historical trajectories.

The role of entanglement in the formation of historical trajectories can be observed as the gathering of relations and interactions where things and people depend on other things and people, thus forming nondirectional processes that become entwined through time. In this view, the focus is on the situated responses that develop from these interactions and the further implications these responses entail. Moving away from unitary approaches that emphasize social, economic, or political aspects of society, entanglement presupposes that historic events do not simply affect each other through bounded spheres; rather, they are a messy tangle of interactions of elements, forces, agents, spatial scales, and temporalities that shape one another (Mitchell 2002). Hence, these trajectories are understood through a heterogeneity of meaning, resisting explanation and avoiding rigid definitions. An example of such a multiscalar approach is highlighted in this volume by Jennings and Yépez Álvarez (chapter 3) as they explore the dynamism that characterizes Imperial expansion in the Andes ca. VII AD, where local and global histories of things reveal the unstable yet accretive nature of historical pathways.

A crucial aspect of such trajectories relies on the temporal aspects of human-thing relations and the way they develop through time. Temporality is key to our understanding of the dependences and dependencies that people-thing relations create in contrast to Latour's ANT or Knappett's network analysis. Time for things, such as houses, rocks, or cloth, holds different meanings and is often in contrast with conventional human measures of time. Temporality is fluid, situational, and contingent, and thus time is not only understood in its absolute perception but also in terms of moments (Nuttall 2009). An example that comes to mind is Joseph-Achille Mbembe's "time of entanglement" (2001:17) during the South African apartheid where the relations established between people with different categories for time became entwined and their social and physical boundaries were permeated. Time in this sense encloses multiple *durées* made up of discontinuities, reversals, inertias, and swings that overlay one another and that define which paths of action persist, evolve, or fade (Mbembe 2001).

This heterogeneous concept of time is intrinsically bound to the incommensurable character of space and the different scales that comprise a multifaceted concept of the past too often dismissed as unassailably complex and impossible to tackle. Mitchell's analysis of the materialization of territoriality through rules, techniques, maps, and institutions during the creation of the Egyptian "nation" presents us with an interesting example of how one can conceivably internalize different relations with space (2002). Building on this idea, Morozowski (chapter 8) uses entanglement as a tool to trace the threads that entwine landscape and history by understanding how space and place gather different meanings through time. Thus, historical gravity is accrued through the intricate association between events, emotion, and memory.

To understand how historical trajectories are created, it is necessary to explore the role things have in bringing humans and nonhumans together in heterogeneous mixes that throughout time become tangled and entrapped in the maintenance and sustenance of their material world (Hodder 2012). Following the historical-processual paradigm called for by Pauketat (2001), entanglement scrutinizes not just the *why* of the social sphere but also the *how*. Expounding on the groundbreaking work of the sociocultural anthropologist Appadurai (1986) and literature scholar Brown (2003), entanglement theory goes beyond simple connections between people and things to understanding how the relationships between people and things are embedded in and underlie social processes. Thus, the focus changes from how things *make* society to the thing *itself* and its multiple relationships. It's at once a perceptual and conceptual flip. Key to understanding the concept of entanglement is to take into consideration that while things appear as durable and unchanging objects that stabilize human life (Arendt 1958), we actually take them for granted, failing to see them for their own characteristics, connections, dependencies, and temporalities. There is a spatial and temporal forgetting of the unstable connections of things that allows people to depend on their apparent durability (Hodder 2012). The metaphor of entanglement allows for the acknowledgment of the indecipherability of things as they are transformed into charged objects, at the same time shifting the attention from the object itself onto the symbolic processes it provokes on the beholder (see also Fernandini in chapter 4).

Recognizing the multifaceted historicities of time and space, entanglement as a metaphor provokes a powerful and kaleidoscopic relational approach. The advantage of such a metaphor is precisely in its allowance for dissonant contexts, subjects, processes, and events. This metaphoric use of entanglement is intended for use in conjunction and collaboration with a variety of theoretical perspectives to elucidate a deeper understanding of past lifeways through nuanced archaeologies. This is the precise advantage of entanglement: its ability to speak to the data across a diversity of archaeological perspectives, both methodologically and theoretically, so that archaeologists working in postcolonial contexts may find it just as applicable as those who work in the prehistoric Old World. As such, this volume portrays how the archaeology of entanglement moves away from the outcome of events onto the processes behind, during, and after lived experiences; that is, the everyday practices and contingencies that develop through the interactions between things and people, things and things, and people and people (Hodder 2011, 2012). This flexible framework allows scholars to trace the paths developed between and among these interfaces in conjunction with the way beings, both animate and inanimate, develop dependences and dependencies on different things, therefore entrapping themselves within their own histories. Entanglement reconfigures the way that archaeologists examine the relationships between people and things. It is a shifting of agency and—in some respects—even power, as it argues that things are just as capable of ensnaring people into particular situations as people are of enslaving things. And it is this realignment which makes entanglement as a metaphor uniquely "good to think and good to think with" (Silliman, chapter 1).

The Chapters

This volume builds on the intersections between science, the humanities, and ecology to provide a more fine-grained, multiscalar treatment that benefits from the long-term perspective that characterizes archaeological research. Accordingly, the chapters in this volume are organized around three main themes with the objective of highlighting the breadth, both in terms of various topical and regional areas, with which entanglement can engage. Throughout the book, we hope readers will recognize recurring ideas of entrapment, dependency and dependence, historical trajectory, and human-thing interaction as both the underlying strands binding these chapters together as well as touchstones for entanglement applications in archaeology.

The first theme, "Local and Foreign: Entanglements of Colonial Encounters and Social Inequality," examines the more common practice of using entanglement studies in archaeologies of colonialism. In "Disentangling the Archaeology of Colonialism and Indigeneity" (chapter 1) Silliman reviews how entanglement has been approached within the archaeology of colonialism in the past two decades. The author examines how colonialism, with its intersections of people and things, local and nonlocal, has led different authors to conceptualize the term into models, metaphors, methodologies, and theories. Silliman emphasizes the importance of these advances in the study of colonialism, stressing the effective use of entanglement as a metaphor and as a useful heuristic for thinking. In Silliman's view, entanglement does not require a precise theoretical framework, but rather should be used as a guide to think about networks, linkages, practices, consumption, and affordances. Similarly, in chapter 2, "'Is this the Gold that You Eat?' Coins, Entangled Subjects, and Early Colonial Orderings in the Andes," Corcoran-Tadd explores the multiple scales of interdependency that persisted as Spanish and Andean communities became mutually entangled in the early colonial period. Corcoran-Tadd reconsiders the role of the coin as a "thing" to engage in a discussion of the asymmetrical relationships between humans, objects, and discourses that generate the immutable cycle of human-thing relations. In this way, the author traces the socio-material linkages of coins to provide a wider context for understanding the complex regional context that characterized the colonial project in the Andes. He examines how heterogeneous concepts of wealth permeated the unbalanced introduction of metal as currency. The subsequent entanglements entrapped indigenous and Spanish people, revealing the constant tendency of the material to resist, mutate, fail, and even subvert.

Expanding on colonial applications to a consideration of the way that different societies and cultures interact in general, this section also presents two chapters dealing with entrapments and the social inequality that result when foreign and local elements come together. Jennings and Yépez Álvarez (chapter 3) bring forward the interregional, regional, and local entanglements that ensnared a group of elite members whose funerary remains were destroyed by their contemporaries. Through this multiscalar approach, the authors address the entrapments generated by the reordering of local social structures under foreign concepts. They propose that the connections between elite members and the foreign Wari Empire generated a series of unintended consequences that led to a complete rupture between the local elite and general populace, culminating in the desecration of their own leaders. Along the same lines, Fernandini (chapter 4) traces the introduction of exotic objects into a conservative material context and the subsequent consequences. She proposes that as elite members became entangled with long-distance trade, emulation, and hybridization processes they were inadvertently ensnaring themselves into a social trap from which they were not able to disentangle. Ultimately, Fernandini moves away from concepts of intentionality and political strategy by emphasizing the role of contingent situated practices in the formation of historical trajectories, social inequality, and power.

The second theme, "Entanglements with the Natural World: Landscapes and Agriculture," explores how archaeologists might use entanglement to understand and conceptualize relationships between nature and society, a concept Darwin considered with his metaphoric use of an "entangled bank," which evokes the contradiction of disparate and diverse life forms being simultaneously entwined in dependencies and competition with one another, entwining nature and society in a seemingly organic manner (Darwin 1860). Entanglement takes this metaphor further, moving beyond just complicated webs between species and instead emphasizing the emergent practices, meanings, and relations that lie between and within these interactions. In "Entangled Banks and the Domestication of East African Pastoralist Landscapes" (chapter 5), Lane questions dichotomous perceptions of human and natural processes in the production of landscapes over time by bringing to light the interconnections and even dependencies that different timescales and places produce. Lane's argument focuses on dung as a way to interrogate the evolving human-thing relations that co-produce East African landscapes and which in some way transcend time by linking the past to the present. His view challenges conventional taxonomies of landscapes as wild spaces that accommodate human presence, instead thinking of them as continuous cycles of colonization and recolonization by both human and nonhuman things so that both the cultural and natural spheres are presented as co-producers of a shared history.

Likewise, Hegmon et al. (chapter 7) and Fuller et al. (chapter 6) in this section also explore entanglements as dynamic processes that fluctuate and are even self-reinforcing. Fuller et al.'s chapter on the multidirectional dependencies between humans and plant (plants for management and reproduction; humans for subsistence and culture), like Lane's, focuses on the domestication of the natural world. The authors look at four regions representing a variety of ecologies, including the Levant, northeast Asia, the Yangtze Basin, and southern India, and the ways that plant physiology, human behavior, and resource availability result in real and unforeseen repercussions for social, economic, ideological, technological, material, and environmental aspects of life. They argue that cereal domestication processes adhere to a basic path rigidity but diverge in the manner the path is followed and manifested due to local cultural traditions and ecologies. They demonstrate that the unintended consequences of plant domestication are numerous and far reaching, from the restriction of people's movements within the landscape to the abandonment of wild staples and evolutionary trends favoring greater seed size.

Moving too beyond notions of entanglement as relegated to the material realm, Hegmon et al. reflect on the intertwinement of canal system construction, population growth, and agricultural yields in their case study of Hohokam large-scale irrigation systems in the American Southwest as part of the "Change is Hard: The Challenges of Path Dependence" research project. The authors contend that increasing dependence on irrigation canals to support a rising population resulted in "labor traps" and "lock-in" so that people were forced to continue along a historical trajectory of ever-expanding irrigation. This argument is not unlike Fuller et al.'s, who maintain that plant domestication altered people's behavior to the point that they became trapped in laborious activities such as fertilizing fields. For Hegmon et al., considerations of path dependencies in archaeological research has significant potential since this approach "asks questions about both the actions and motivations of the people who set the trajectory into motion." They argue that this knowledge, in turn, may inform contemporary practices and choices.

The third and final theme of this volume, "Rethinking Dependences and Dependencies: Contemporary Perspectives on Entanglement in Archaeology," is a set of three chapters that take on broader discussions of the nature of dependencies and how they are created and have long-lasting and unpredictable effects beyond initial intentionality. In many ways, the chapters in this section reiterate and reconceptualize many of the key ideas underlying the preceding sections. In "Entangled Histories, Entangled Worlds: Reflections on Time, Space, and Place" (chapter 8), Mrozowski rethinks traditional archaeological applications of entanglement studies to elucidate how space and history are interwoven in such a way as to result in "historical gravity."

Interested in places of deep memory, he builds upon Lane's observations that people use material culture to link the past to the future (chapter 5) by looking at how people connect place to history in mechanisms of memorialization, as a means of keeping the past alive. They did not anticipate these ties would still exist in a sort of "historical gravity" hundreds or thousands of years later and have far-reaching effects such as gathering people into urban centers. His multiscalar comparative approach spans from the smaller settlements of Magunkaquog and Hassanamesit in New England to the larger and more imposing Stonehenge in the United Kingdom. In addition, Mrozowski touches upon how archaeologists themselves are embedded within these entanglements, often unintentionally endowing certain sites with "historical gravity" through the mere act of rediscovering them.

Der also takes up the issue of the entwinement of archaeologists in the past and re-creations or reimaginings of the past in a study of looting as an unintentional outcome of archaeology (chapter 9). Der argues that archaeology effectively valorizes ancient material culture, thus making cultural objects desirable in an entangled web that also features museums, collectors, organized crime, and commercial entities, namely auction houses. At the same time, assigning value to the past, and knowledge of it, is what enables archaeology as a discipline to survive and have merit both financially and academically. Thus, the relationship between archaeology and looting is complex, messy, and multidirectional.

The final chapter by Hodder is a deeper examination of dependences and dependencies, using a case study of pottery at the Middle Eastern site of Çatalhöyük. Although Hodder touches on many aspects of entanglement that appear earlier in this volume, such as labor traps (see Fuller et al. in chapter 6 and Hegmon et al. in chapter 7), the inability of things and people to be self-sufficient (Silliman, chapter 1), relationships to space (Mrozowski, chapter 8), and social inequality (Jennings and Yépez Álvarez in chapter 3 and Fernandini in chapter 4), his main interest is in differing degrees of dependency or insufficiency fluctuating through time. Hodder emphasizes the way that something—for instance, pottery—can become increasingly important and central to a way of life while at the same time becoming rapidly less self-sufficient. Greater entanglement has the consequence of increased reliance, decreased independence, a possible loss of control, and sometimes even repurposing or the shifting of roles. This last chapter provides a satisfying end to the case studies presented here as it gathers together many of the conceptual threads woven through the other chapters in a theoretical way.

All the authors in this volume, while dealing in a variety of ways with the entanglements of objects and people, are at the same time interested in how archaeologists think about entanglements. They recognize the ability of the metaphor of entanglement to capture particular kinds of complexities and the irreducible consequences of life that theoretical approaches alone, such as

ANT, often do not completely address. An entanglement framework provides us with unexplored understandings of how the past is wrapped up in the future and vice versa. It can illuminate new insights into temporalities, space, and historicities. It recognizes that interaction between and among humans and nonhumans is not simply a no-strings-attached affair, but often comes with entrapment and unpredictable consequences. This multifaceted volume, which covers a wide array of regions and time periods, demonstrates that entanglement as a metaphor of study is applicable to a broad range of topics, including archaeological science, heritage, and more theoretical discussions. We hope this volume will provoke new thoughts on the subject and treatment of entanglement perspectives in the discipline, and that the case studies here resonate with readers in their own research, wherever that may be.

References

Appadurai, Arjun, 1986. Introduction: Commodities and the Politics of Value. In *The Social Life of Things: Commodities in Cultural Perspective,* edited by Arjun Appadurai, pp. 3–63. Cambridge University Press, Cambridge, UK; New York.

Arendt, Hannah, 1958. *The Human Condition.* University of Chicago Press, Chicago, IL.

Boivin, Nicole, 2008. *Material Cultures, Material Minds.* Cambridge University Press, Cambridge, UK; New York.

Bourdieu, Pierre, 1977. *Outline of a Theory of Practice.* Cambridge University Press, Cambridge, UK; New York.

Brown, Bill, 2003. *A Sense of Things: The Object Matter of American Literature.* University of Chicago Press, Chicago, IL; London.

Darwin, Charles, 1860. *On the Origin of Species by Means of Natural Selection, or the Preservation of Favoured Races in the Struggle for Life.* Murray, London.

Dietler, Michael, 1998. Consumption, Agency, and Cultural Entanglement: Theoretical Implications of a Mediterranean Colonial Encounter. In *Studies in Culture Contact: Interaction, Culture Change, and Archaeology*, edited by James G. Cusick, pp. 288–315. Center for Archaeological Investigations, Southern Illinois University, Carbondale, IL.

Dietler, Michael, 2010. *Archaeologies of Colonialism: Consumption, Entanglement, and Violence in Ancient Mediterranean France.* University of California Press, Berkeley.

Gosden, Chris, 1994. *Social Being and Time.* Blackwell, Oxford, UK; Cambridge, MA.

Gosden, Chris, 2004. *Archaeology and Colonialism: Cultural Contact from 5000 BC to the Present.* Cambridge University Press, Cambridge, UK.

Gosden, Chris, 2005. What Do Objects Want? *Journal of Archaeological Method and Theory* 12(3):193–211.

Hegmon, Michelle, Matthew A. Peeples, Ann P. Kinzig, Stephanie Kulow, Cathryn M. Meegan, and Margaret C. Nelson, 2008. Social Transformation and Its Human Costs in the Prehispanic U.S. Southwest. *American Anthropologist* 110(3):313–324.

Heidegger, Martin, 2002. The Origin of the Work of Art. In *Heidegger: Off the Beaten Track,* edited and translated by Julian Young and Kenneth Haynes, pp. 1–56. Cambridge University Press, Cambridge, UK.

Heidegger, Martin, 2008. *Being and Time.* HarperOne, New York.
Hodder, Ian, 2011. Human-Thing Entanglement: Towards an Integrated Archaeological Perspective. *Journal of the Royal Anthropological Institute* 17(1):154–177.
Hodder, Ian, 2012. *Entangled: An Archaeology of the Relationships Between Humans and Things.* Wiley-Blackwell, Malden, MA.
Ingold, Tim, 2000. *The Perception of the Environment: Essays on Livelihood, Dwelling and Skill.* Routledge, London.
Ingold, Tim, 2010. Bringing Things to Life: Creative Entanglements in a World of Materials. *ESRC National Centre for Research Methods, NCRM Working Paper Series* 15:1–15.
Johnson, Jim, 1988. Mixing Humans and Nonhumans Together: The Sociology of a Door-closer. *Social Problems* 35(3):298–310.
Knappett, Carl, 2005. *Thinking Through Material Culture: An Interdisciplinary Perspective.* University of Pennsylvania Press, Philadelphia.
Latour, Bruno, 1992. Where Are the Missing Masses, Sociology of Mundane Artefacts. In *Shaping Technology/Building Society: Studies in Sociotechnical Change,* edited by W. E. Bijerker and J. Law, pp. 255–258. MIT Press, Cambridge, MA.
Latour, Bruno, 1999. On Recalling ANT. *The Sociological Review* 47(S1):15–25.
Latour, Bruno, 1987. *Science in Action: How to Follow Scientists and Engineers Through Society.* Harvard University Press, Cambridge, MA.
Latour, Bruno, 2005. *Reassembling the Social: An Introduction to Actor-Network-Theory.* Oxford University Press, Oxford, UK; New York.
Mahoney, James, 2000. Path Dependence in Historical Sociology. *Theory and Society* 29(4):507–548.
Malafouris, Lambros, and Colin Renfrew, 2010. *The Cognitive Life of Things: Recasting the Boundaries of the Mind.* McDonald Institute for Archaeological Research. Distributed by Oxbow Books; David Brown Co., Cambridge; Oxford, UK; Oakville, CT.
Martindale, Andrew, 2009. Entanglement and Tinkering: Structural History in the Archaeology of the Northern Tsimshian. *Journal of Social Archaeology* 9(1):59–91.
Mbembe, Joseph-Achille, 2001. *On the Postcolony.* University of California Press, Berkeley.
Mitchell, Timothy, 2002. *Rule of Experts: Egypt, Techno-politics, Modernity.* University of California Press, Berkeley.
Nuttall, Sarah, 2009. *Entanglement: Literary and Cultural Reflections on Post-apartheid.* Wits University Press, Johannesburg, South Africa.
Olsen, Bjørnar, 2003. Material Culture after Text: Re membering Things. *Norwegian Archeological Review* 36(2):87–104.
Olsen, Bjørnar, 2007. Keeping Things at Arm's Length: A Genealogy of Asymmetry. *World Archaeology* 39(4):579–588.
Olsen, Bjørnar, 2010. *In Defense of Things: Archaeology and the Ontology of Objects.* AltaMira Press, Lanham, MD.
Orser, Charles E., 1996. *A Historical Archaeology of the Modern World.* Plenum Press, New York.
Ortner, Sherry B., 1984. Theory in Anthropology Since the Sixties. *Comparative Studies in Society and History* 26(1):126–166.

Ortner, Sherry B., 2006. *Anthropology and Social Theory: Culture, Power, and the Acting Subject.* Duke University Press, Durham, NC.

Pauketat, Timothy R., 2001. Practice and History in Archaeology. *Anthropological Theory* 1(1):73–98.

Pierson, Paul, 2000. Increasing Returns, Path Dependence, and the Study of Politics. *The American Political Science Review* 94(2):251–267.

Renfrew, Colin, 2004. Towards a Theory of Material Engagement. In *Rethinking Materiality: The Engagement of Mind with the Material World,* edited by Elizabeth DeMarrais, Chris Gosden, and Colin Renfrew, pp. 23–32. McDonald Institute for Archaeological Research, Cambridge, UK.

Renfrew, Colin, Chris Frith, and Lambros Malafouris, 2008. Introduction. The Sapient Mind: Archaeology Meets Neuroscience. *Philosophical Transactions of the Royal Society B: Biological Sciences* 363(1499):1935–1938.

Stahl, Ann B., 2009. The Archaeology of African History. *The International Journal of African Historical Studies* 42(2):241–255.

Stein, Gil, 2005. *The Archaeology of Colonial Encounters: Comparative Perspectives.* School of American Research Press, Sante Fe, NM.

Strathern, Marilyn, 1988. *The Gender of the Gift: Problems with Women and Problems with Society in Melanesia.* University of California Press, Berkeley.

Thomas, Nicholas, 1991. *Entangled Objects: Exchange, Material Culture, and Colonialism in the Pacific.* Harvard University Press, Cambridge, MA.

Thomas, Julian, 1999. *Time, Culture, and Identity an Interpretative Archaeology.* Routledge, London; New York.

Tilley, Christopher Y., 1994. *A Phenomenology of Landscape: Places, Paths, and Monuments.* Berg, Oxford, UK; Providence, RI.

Local and Foreign: Entanglements of Colonial Encounters and Social Inequality

Chapter 1

Disentangling the Archaeology of Colonialism and Indigeneity

Stephen W. Silliman

Introduction

The idea of entanglement has been announced recently in archaeology as a remedy to a host of interpretive problems. Most notably, Hodder (2011, 2012) suggests that a notion of entanglement permits a redirection of archaeological inquiry away from agency, practice, and materiality into the relations, affordances, and dependences that bind and propel them. It parallels some developments in actor-network theory and related "symmetrical archaeology" and in social network analysis, but it has a unique approach as a methodology for disentangling the various strands and as an interpretive model for long-term patterns in human history and evolution. Stockhammer (2012, 2013) has also proposed a notion of entanglement in archaeology to replace the political and biological layers embedded in the term "hybridity." An idea of entanglement has also caught on slightly in the archaeology of colonialism and "culture contact" (Dietler 2010; Jordan 2009, 2014; Martindale 2009; Silliman 2005; Stahl 2002), as it often picks up some of the direction initially suggested by Thomas (1991), Dietler (1998), and Alexander (1998) in the 1990s to account for a variety of material and cultural intersections.

In this chapter, I examine the potential ability of "entanglement" to resolve some problems in the archaeology of colonialism. What has it meant, and what could it mean for archaeologists who work on these issues? This requires some historical perspective, albeit not comprehensive, and some projection for the future. Perhaps most significantly, I ask: Is "entanglement" a metaphor, model, or method? That is, does it provide a heuristic perspective to frame certain historical and social/material understandings (metaphor), does it serve as a theory or concept to guide analysis once particular issues have been identified (model), or does it provide a technique for tracking networks, objects, and trajectories that require an additional theoretical framework to interpret

Archaeology of Entanglement edited by Lindsay Der and Francesca Fernandini, 31–48

appropriately (method)? I provide some tentative answers here that highlight both the strengths and weaknesses of an entanglement framework in archaeologies of colonialism and hopefully archaeology more broadly.

Entanglement in the Archaeology of Colonialism

According to Martindale (2009:61), entanglement owes its origins in the anthropology of colonialism to Thomas's (1991) foundational work on the colonial encounter and the ways that material objects underwent recontextualization within it (see Hodder 2012:90). Yet, despite that important book setting the trajectory for Thomas's own later work (Thomas 1994), which has informed postcolonial archaeologists in important ways, an idea of entanglement as a term or an idea has not enjoyed a rich history in the archaeology of colonialism (see Cobb and Loren 2008:15). This is despite arguments, such as those by Gosden (2004), that tend to emphasize the often-entangled relationships between material culture, places, and people that actually define colonialism.

Entanglement next appears in two key chapters in Cusick's (1998) volume *Studies in Culture Contact*, in which Dietler (1998) argues that "contact encounters" are contexts in which Indigenous people—in this case, local Europeans facing increasing Hellenistic influence—had consumption practices of alien goods entangled within their own socially relevant demands and resistances. In Dietler's piece, entanglement is presented more as an analytical metaphor about consumption practices rather than something to be identified per se. However, recently he has argued that entanglement stands apart from processes of creolization and hybridity because it does not entail the "very different asymmetries of power" that characterize full-blown colonialism (Dietler 2010:53,74). He states, "In using the term *entanglement*, I want to signal my interest in pursuing the complex webs of economic, political, social, and cultural linkages that can result, often inadvertently, from the consumption of alien material culture" (Dietler 2010:53, emphasis in original). This acknowledges entanglement's fundamental role in colonialism, but suggests that entanglement is more about material consumption, specifically "alien" objects, in larger networks and the intended and unintended consequences of those consumption practices.

Alexander (1998), in her chapter reflecting on the larger Cusick (1998) volume, takes on the task of navigating the various paths and perspectives of "culture contact" studies to reach a series of generalizations about how these might be understood and classified. As part of this discussion, she settles upon a notion of "cultural entanglement" to describe certain situations of interaction that were not a fully developed colonialism, drawing in part on Dietler's (1998) chapter. She defines it as "a process whereby interaction with an expanding territorial state gradually results in change of indigenous patterns of production, exchange, and social relations" that she further describes as "long-term, gradual, and nondirected" (Alexander 1998:485). The "non-directed" element resurrects Spicer's (1961) earlier attempts to highlight a kind of contact, within an acculturation model, that did not involve top-down imposition of colonial or other policies on another group. Contrary to Dietler's emphasis on metaphor, Alexander sets up entanglement as a particular kind of "culture contact," albeit part of a continuum from interaction to colonization. That is, she presents a more model-like use of entanglement since, according to her formulation, it should be used to describe a particular *state* of cross-cultural interaction and a certain set of *processes*.

It took several years before entanglement appeared again in a noticeable way in the archaeological literature on colonialism, which it has done in three ways. First, Stahl (2002) and I (Silliman 2005) were inspired by Thomas's (1991) work to refer to *colonial entanglement*, which we found a helpful variation on simply colonialism, to accentuate the complexities of interactions, objects, meanings, and identities involving Indigenous people confronting European people, ideas, and material culture in the last 500 years (see also Quimby 2011). It was not proposed as a theoretical intervention as much as a terminological acknowledgment of networks of materials, people, and consumption (after Dietler 1998). It also drew, in part (Silliman 2005), on the work of Australian archaeologists regarding "shared histories" and the entanglement this implies (Byrne 2003; Harrison 2004; Murray 1996, 2004; see also Paterson 2008:45). These Australian scholars have rightly criticized the tendency of archaeologists and heritage professionals to separate Indigenous and colonial histories and sites/objects of heritage rather than consider their inextricability and how this leads to particular discourses of difference and sameness for political purpose.

Second, Martindale (2009) advanced an idea of *contact-as-entanglement*. He situates this in the same trajectory highlighted here (minus Alexander 1998), but prefers to consider the idea of entanglement as a way to link colonial encounters with much larger concepts of cultural contact. This follows very much in the spirit of Cusick's (1998) overall volume and Alexander's (1998) concluding chapter, but may diminish the ability to focus on colonialism specifically. For instance, Martindale (2009:61) claims that entanglement

> ... advances the thesis, advocated here, that the European colonial encounter with Indigenous communities was a variant of the larger concept of cultural contact. While the history of European colonialism has its own character, it is not the only example of colonial contact or fundamentally different from contact between Indigenous communities themselves.

For Martindale, entanglement centers the focus more on cultural entanglement rather than colonial entanglement, but set within Indigenous structural histories and object relations and their culturally situated abilities to "tinker." He uses this as an entry point for topics such as resistance, autonomy, resilience, and identity (Martindale 2009:61).

Third, Jordan (2009, 2014) joined the discussion by drawing heavily on Alexander (1998) to advocate a focus on *cultural entanglement*. The adjective is important, as it intentionally creates a distinction vis-à-vis "colonial entanglement." He uses this to characterize relationships between Europeans and Native Americans, broadly defined, that are more involved and layered than mere "contact" would suggest but, at the same time, display more autonomy and power equity between groups than colonialism might normally entail. His proposal not only highlights, again, the nature of entanglement linking people, places, and things and a need to consider intercultural interactions (especially those outside of domination), but also tries to propose a category of "cultural entanglement" that can be distinguished from outright colonialism. Following Alexander (1998), Jordan undertakes this latter move to counter both notions of analytically and politically neutralized notions of "culture contact" and seemingly deterministic and retroactive attributions of colonialism with its unequal power relations, dispossession, and territorial and demographic overturns. Jordan (2009) wants more attention to contexts that were not explicitly colonial at the time, even if they became such later, so that those who engage with social, political, and economic processes can better understand them on their own terms. For him, entanglement is both metaphor and model.

This summary has been brief, largely because the use of entanglement in the archaeology of colonialism has itself been brief and not particularly uniform. It does, however, begin to resolve the question of whether entanglement has been metaphor, model, or method. To date, it has been largely metaphor, a use that gives it flexibility to describe process but also an inability to offer sharp analytical clarity. A few archaeologists have tried to develop an actual model, albeit one mobilized by the metaphor of entanglement, but in doing so they have not articulated an explicit theory of or about entanglement and have instead created a category in a continuum of political economic and interaction models (Alexander 1998; Jordan 2009). Their use reduces its flexibility as a heuristic, but clarifies it as an analytical device, especially if one wants to avoid applying the term "colonialism" to all interactions between Europeans and Indigenous people. The next step is to consider how or if these have advanced archaeological studies of colonialism and indigeneity.

Entanglement as Model

Only Jordan (2009, 2014) and Alexander (1998) trend toward model building in the archaeology of colonialism, although Stockhammer (2012), apparently rather independently given his lack of reference to the others, has recently proposed two "states" of cultural entanglement—relational and material—that would apply to processes by which alien objects are brought into a cultural context that may or may not be colonial. As currently conceived, the proposal of "cultural entanglement" has both potentials and problems for the study of colonialism, which is its rightful disciplinary home even if its proponents draw a distinction. On the positive side, Jordan's (2009, 2014) conceptual discussions help to ensure that contexts that are eventually deemed colonial are not considered so from the beginning, at least not necessarily. This prevents retrodicting the outcome as an immutable trajectory from select features in the past and asks instead that we consider the multiplicity of paths forward from those times that social actors had to consider. It reminds us that not everything in the past is on a linear trajectory to the present. For example, Kulisheck (2010) argues similarly that population decline and increase among the Pueblos and Navajos in New Mexico need to be understood from their past going forward rather than from a projection backward from an assumed "endpoint" of major demographic collapse. In addition to power and temporal context, Jordan's (2009, 2014) perspective on entanglement also better accounts for complexity in the interstices between categories of "colonizer" and "colonized" to avoid stereotyped perceptions of power and colonial inevitability.

On the other hand, Jordan's (2009, 2014) conceptualization poses problems since it takes a process of entanglement and moves it closer to an actual category. Labeling some of these supposed "no-longer-contact" and "not-yet-colonial" contexts as entanglement confuses two different valences: carrying forward colonialism and actively colonizing. Much of Jordan's concerns are about not projecting the latter onto the situations when those who wanted or tried to colonize did not have the power to make it actually happen. However, the former can be understood in a variety of ways that makes many of the situations Jordan labels as "cultural entanglement" actually worth calling colonialism. Thomas's (1994) notion of "colonial projects" captures this meaning when he argues that Europeans and Indigenous people alike often did not know what the consequences of their actions—trade, intimacy, settlement, conflict, alliance—would be. They often did not even think to consider themselves as either "oppressive colonizers" or "dominated colonized." For example, the Mohegan and Narragansett warriors who sided with the English in their 1636 attack on the Pequot village at Mystic in what is now southern Connecticut did not participate as the "colonizers" or as the "colonized," but they certainly participated in a "colonial project" that had long-term ramifications. Colonialism is not simply top down, European driven, and ubiquitously powerful in its process. Colonialism happens because of both colonizer and colonized—the duality is required (but see below)—rather than simply because of the imposition of colonial rule. Moreover, we must remember that the mere presence of Europeans in the American landscape resulted from acts of colonization and often explicit crown and mercantile efforts at colonizing, whether at the metropole or on the frontier. We proceed perilously if we do not situate these cases within that context.

Finally, turning process into category may create a stumbling block. We face the dilemma of asking when cultural entanglement ends and colonialism begins, much like that interrogated already for the "contact period" (Silliman 2005:62). My suspicion is that this break will be hard to identify, despite Jordan's (2014) optimism about being able to make the analytical distinction between cultural entanglement and colonialism. Besides, we can surely expect cultural entanglement to continue, even the kind outlined by Jordan, within even the later stages of colonialism. In addition, we run the risk of isolating archaeology from other disciplines as earlier terminologies of "culture contact" did (e.g., Silliman 2005:62–63). Just as there are no longer (if ever) "contact period" studies in other disciplines such as history, comparative literature, material culture studies, and sociology after the demise of acculturation approaches, there are also no "cultural entanglement" studies either. Instead, the processes that Jordan (2009, 2014) highlights already exist as topics within studies of colonialism, and we should encourage more interdisciplinary dialogue about processes and patterns of entanglement therein. He has done well to draw attention to them, much like Dietler (1998, 2010), but at the level of political economy rather than consumption.

Entanglement as Metaphor

Thus far, entanglement has worked best in archaeology as a metaphor to capture the nature of particular processes and interactions in the past. It has not offered solid theoretical advancement on its own, but when coupled with other perspectives such as those on practice and postcolonialism, it can provide a useful heuristic to open up new lines of inquiry.[1] For instance, Martindale's (2009) argument for "contact-as-entanglement" acknowledges cultural processes operating at different material, temporal, and cultural scales, which situates colonialism and contact in ongoing trajectories in Indigenous societies (see also Hart et al. 2012). In addition, entanglement has been and may continue to be a useful way to avoid a trap lingering in the notion of shared histories, to highlight the limitations of dichotomous categories that derive from colonialism itself, and to provide a likely better alternative than hybridity to talk about process rather than product. These are considered in more depth below.

Entanglement may provide a better term for the process otherwise inherent in the Australian notion of "shared" histories. Both are about intersection, overlap, and intertwinement in realms such as material culture, land, labor, and national narratives of history, but entanglement as a term—not a model—may prove more effective. For one, *entanglement* implies messiness, potential entrapment, and the weaving together of strands, whereas *sharing* could be interpreted as more equitable in its give-and-take and more about hybridization to produce something more singular. Entanglement as a metaphor can result in a variety of terminological/conceptual outcomes such as unraveling, trapping, strengthening, burdening, and even choking, but sharing tends to not offer permutations other than sharing/not-sharing. Admittedly, not a single one of its academic proponents has been guilty of this flattening (e.g., Byrne 2003; Harrison 2004; Murray 1996, 2004), and I do not have any problems with its usage. I merely consider here the different options provided by the two terms since the potentials for different understandings and permutations of these metaphors by other archaeologists, politicians, and the general public are worth considering.

Entanglement has served a useful terminological purpose in its ability—not uniquely, but among more direct terms and critiques—to highlight the problems of dichotomous thinking that have hindered archaeological understandings of colonialism and the experience of Indigenous people therein. Advances have been made in recent years on this problem, with archaeologists tackling a variety of classic binarism such as Native/European (Loren 2008; Silliman 2009), colonized/colonizer (Dietler 2010; Given 2004; Liebmann 2010; Loren 2008; Voss 2005, 2008), change/continuity (Ferris 2009; Silliman 2009, 2012), and prehistory/history (Hart et al. 2012; Lightfoot 1995; Schmidt and Mrozowski 2013; Scheiber and Mitchell 2010). Many of these critiques have sprung, in part, from explicit and implicit recognitions of entanglement.

The problem with such dualistic thinking is that even though these states or categories may be analytically useful at certain moments or may have even had salience for people negotiating their own historical times, these opposing states are not natural, nor are they required. Lives, objects, and things are more entangled than dichotomies can express. Instead, we have developed them, now and in the past, to account for and to create difference in politics and analytics. Like the proverbial "two sides of the coin," we treat these kinds of categories in an either/or way. An artifact is either Native or European, a practice is either indigenous or colonial, a site component is either historic or prehistoric, a culture shows either change or continuity: heads or tails.

Yet, as historical archaeologists especially can appreciate, a coin is not composed of two sides. It is one object; one with two distinct faces, but also with a circumferential face as well. And the two primary faces are not separate; they connect through the center of the coin in the same materiality. That connection—a kind of material and ontological entanglement—is as fundamental to the coin as the two faces. The ability to only see one face at a time is a problem of perspective, not a problem for the coin's character or for the existence or necessity of the other face. It is not about which face we see depending on our analytical perspective, or about reducing someone or something as the obverse of the other since that only reifies the dichotomy, or about just repeatedly flipping over the coin. It is more about the totality of the coin itself; that is, how the different sides connect and structure the other while also recognizing difference across and within the context. The components of the dichotomies mentioned before—Native/European, colonized/colonizer, change/continuity, and prehistory/history—exist in relation to one another,[2] and we must account for that coexistence, not just in how we interpret such things in the past, but also in how we structure our interpretations of that past. This is entanglement at its most fundamental.

The critique of dichotomies has been successful in part because of the concept of hybridity, which has flourished a bit more in the archaeologies of colonialism than has the slightly less developed idea of entanglement. They do have some overlap in purpose and origin: both surfaced in postcolonial theory developed by Thomas (1991, 1994) and Bhabha (1994), among others, but they have different referents. In other words, hybridity and entanglement can both serve to highlight problems of interpretation and to emphasize intersection, but they are not interchangeable. In fact, Stockhammer (2012, 2013) argues that cultural hybridization should be replaced by entanglement.

Hybridity has its origin in several different theoretical trajectories such as evolutionary biology, actor-network theory, and postcolonialism (Silliman 2013, 2015). This eclectic mix has produced a concept that has considerable slippage and disunity, despite its initial promise to describe people, practices, and things that elude simple characterization within binary categories and that may be liminal rather than essential as they transgress those binarisms. For that it should be commended, especially when properly situated in postcolonial theory. For example, Liebmann (2008:5) defines hybridity in an archaeological context as the "new, transcultural forms produced through colonization that cannot be neatly classified into a single cultural or ethnic category." Here, hybridity permits the rethinking of dualities, and it demonstrates that leaving behind dichotomies does not require leaving behind difference or a kind of Bhabhian "thirdspace."

Where hybridity fails in archaeological analysis, though, is its potential creation of an untenable category, much like the problem facing "cultural entanglement" (Silliman 2015). Once something or someone has become a hybrid—a mixture of two or more previous states, a new entanglement—how long does it retain that status? Is everything not falling into old dichotomous categories still a hybrid, even today? How does a hybrid then become an "authentic" state from which to hybridize again, and does it do so as a segment of a new dichotomy? For example, how does one handle the projectile point made with lithic technology using bottle glass? It can be described as a hybrid object resulting from hybrid technological and cultural practices in certain circumstances, but are *all* glass points hybrids from this origin onward? This reveals the problem with interpretive applications of hybridity; that is, reifying the dichotomies it seeks to resolve. Ultimately, the larger problem facing hybridity is its reliance on a biological metaphor, its potential rendering of all processes of colonialism as cultural ones (Dietler 2010:52), and its tendency to accentuate the phenomenon of "mixture" (Stockhammer 2012:46).

I have proposed some resolution to this conceptual predicament elsewhere (Silliman 2015), but similar to Stockhammer (2012), I want to suggest here that a heuristic of entanglement may provide a better alternative to hybridity, even though the latter currently carries more theoretical backing. Unlike hybridity, entanglement can provide a view of how things, peoples, and practices intertwine to produce new forms without requiring them to remain that way, and without applying a term to the product that binds it to an entangled state (e.g., a "hybrid"[3] versus a "tangle"). This is a good lexical prohibition to keep interpretation out of problematic realms. Instead, one discusses components—both practical and narrative—in processes of entanglement: ones that intersect, come apart, braid together, and venture in new directions with and without other intertwined strands. In addition, knowing that everything can be entangled (in different ways, of course) is a helpful starting point for analysis to trace lineages and connections, but finding that everything is hybridizing could create categories that rely on "purer" antecedents and that are often considered "less than one and double" (Bhabha 1994:139). Entanglement permits different starting and ending points depending on the question asked, but hybridity usually requires clear starting points to identify something before and after hybridization. Moreover, entanglement, as opposed to hybridity, may better draw out the analytical potential of the metaphor of "roots and routes" introduced first by Clifford (1994, 1997) and critically examined or applied by Friedman (2002), Hauser (2011) and Liebmann (2008). It can do this by addressing the routes of entanglement, rather the roots of hybridization, without getting caught in the celebration of movement and unrootedness of transnationalism (see Friedman 2002).

Entanglement as Method and Theory

As the review of entanglement has highlighted thus far, the successes of the term and associated ideas have been primarily in the realm of metaphor. So far, it has not worked as a true theory or model; it has not provided a clear method, either. This could be a healthy and helpful conclusion, knowing that we should use the word to describe, guide, criticize, interrogate, and represent the past, but perhaps should not look to it to help explain, interpret, or categorize it. However, Hodder (2011, 2012) argues that a kind of "entanglement theory" could be a panacea for archaeological method and theory and could help unify what he feels are disparate and limited theoretical realms ranging across agency, practice, evolution, history, and network approaches. This has involved both a theoretical program about things and people—including their relationships, networks, affordances, dependences, and dependencies—and a methodological perspective on how to identify and trace those dimensions through what he calls "tanglegrams." I conclude this chapter by considering the possibilities and prospects of such a proposal for the archaeologies of colonialism, which is an area he mentions briefly in his work to develop these particular ideas. Will it offer helpful method and theory, or perhaps just an accentuation of the entanglement metaphor?

Applying Hodder's entanglement model fully to an archaeological case study of colonialism to check its applicability and robustness is not possible in the short space of a chapter, so I opt instead to draw out some of its implications and inspirations as they have helped me better refine my own use of entanglement as an analytical device. Three key aspects of Hodder's approach have heuristic value, at least for archaeologies of colonialism, beyond his own suggestion that the entanglement approach can remedy some problems with yet another dichotomy plaguing research on colonialism: domination/resistance (Hodder 2012:222). First, the entanglement idea situates things (literal and figurative) in their proper place in social life, in the physical world, and in social theory. It pays attentions to object worlds, how they depend on and are depended on by other things and people, and what they afford. Second, it calls attention to networks and relationships. In some ways, this aspect parallels other approaches to colonialism that have favored an orientation to social and global networks (Orser 1996), but it differs in its insistence that networks are not, in the end, the final locus of analysis. Third, it historicizes things by tracing out their lineages, intersections, and tautness of relations with other things and people. For those who have appreciated approaches on the biography of things (e.g., Turgeon 1997), this may have some resonance.

The latter two elements have been considered in archaeologies of colonialism in a variety of frameworks, and Hodder's proposition may further promote these particular realms of study by refining the language used to describe and represent them. The discussion of affordances, however, is a more novel introduction, one that I would like to push further here to see if it might bring clarity to particular kinds of entanglements. The concept of affordances draws upon the early work in ecological psychology and perception developed by Gibson (1979), but Hodder has revisited this to make it resonate with the material and the social. Affordances are simply what the material world and the objects within it make possible, an idea that takes on particular meaning in Hodder's theory of entanglement because it returns attention to "thingness." It may be a simple definition, but it encourages an important observation. I consider it here with respect to the search for identities in the entanglements of Indigenous people and colonialism.

A highlight of the archaeology of colonialism, from its origins in acculturation approaches of the early twentieth century to its postcolonial manifestations of the last 20 years, has been a focus on identity. Earlier interpretive attempts assumed that objects reflected existing identities—usually cultural—that could be indexed in their strength and trajectory by material culture.

More recent attempts posit that identities are made in the context of material culture and seek to find their active expressions in the object worlds that people inhabit by choice and by force. Normally in the archaeological study of colonialism, these are framed in a context of dichotomy: things, people, and practices are Native American/Indigenous/colonized/subaltern or European/colonizer/dominant. Thanks to postcolonial thinking, and now the infusion of ideas of entanglement described in this chapter, these binarisms are being carefully unpacked. A notion of affordances permits that kind of rethinking in a unique way.

In the rush to assign identities to archaeological remains, archaeologists frequently overstep their reach, particularly when studying Indigenous people in colonial contexts. Archaeologists tend to assume that social identity, especially cultural identity, had a significant influence on an individual's choices to use a particular object, and that particular artifacts had cultural identities of their own based on the origin of manufacture or original use (e.g., stone tools are Native American, whereas factory-produced ceramics are European). These assumptions work in some instances, but they cannot be assumed universally or even considered sufficient since they do not attend to the entanglements that permeate them (see Silliman 2009). The transgressions of these assumed dichotomies by people in the past—such as Native Americans using pottery made in England or adorning themselves with glass beads from Italy, or Spanish settlers using corn and Italians adopting the tomato into their cuisine—are not the "exceptions that prove the rule." Instead, they reveal its fundamental flaws.

What if people do not always choose objects as a result of their identities or, more interestingly, sometimes actually choose them *despite* those identities and object origins? What if they choose items for practices that these things first and foremost *afford*, especially in contexts when people lose control over production, distribution, and access of material items, as happens in many colonial contexts around the world? Archaeologists have to remember that identities do not inhere in objects, that these objects do not afford identity in a straightforward way, and that identity is not always directive even when informative. Instead, objects afford practices of consumption, like that argued by Dietler (2010) and somewhat by Stockhammer (2012), and these can be brought into or narrated as part of identity. Rather than assuming that ceramic and glass vessels from Europe were first and foremost European objects in the hands and lives of Native Americans (and labeling them as such when they come out of the ground during excavation and move through laboratory analysis), entanglement perspectives leave this as a question to be answered by first asking a different question. Instead of asking "Who is this?" (or "Whose is this?") to the archaeological materials that filled out people's lives, archaeologists should ask "What did these objects afford?" and "Is 'who' part of that affordance?"

This leads more directly to answers about preparing food, storing food and drink, feeding families, serving guests, decorating tables and shelves, having access to market goods rather than relying on local production, passing down heirlooms, acquiring raw material for other purposes, producing trash that requires disposal, and many other dimensions. All of these can be considered entanglements. For example, perhaps using a store-bought ceramic bowl from England permitted the same cooking of shellfish for a Native American household as did hand-crafted, low-fired ceramics in an earlier generation, and maybe in those cases cooking and eating shellfish meant more than the bowls in which they were prepared. Perhaps in a surprising cost-benefit way, these particular consumption practices then afforded time or energy for other pressing tasks. This is hypothetical, of course, but it encourages a different thinking about entanglement. If materials afford practices, if different materials can afford the same practices, and if practices anchor identity more than simply objects themselves, then this builds up interpretation more properly, often starting with the "thingness" of objects as Hodder (2012) has advocated, but anchoring it in the practices that employ those things.

Affordance may yet offer another insight into past entanglements and colonialism, yet in a somewhat counter temporal way to that advocated by Hodder (2012) but somewhat more akin to Jordan's (2009, 2014) perspective on cultural entanglement. Piecing together networks and affordances in a tanglegram offers a strong method for delineating how the past "moved forward" in and because of its entanglements, but an idea of affordances also points toward the usefulness of not simply looking back from already concluded lineages of entanglement, but also looking forward from past moments from the perspective of those embarking on—or rather making—those lineages. If we orient to affordances as the possibilities of objects, archaeologists are encouraged to think about not only what *actually* happened in the past, but also about what *could have* happened. This does not mean an exercise in a kind of "what if" history with "alternate endings," but rather is an explicit attempt to ascertain what social actors could have or could not have done with the affordances in their social and physical environment. Entanglements are not simply about ever-increasing bundles, but sometimes about choking out and truncating particular trajectories. People tend to do only a small range of actions afforded by things in their environment. Knowing these options at any given moment gives more direct access to choice among alternatives, which I feel is a stronger basis for understanding agency as the ability to act otherwise, rather than agency as "simply the ever-present force of things: the life force of humans and all organic things, and the forces of attraction, repulsion, etc., of all material things and their interactions" (Hodder 2012:215). An idea about affordances may help to identify what those "otherwise" options were.

Subsequently, the affordances and the agencies enacted around objects may lead to new entanglements. A relevant example is the ways that Indigenous people in the sixteenth through nineteenth centuries engaged with and frequently developed dependencies on mass-produced "Old World" consumer goods such as ceramic vessels, metal tools, and glass bottles. Choosing to add novel objects to material practices and technologies, especially those substituting for more local craft products, can lead to entanglements at different scales. Spatially, people become distanced from the production of these goods, and they must rely on systems of credit, markets, and distributors. This is nothing new to students of capitalism and alienation, but it does add a perspective on the practicality of entanglements on the ground that led to broader enmeshments. Longitudinally, these new goods entrap subsequent actions that archaeologists often identify as both change and continuity. They may work against preservation of craft traditions and technical knowledge systems, which sets up a likelihood of cultural change, but they may be adopted and encouraged because they solve particular material, technological, or social problems pertinent to a cultural context, which establishes a way for these new goods to promote continuity. This demonstrates permutations of effective "fittingness" (Hodder 2012) and "tinkering" (Martindale 2009).

However, many of these dimensions play out only in the moments of adoption, not in the entanglements that develop as a result. Children who engage with what were new items for their parents tend to treat them as their own items, as ones without different histories or origins at least as far as their own life histories are concerned. This promotes intergenerational strands of continuity rather than stark breaks of change (see Silliman 2009), or what might be a function of the "forgetness of things": the hiding of the entanglements that make them possible or accessible (see Hodder 2012). Ideas of entanglement permit some puncturing of the politics that surround such assessments of cultural trajectories by equalizing the frameworks of comparison. Consider how many Native Americans were "changing" (or worse, becoming less "Indian") according to archaeologists, historians, and the general public when they adopted beef or wheat into their diets in the late eighteenth century, whereas Italians of the same time period were supposedly becoming more "Italian" as they developed tomato-based sauces from this New World (or Native American) vegetable-like fruit. If treated as entanglements, these become much easier to view as comparable cultural processes involving large networks, individual practices, material limitations and opportunities, and a globalizing world.

Despite the positive aspects of Hodder's (2012) entanglement ideas outlined here, I do worry about importing the perspective wholesale given some unresolved problems. Some of these are particularly relevant to archaeologies of colonialism. First, although his proposition is to create a "theory of things" or a "theory of entanglement," the model falls short of well-defined theory because, ironically, of its far reach. It does not offer clear ways to evaluate or resolve discrepancies or trajectories, relying mainly on inductive data gathering and entanglement tracing. In this way, it may revert to being primarily a heuristic instead of a theory. Second, the otherwise rigorous and expansive methodology of tracing as many entanglements as possible leads to a conceptual impasse. Although all entanglements might be discernible, not all of them matter. Yet, the theory offers no guide to identify those that do and those that do not. Just because connections can be found—and likely in superabundance—does not mean that they each deserve the same analytical attention. This is particularly true in the study of colonialism, given its powerful legacies in the contemporary world. Third, too much emphasis on entanglements and networks could result in decentering the things themselves, and, particularly, the people who activated and gave meaning to those objects through their practices. It has taken some time to restore the dignity and agency of Indigenous people struggling with and negotiating colonial worlds, and certain models of entanglement disempower by distributing the drive of those struggles and negotiations into a variety of human-object relations represented by formulas. Fourth, my worry is that an overemphasis on entanglement *as theory* in colonial contexts, even when these might be some of the most entangled in all of the millennia of human history, could produce the undesirable effect of minimizing difference in place of ever-growing intertwinements. We do not want more entanglement to translate simply into more mixing or (as is often rendered in problematic political turns) more homogeneity, an outcome I have cautioned could result in a "short purée" model (Silliman 2012). Entanglement can produce discourses and practices of differentiation as much as it can promote sharing, overlap, and networking.

Conclusion

Although the dimensions and applications of entanglement are still in their infancy, in large part due to intermittent use and development in only two decades, the idea of entanglement has brought new insights, refined methods, and theoretical clarification to archaeology generally and to archaeologies of colonialism specifically. Entanglement has proven to be an effective metaphor and useful heuristic for thinking about the many intersections of people and things, especially the intersections that come about when the local meets the nonlocal, the unfamiliar, the alien. It has accentuated networks and linkages, put practices and consumption in the forefront, given objects their rightful materiality but diminished their uncritically assumed identities, demonstrated further that dichotomies are problematic ways to think, and improved upon hybridity and its problematic attribution of mixture to people and objects. Here may lay a real power of entanglement ideas for studies of indigeneity and colonialism. Much more so than the loose notions of mixture present within hybridity, heavy frameworks of colonialism, overweighted politics of identity, or even the uncritically valued poles of change and continuity, entanglement may permit a clearer view of cultural persistence because of the weaving and unweaving of strands in ongoing practices that acknowledge both routes and roots.

At the same time, entanglement has provided an ambiguous concept with an uncertain future as both method and theory. Hodder (2012), Jordan (2009, 2014), and Stockhammer (2012) seek to move entanglement from metaphor to actual model, albeit from different theoretical foundations and for different interpretive reasons, but the path is not yet clear. This might be a case where too much attention to semantics could detract from interpretive work and analytical clarity. That is to say, we may not want to spend too much time unpacking the word if its role is mainly to guide rather than explain. Entanglement does not need to develop as a precise theoretical term to remain useful, nor should it become a particular category of events, things, or people. As a metaphor, it simply works to draw attention to other issues that require close theoretical attention. With a nod to Claude Lévi-Strauss: entanglement may be good to think and good to think with.

Notes

1. However, not all agree. The first time that I presented on this topic of colonialism and entanglement prior to the publication of my 2005 article, the discussant for the session hinted that "entanglement" had limited utility since it mainly reminded him of the contents of his sock drawer.
2. I mean simply that dichotomous thinking requires dichotomous categories. I do not imply here at all that Indigenous people and their unique cultures and long-term histories somehow exist only in relation to Europeans and their colonial efforts. They can be studied in their own right, sometimes using colonialism as only one inflection on their historical curve (e.g., Hart et al. 2012; Scheiber and Mitchell 2010). Instead, I mean that in studying colonialism with its various participants, victims, proponents, etc., we have to be cautious not to dichotomize what are otherwise messy, intersecting relations of material culture, bodies, land, and many other dimensions. Labeling people as "the colonized" or "Native American" may not even capture their own historical realities and identities.
3. This not universally true, of course, among critical scholars. Friedman (2002:24) notes that hybridity is not a real state for people in the past: "This hybridity is simply *our* identification of 'matter out of place,' *hybrids-for-us*" (emphasis in original). Similarly, Liebmann (2008:85; see also Liebmann 2015) comments that "Hybridity is not an ethnographic object in and of itself but, rather, a theoretical lens that can prove useful for viewing familiar ethnographic objects in a new light." Yet the tendency remains for anthropological identifications of hybridity to generate in museums and the public eye the notion of actual and identifiable hybrid things, people, and cultures in the past.

References

Alexander, Rani T., 1998. Afterword: Toward an Archaeological Theory of Culture Contact. In *Studies in Culture Contact: Interaction, Culture Change, and Archaeology*, edited by James G. Cusick, pp. 476–495. Center for Archaeological Investigations, Southern Illinois University, Carbondale.

Bhabha, Homi, 1994. *The Location of Culture*. Routledge, New York.

Byrne, Denis, 2003. The Ethos of Return: Erasure and Reinstatement of Aboriginal Visibility in the Australian Historical Landscape. *Historical Archaeology* 37(1):73–86.

Clifford, James, 1994. Further Inflections: Toward Ethnographies of the Future. *Cultural Anthropology* 9(3):302–338.

Clifford, James, 1997. *Routes: Travel and Translation in the Late Twentieth Century*. Harvard University Press, Cambridge, MA.

Cobb, Charles, and Diana DiPaolo Loren, 2008. The Earth of the Modern. *Archaeologies* 4(1):11–23.

Cusick, James G., ed., 1998. *Studies in Culture Contact: Interaction, Culture Change, and Archaeology*. Center for Archaeological Investigations, Southern Illinois University, Carbondale.

Dietler, Michael, 1998. Consumption, Agency, and Cultural Entanglement: Theoretical Implications of a Mediterranean Colonial Encounter. In *Studies in Culture Contact: Interaction, Culture Change, and Archaeology*, edited by James G. Cusick, pp. 288–315. Center for Archaeological Investigations, Southern Illinois University, Carbondale.

Dietler, Michael, 2010. *Archaeologies of Colonialism: Consumption, Entanglement, and Violence in Ancient Mediterranean France*. University of California Press, Berkeley.

Ferris, Neal, 2009. *The Archaeology of Native-Lived Colonialism: Challenging History in the Great Lakes*. University of Arizona Press, Tucson.

Friedman, Jonathan, 2002. From Roots to Routes: Tropes for Trippers. *Anthropological Theory* 2(1):21–36.

Gibson, James J., 1979. *The Ecological Approach to Visual Perception*. Houghton Mifflin, Boston, MA.

Given, Michael, 2004. *The Archaeology of the Colonized*. Routledge, London.

Gosden, Chris, 2004. *Archaeology and Colonialism: Cultural Contact from 5000 BC to the Present*. Cambridge University Press, Cambridge, UK.

Harrison, Rodney, 2004. Shared Histories and the Archaeology of the Pastoral Industry in Australia. In *After Captain Cook: The Archaeology of the Recent Indigenous Past in Australia*, edited by Rodney Harrison and Christine Williamson, pp. 37–58. AltaMira Press, Walnut Creek, CA.

Hart, Siobhan M., Maxine Oland, and Liam Frink, eds., 2012. *Decolonizing Indigenous Histories: Exploring "Prehistoric/Colonial" Transitions in Archaeology*. University of Arizona Press, Tucson.

Hauser, Mark, 2011. Routes and Roots of Empire: Pots, Power, and Slavery in the 18th-century British Caribbean. *American Anthropologist* 113(3):431–447.

Hodder, Ian, 2011. Human-Thing Entanglement: Towards an Integrated Archaeological Perspective. *Journal of the Royal Anthropological Institute* 17(1):154–177.

Hodder, Ian, 2012. *Entangled: An Archaeology of the Relationships Between Humans and Things*. Wiley-Blackwell, Malden, MA.

Jordan, Kurt A., 2009. Colonies, Colonialism, and Cultural Entanglement: The Archaeology of Postcolumbian Intercultural Relations. In *International Handbook of Historical Archaeology*, edited by Teresita Majewski and David Gaimster, pp. 31–59. Springer, New York.

Jordan, Kurt A., 2014. Pruning Colonialism: Vantage Point, Local Political Economy, and Cultural Entanglement in the Archaeology of Post-1415 Indigenous Peoples. In *Rethinking Colonial Pasts Through Archaeology*, edited by Neal Ferris, Rodney Harrison, and Michael Wilcox, pp. 103–120. Oxford University Press, Oxford, UK.

Kulisheck, Jeremy, 2010. "Like Butterflies on a Mounting Board:" Pueblo Mobility and Demography before 1825. In *Across a Great Divide: Continuity and Change in Native North American Societies, A.D. 1400–1900*, edited by Laura S. Scheiber and Mark Mitchell, pp. 258–276. Amerind Studies in Archaeology 4. University of Arizona Press, Tucson.

Liebmann, Matthew, 2008. Postcolonial Cultural Affiliations: Essentialism, Hybridity, and NAGPRA. In *Archaeology and the Postcolonial Critique*, edited by Matthew Liebmann and Uzma Z. Rizvi, pp. 73–90. AltaMira Press, Lanham, MD.

Liebmann, Matthew, 2010. The Best of Times, the Worst of Times: Pueblo Resistance and Accommodation during the Spanish *Reconquista* of New Mexico. In *Enduring Conquests: Rethinking the Archaeology of Resistance to Spanish Colonialism in the Americas*, edited by Matthew Liebmann and Melissa S. Murphy, pp. 199–221. School for Advanced Research Press, Santa Fe, NM.

Liebmann, Matthew J., 2015. The Mickey Mouse Kachina and Other "Double Objects": Hybridity in the Material Culture of Colonial Encounters. *Journal of Social Archaeology*. 15:319–341.

Lightfoot, Kent G., 1995. Culture Contact Studies: Redefining the Relationship between Prehistoric and Historical Archaeology. *American Antiquity* 60(2):199–217.

Loren, Diana DiPaolo, 2008. *In Contact: Bodies and Spaces in the Sixteenth- and Seventeenth-Century Eastern Woodlands*. Rowan & Littlefield, Lanham, MD.

Martindale, Andrew, 2009. Entanglement and Tinkering: Structural History in the Archaeology of the Northern Tsimshian. *Journal of Social Archaeology* 9(1):59–91.

Murray, Tim, 1996. Contact Archaeology: Shared Histories? Shared Identities? In *SITES: Nailing the Debate: Archaeology and Interpretation in Museums*, pp. 201–213. Museum of Sydney, Sydney, Australia.

Murray, Tim, 2004. The Archaeology of Contact in Settler Societies. In *The Archaeology of Contact in Settler Societies*, edited by Tim Murray, pp. 1–16. Cambridge University Press, Cambridge, UK.

Orser, Charles E., 1996. *A Historical Archaeology of the Modern World.* Plenum Press, New York.

Paterson, Alistair G., 2008. *The Lost Legions: Cultural Contact in Colonial Australia.* AltaMira Press, Lanham, MD.

Quimby, Frank, 2011. The Hierro Commerce: Culture Contact, Appropriation and Colonial Entanglement in the Marianas, 1521–1668. *The Journal of Pacific History* 46(1):1–26.

Scheiber, Laura S. and Mark Mitchell, eds., 2010. *Across a Great Divide: Continuity and Change in Native North American Societies, A.D. 1400–1900*. Amerind Studies in Archaeology 4. University of Arizona Press, Tucson.

Schmidt, Peter R., and Stephen A. Mrozowski, eds., 2013. *The Death of Prehistory*. Oxford University Press, Oxford, UK.

Silliman, Stephen W., 2005. Culture Contact or Colonialism? Challenges in the Archaeology of Native North America. *American Antiquity* 70(1):55–74.

Silliman, Stephen W., 2009. Change and Continuity, Practice and Memory: Native American Persistence in Colonial New England. *American Antiquity* 74(2):211–230.

Silliman, Stephen W., 2012. Between the Longue Durée and the Short Purée: Postcolonial Archaeologies of Indigenous History in Colonial North America. In *Decolonizing Indigenous Histories: Exploring "Prehistoric/Colonial" Transitions in Archaeology*, edited by Siobhan M. Hart, Maxine Oland, and Liam Frink, pp. 113–132. University of Arizona Press, Tucson.

Silliman, Stephen W., 2013. What, Where and When Is Hybridity? In *The Archaeology of Hybrid Material Culture*, edited by Jeb Card, pp. 486–500. Center for Archaeological Investigations, Southern Illinois University, Carbondale, IL.

Silliman, Stephen W., 2015. A Requiem for Hybridity? The Problem with Frankensteins, Purées, and Mules. *Journal of Social Archaeology*. 15:277–298.

Spicer, Edward H., 1961. Types of Contact and Processes of Change. In *Perspectives in American Indian Culture Change*, edited by Edward H. Spicer, pp. 517–544. University of Chicago Press, Chicago, IL.

Stahl, Ann B., 2002. Colonial Entanglements and the Practices of Taste: An Alternative to Logocentric Approaches. *American Anthropologist* 104(3):827–845.

Stockhammer, Philipp Wolfgang, 2012. Conceptualizing Cultural Hybridization in Archaeology. In *Conceptualizing Cultural Hybridization: A Transdisciplinary Approach*, edited by Philipp Wolfgang Stockhammer, pp. 43–58. Springer, New York.

Stockhammer, Philipp Wolfgang, 2013. From Hybridity to Entanglement, from Essentialism to Practice. *Archaeological Review from Cambridge* 28:11–28.

Thomas, Nicholas, 1991. *Entangled Objects: Exchange, Material Culture, and Colonialism in the Pacific.* Harvard University Press, Cambridge, MA.

Thomas, Nicholas, 1994. *Colonialism's Culture: Anthropology, Travel, and Government.* Princeton University Press, Princeton, NJ.

Turgeon, Laurier, 1997. The Tale of the Kettle: Odyssey of an Intercultural Object. *Ethnohistory* 44 (1):1–29.

Voss, Barbara L., 2005. From Casta to Californio: Social Identity and the Archaeology of Culture Contact. *American Anthropologist* 107(3):461–474.

Voss, Barbara L., 2008. *The Archaeology of Ethnogenesis: Race and Sexuality in Colonial San Francisco*. University of California Press, Berkeley.

Chapter 2

"Is this the Gold that You Eat?" Coins, Entanglement, and Early Colonial Orderings in the Andes (AD 1532–ca. 1650)

Noa Corcoran-Tadd

Introduction

In his influential work on the Spanish conquest of Peru, *The Vision of the Vanquished*, French historian Nathan Wachtel writes, "The introduction of money did not transform the native economy into a monetary economy: it played only a destructive and negative role" (1977:122). Historical anthropologist Karen Spalding comes to a similar conclusion in her ethnohistorical account of colonial Huarochirí: "The expansion of commerce and the growing participation of the members of the Andean communities in the European market system, both through compulsion and through choice, further pushed the fragmentation and eventual dissolution of the Andean rural community" (1984:299).

Yet, despite this apparent impact, Andean historians, anthropologists, and archaeologists all tend to ignore the coins themselves. I respond to this particular lacuna in three ways. First, drawing on the emergent entanglement perspective and postcolonial material culture studies, I outline a theoretical framework with which to situate objects such as coins within their wider colonial context. Second, using archaeological, historical, and modern ethnographic sources, I consider the multiple scales at which coins, colonial subjects, and other actors found themselves increasingly interdependent as the Peruvian viceroyalty began to stabilize. Third, I explore the ways in which these bodies of evidence complicate existing historical understandings of the processes of colonial change in the Andes. In revisiting colonial coinage as a contested material genre that brought together materials, human actors, and regimes of value, this approach hopefully provides an insightful, alternative viewpoint on the uneven processes by which Spanish and indigenous communities became mutually entangled during the early phases of the colonial project.

Archaeology of Entanglement edited by Lindsay Der and Francesca Fernandini, 49–76

Figure 2.1 CONQUEST / GUAINA CAPAC INGA / CANDIA, SPANIARD / Is this the gold that you eat? [*Quechua*] / This is the gold we eat [*Spanish*] / in Cuzco. GKS 2232 4°, Guaman Poma de Ayala, *Nueva corónica y buen gobierno* (1615), p. 369 [371], Drawing 147 (The Inka asks what the Spaniard eats). Reproduced with permission from the Royal Library, Copenhagen, Denmark.

Approaches to Colonial Materials

While much has been written on the discursive practices of the colonial and the complex, contextual negotiations of new hybrid identities (e.g., Bhabha 1990; Mignolo 2005), colonialism is also a fundamentally *material* phenomenon. If one considers Gosden's evocative archaeological redefinition of colonialism as "a particular grip that material culture gets on the minds and bodies of people, moving them across space and attaching them to new values" (2004:3), the interpretive possibilities of the notion of *entanglement* are particularly clear. Evoking an *a priori* mixed world by moving beyond a focus on the "purified" sociocultural domain to consider the heterogeneous connections between people, environments, ideologies, and object worlds, entanglement has proven an

Figure 2.2 NOTARY / NOTARY OF THE MUNICIPAL COUNCIL or royally appointed [official] or receiver of this kingdom / Pay [*Spanish*] / Here you are, sir [*Quechua*] / don Diego de Mendoza, governor of this province / in the provinces. GKS 2232 4°, Guaman Poma de Ayala, *Nueva corónica y buen gobierno* (1615), p. 521 [525], Drawing 210 (The royal administrator's notary receives a payoff from a tributary Indian). With permission from the Royal Library, Copenhagen, Denmark.

increasingly popular metaphor for situations of "culture contact" (e.g., Jordan 2009; Martindale 2009).

It is worth contrasting entanglement with some of the other key metaphors about connection and difference that scholars across the social sciences have used increasingly in the last few decades. The popular models of "creoles" and "creolization" are ultimately linguistic in origin and, with their implications of grammars and lexicons, they still retain a particularly sociocultural flavor. Another favorite metaphor for postcolonial theorists has been the "hybrid," with its biological intimations of mixture and a "neither/nor" logic. A rather different set of authors has tended to favor the "network," an image that emphasizes topological relations with relatively stable connections and often a restricted range of what may considered nodes (see discussion in Latour 1999).

Despite frequently casual use, entanglement arguably has its own characteristics worth clarifying. First, in suggesting a *gathering of material strands* knotted together yet still partly separate, it implies a "both/and" logic that differs, for instance, from other senses of hybridity. Second, the term conveys a sense of *process*: entanglements are always in the process of becoming entangled. Finally, entanglement also hints at some of the ambiguities of human-thing relationships, encouraging a focus on the unintended consequences and, indeed, *entrapments* of material routines and projects (Hodder 2012).

In working through the literatures on entanglement, colonial material culture, and early colonial Peru, several authors stand out as particularly influential. The development of actor-network theory by Latour and others has been an important springboard for thinking about the connections between humans and nonhumans, as well as the dynamics of controversies and breakdowns (Latour 1999, 2005; Law 1994). Preda's examination of material and textual translations of money and markets follows this approach and provides a particularly useful exploration of the mundane "technologies that pervade everyday life, regulating and standardizing the possibilities for human action" (1999:362).

In recent writings, Hodder (2012) has taken a somewhat different approach that considers the unanticipated consequences of our engagements with things, often leading us to entrapment in relations of mutual dependence. Drawing on the Heideggerian notion of the "thing" as a gathering together, Hodder also emphasizes the ways in which things always depend on other things and persons in projects of maintenance, reinforcement, and repair.

Entanglement has also played a growing, if not always fully explicated, role in retheorizing the specific dynamics of colonial encounters. Thomas's (1991) account of evolving entanglements in colonial Melanesia created by the combination of existing social forms, new economic demands, and new "colonial objects" has proved particularly inspirational, while Stahl's (2002) work on the archaeology of consumption and taste in colonial West Africa highlights the multiple spatial and temporal scales of these encounters.

As both Thomas (1991) and Gosden (2004) have noted, a focus on the material side of things leads one to consider the nonlinear aspects of colonial histories. Rather than starting *ab initio*, colonial projects always begin in the middle of things; that is to say, with accumulated entanglements of people, practices, and objects; commitments to pre-existing projects; and flourishing ideas about the values and utilities of certain kinds of persons and materials. Hence, the emergence of a "colonial Andes" must be understood not only in terms of the conjuncture of two worldviews, but also the complex and continued engagement of multiple "things" (e.g., models of divine authority, llamas, swords, human actors, coins). The resulting approach begins to destabilize previous assumptions about self-evident agents and patients (indigenous and Spanish, people and coins) in ways that hopefully provoke a deeper understanding of historical process.

Historical Contexts

Just prior to contact, the central Andes was in a state of considerable flux. Rapidly unified through conquest and the co-option of local elite (the *kurakas*), by 1529 the Inka Empire of Tawantinsuyu was in the throes of a civil war (Andrien 2001). Nevertheless, the achievements of the empire—from a vast network of paved roads and *tambos* (roadside stations) to a complex of tributary labor systems (including the *mita*)—had already had a considerable impact on the region. One of the most striking aspects of Tawantinsuyu, as with earlier Andean societies, was the apparent absence of any market mechanisms. As Murra and others have argued, the imperial polity functioned entirely through institutions of politicized reciprocity and redistribution (La Lone 1982; Murra 1972).

While hardly analogous, Spain was also in the midst of considerable change during this period: following the unification of Castile and Aragon in 1469 and the fall of Granada in 1492, the Spanish state underwent a series of reorganizations that led to what some consider an important forerunner of the modern integrated European state (see Lockhart and Schwartz 1983). With the passing of the Royal Edict of Medina del Campo in 1497, Spanish mints were producing a relatively unified currency of gold, silver, and *vellón* (cheap copper alloy) coinage (Paoletti et al. 2006). These political changes were paralleled by socioeconomic shifts as well: although the nobility remained a significant force in Spanish society, a growing mercantile class was gaining increasing economic clout during this period.

These two worlds began to come together in 1532; although the colonial order in the Andes gradually consolidated through the sixteenth and seventeenth centuries, the earliest phases were punctuated by episodes of civil war (in 1538–1541, 1544–1548, and 1554), indigenous rebellion (in 1539, 1564, and 1572), and overall political uncertainty (Andrien 2001). This was also a period of incredible economic change as the Spanish colonial market system quickly expanded and established itself in burgeoning towns and cities, ports, mining complexes, and rural estates. Following the initial conquest and the accompanying wave of pillaging *huacas* (indigenous sacred objects or places), more permanent economic institutions emerged that increasingly engaged with local communities. Perhaps most important was the collection of tribute through the system of *encomiendas* (grants to Spanish citizens allowing them to appropriate the labor of certain local communities): not only were communities required to provide labor and local products to their *encomendero* masters, but they were also increasingly required to pay with money (Ramírez 1996).

Weekly markets and urban craft production were also increasingly important for Spanish and indigenous communities alike (Ramírez 1995).

The extraction of precious metals was key to this dramatic economic boom: in both Peru and Mexico, "mines provided the basic economic motor" for the early internal colonial economy (Lockhart and Schwartz 1983:146). By the 1540s, mines and mints under the royal monopoly began to appear: the discovery of rich silver deposits at Cerro Rico near Potosí in 1545 provoked further exploration, and royal mints began producing silver coinage at Lima (1568–1588) and Potosí (1576–1825).[1] Convoys (*flotas*) sailed twice a year, bringing European commodities to Peru via Portobello, Panamá, and transporting much of the extracted metal back to Spain.

Further change arrived with Viceroy Francisco de Toledo's reforms in the 1570s, introducing innovations such as a reorganized system of labor tribute (the famous *mita*), the resettlement of indigenous populations into *reducciónes* (formal nucleated settlements), and the "rationalization" of tribute lists, all of which began to increase the state's control over the internal colonial economy. Combined with the introduction of amalgamation (the use of mercury to process silver ore more efficiently) in the 1570s, these changes led to a huge influx of Andean silver bullion and specie into the colonial and European markets. The figures are often staggering: by 1640, the Peruvian mining system was at peak capacity, producing 54% of the world's silver (TePaske 2010).

The social, political, and economic dynamics of the colonial encounter and its legacies in the Andes have proved a persistent and much-debated topic for historians, political economists, and anthropologists. Historians and political economists such as Wachtel and Assadourian have tended to take a globalizing approach by emphasizing "the transformative power of mercantile capitalism that battered Andean communities" (Larson 1995:17) and placing great importance on the moment of rupture "when the Andean world was forcibly incorporated into the Western economic model" (Luque Luque 2005:567; my translation).

This contrasts with the more localizing approaches of historical anthropologists, who have often focused on the "unique structural properties of an Andean social and mental world that seemed impervious to change" (Larson 1995:17). The region is often considered geographically and historically unique, and the pre-conquest central Andes is often understood as a striking case of sociopolitical complexity based on a radically different, nonmarket economic logic (La Lone 1982; Ramírez 1995). This notion of a unique, almost geological Andean pattern of ecological complementarity, moiety divisions, personified mountains, and tenacious traditionalism is often termed *lo andino* and is further rooted within a complex genealogy of nationalist and North American anthropological scholarship in the Andes (Jamieson 2005; Van Buren 1993). In the past 25 years, however, a number of revisionist scholars (e.g., Ramírez 1996; Stern 1995) have begun to question both models by introducing ideas about social agency, cultural hegemony, and coexisting (even hybridizing) economic logics in the colonial Andes.

In the past 30 years, historical archaeologists have engaged substantially with these issues in other regions in the Spanish empire. In her recent review of Spanish colonial archaeology, Van Buren notes an increasing acknowledgement of "the highly variable ways in which people negotiated, embraced, resisted, and were transformed by their incorporation into a new [colonial] world order" (2010:152). And yet, Andean archaeology generally has had little to contribute to these debates. Historical archaeology in the region has had a tendency towards parochialism (Jamieson 2005), with researchers generally focusing on local scales within the historical context of a wider but vague "Spanish colonial project." While much of this research continues to focus on questions of "culture change" and the emergence of new identities (albeit increasingly informed by practice theory and postcolonial perspectives), Van Buren has suggested that "the kind of obsessive concern with identity that has occurred in other fields could inhibit investigation of the multitude of processes that were touched but not determined by the relationship between colonizers and colonized" (2010:159).

One alternative avenue of investigation is clearly refocusing on the multiscalar connections of colonialism, investigating the "environmental factors, economic systems, institutional regulations, and labor and tribute regimes" (Voss 2008:867) of the emerging Spanish colonial order by moving between "the 'small things forgotten' of daily life and particular individuals and the global system of distribution characteristic of modernity" (Hall and Silliman 2006:8). As Mignolo notes, "The current and available production under the name of postcolonial studies ... starts from the 18th century, leaving aside the crucial and constitutive moment of modernity/coloniality that was the 16th century" (2000:xi). Following Mignolo, however, it may be useful to reframe early colonialism as constitutive rather than derivative of an *embryonic* capitalism.

Yet even in more nuanced accounts of European colonialism, certain teleological assumptions often link the narrated past to an implicit present following what Carrier (1992) terms the "Occidentalist" move: the projection of an unchanging, homogenous West. He notes, in particular, the anthropological tendency to equate the Occident with a uniform "market mentality," an approach that marginalizes any other social forms (like gift transactions, black markets, personalized credit relationships) as aberrant and marginal. If even in eighteenth-century Europe "capital was what it was in relation to a noncapitalism of immense proportions" (Braudel 1984b:239), the dichotomies of "medieval" and "modern," the Old World and the New World, are insufficiently discriminating to characterize the complexities of a period and a set of social processes in flux. While scholars have begun to explore this problem in more general and abstract terms, it also requires more detailed studies of the localized manifestations of this "former topology of capitalism" (Braudel 1984b:239).

Part of the problem here is that a traditional model of "modernity" as singular moment of rupture is inherent to many of the key social science texts that continue to implicitly inform much historical, anthropological, and, indeed, archaeological scholarship. This is particularly evident in the emergence of a specific academic discourse about the nature of money, initially explicit in classic works by Marx, Weber, Simmel, and Mauss, but continuing as a specter in more recent research (Bloch and Parry 1989).

Histories of Money

In moving away from some of these largely *a priori* models of modernity and money and engaging with the messy specificities of the local, it is vital to reconsider the dynamics of money as it enters *concrete* social contexts; that is, to consider the actual practices of coin production and circulation. There have been a few attempts at such an approach (primarily by sociocultural anthropologists in Africa and Melanesia [e.g., Bloch 1989; Foster 2002; LiPuma 1999; Strathern and Stewart 1999]), although the Andean case is foreshadowed by several interesting approaches in the study of economic history.

Hamilton's pioneering 1930s research on the long-term transatlantic flows of bullion and the subsequent Spanish "price revolution" of inflation and stagnation during the sixteenth and seventeenth centuries was followed by Braudel's work on the history of early capitalism and the specificities of "material life" (1972, 1973, 1984a, 1984b), Wallerstein's (1974) influential model of core-periphery relations, and Stern's (1995) more contextual account of a hybrid system within the New World. Nevertheless, these studies generally concentrate only on the large-scale, long-term flow of precious metals. Apart from the pioneering work of Ramírez (1996, 1997, 1998), few authors have actually examined the concrete ways in which money (especially in the form of coins) moved through the colonial archipelago. Historical claims for currency's role in transforming indigenous society as well as contemporary ethnographic literature on the continued unevenness of monetization and the persistence of money's ambiguities (e.g., Harris 1989; Mitchell 1991) point toward the value of reconsidering colonial coinage.

Despite the role of currency in historical accounts, archaeologists of Spanish colonialism have yet to fully explore the contexts of coinage. Although coins are much studied by numismatists and collectors (Asbun-Karmy 1977; Burzio and Ravignani 1945; Craig 2000; Paoletti et al. 2006), historical archaeologists have typically considered coins interesting for purely chronological purposes (e.g., Beck et al. 1983; Deagan 2002; Weaver 2008) or as essentially irrelevant (e.g., Klaus 2008). Even though approaches to material culture having developed considerably since South's 1970s approach to using artifact patterns to profile contexts and sites (South 1978; compare with Deagan 1983; Van Buren 1999), the conceptual place of coins as a minor contributor to the minor category of "personal" object has often remained unchanged. As Myrberg (2010) suggests, archaeologists in general tend to see coins as a relatively "mundane" and "transparent" technology, with little to contribute to more nuanced interpretations of past social lives. As objects that continue to circulate in the contemporary moment, coins are perhaps particularly subject to what Hodder has called "the forgetness of things" (2012:6).

Coins as "Things"

Following Tarlow's counsel to "de-familiarize" the recent past (cited in Hicks and Beaudry 2006), one might think more critically about the "familiar" coin. One possible way forward is a critical exploration of early colonial coins not only as polysemous objects (Beaudry et al. 1991), but also in terms of the other "hidden" people and things they depended upon. Hence, there is a particularly strong need for an approach that carefully tacks between the coins themselves and their wider material and textual contexts and thus enables one to "delve deep into the interpretation of meaning" (Beaudry et al. 1991:174) and show how rather than existing as singular and coherent objects, colonial coins were unstable "gatherings" of substances, human actors, and regimes of value (Hodder 2012).

There are obviously many ways to approach the material qualities of the coins themselves, but two features salient for those involved in their production—metallurgical composition and techniques of manufacture—provide a useful starting point. Archaeometallurgical and historical studies (Craig 2000) show the considerable variation in the gap between official and actual silver content, sometimes as a result of fraud, in other cases because of differing ore compositions. Each coin was individually hand struck with lead-filled hammers (a practice involving considerable skill and strength); at Potosí, the frequent failures of mis-strikes and embrittlement in the coining process (actually due to accelerated production and the skimping on costly fuel in the treeless Altiplano) were attributed to the silver itself "rebelling" (Craig 2000). These particular practices of silver processing and minting obviously determined to a large extent the degrees of formal variability and weight variability. In turn, these specific qualities of individual coins determined their official status as legal tender and their practical aesthetic/economic "quality" of being "good" coinage, which I discuss later in this chapter.

From one perspective, it was the coin's durability and density that enabled the viability of the early colonial project by allowing a transatlantic translation of condensed value in a manner that few other materials could replicate. At the same time, it is worth contrasting the stabilizing quality of silver's durability with its simultaneous destabilizing qualities of being relatively easy to clip or to forge (compared, for instance, with gold [Craig 2000]). One might even say that the silverness of the coins afforded particular kinds of social actions and relationships, only some of which fulfilled the aims of the coins' makers. Of course, these actions were never simply determined by the coins, but were contextually contingent; that is to say, they always took place in the company of other "things." The actor-network theory argument about the making of "immutable mobiles" that, through their specific durabilities and mobilities, temporarily simplify (or conceal) complex networks of things and people is certainly relevant here. While maintained, such an object or pattern "stands for, conceals, defines, holds in place, mobilizes, and draws upon, a set of juxtaposed bits and pieces" (Law 1994:101), enabling it to circulate and translate between multiple contexts.

Even just focusing on the processes of production, it is soon clear that the very existence of coins depended on a vast array of other "things." Assadourian hints at the immediate networks of Potosí: "The annual cycle of silver extraction using amalgamation fueled a constantly dynamic consumption of high intensity, drawing on a kind of constellation of various material inputs: different types of fuel and timber, materials for construction, pots, working tools, iron and steel, lead, tin, copper, salt, animal and hydraulic power, illumination etc." (1978:13; my translation). And, as Weaver's recent research has shown, the resulting industrial landscape of these heterogeneous materials and activities—dams, reservoirs, mills, storage buildings, and slag heaps—is still clearly visible at archaeological sites such as Ferro Ingenio near Porco in Bolivia (Weaver 2008). Nor was it static: archaeological and textual sources illustrate how the landscape, originally exploited by indigenous communities during pre-Hispanic times, shifted during the colonial era from co-opted knowledge and technologies of local exploitation and smelting (using the wind-driven *huayrachina* furnaces) to the growing industrialization of water-powered mills and mercury-based amalgamation (Tandeter 1993; Van Buren and Mills 2005; Weaver 2008; Zulawski 1995).

The Archaeology of Colonial Coins

The archaeological contexts of colonial coins themselves generally reflect the later, if equally complicated, phases of exchange and loss. Despite "the considerable loss of excavation reports and field records at the [Peruvian] National Institute of Culture … [and the] ignorance in most cases of the location of excavated materials" from colonial sites (Mogrovejo Rosales 1996:25), several archaeological sites in the central Andes have yielded evidence for the flow of coinage during the sixteenth and seventeenth centuries.

Excavations at Ferro Ingenio, a silver-processing site with a stamp mill near Porco in modern Bolivia (Weaver, personal communication, 2008), recovered a half-*real* coin dating between 1596 and 1612 from a mixed deposit near

Figure 2.3 Archaeological sites and other locations mentioned in this chapter

one of the furnaces. Given the presence of possibly early seventeenth-century Inka-style ceramics, the mixture of domestic and industrial material, and suggestive textual evidence, Weaver suggests a pattern of communally organized work with the possible presence of a *yanacona* labor force (indigenous servants detached from ethnic and kin groups).

Van Buren's excavations at the early colonial Lupaqa settlement at Torata Alta in the Moquegua valley recovered "straight pins, beads, coins and thimbles" (1993:355) from floor deposits thought to date between the mid-sixteenth and mid-seventeenth centuries. Her more recent project at Tarapaya (Van Buren, personal communication, 1999) has investigated what was apparently an early seventeenth-century elite Spanish secondary residence outside of the mining center of Potosí. While more than 32 square meters of structures and adjacent middens have been excavated, no coins have been found.

The Colca Valley in the southern highlands of Peru has been another area of considerable archaeological focus. A transect survey across the middle of the valley revealed the presence of several early chapels, with a total of 32 sites with Colonial components (Wernke 2003). Perhaps not surprisingly, surface collection yielded no coins. Subsequent excavations at the site of Malata (Wernke and Guerra Santander 2010) have revealed a pre-conquest settlement with a later short colonial phase of what seem to have been a pre-Toledo *doctrina* (Franciscan doctrinal settlement): while other European metal objects were recovered from the 300 square meters of excavations, no coins have been reported.

On the north coast of Peru, there have been extensive excavations at the late sixteenth-century coastal mission and *reducción* of Magdalena de Cao Viejo in the Chicama Valley (Quilter 2010). Although bells and pins (as well as even textiles and paper) have been recovered, any possible presence of early coinage has not been revealed to date. Coins have been found, however, at the rural chapel of San Pedro de Mórrope further to the north in the Lambayeque valley (Klaus 2008). In use between the sixteenth and eighteenth centuries, the site contains numerous disturbed burials. Associated artifacts include coins (three from the Early Colonial period and two from the Republican period) as well as ceramics, nails, candles, and pieces of flat glass.

Excavations under the Casa Osambela in the center of historic Lima (Flores Espinoza et al. 1981) revealed late sixteenth-century midden deposits and the late seventeenth-century construction of the Santo Domingo Monastery cloisters. More than 40 square meters were excavated, but only one copper centavo dating to 1863 was recovered. Similarly, Jamieson's Ecuadorian project of test pits in house yards (Jamieson 1999, and personal communication) at the two rural sites of Cachaulo and Hacienda Yanuncay Grande and in an elite colonial neighborhood in the urban center of Cuenca has encountered deposits from the sixteenth through nineteenth centuries containing other European metal artifacts, but no coins.

Here one is faced with the classic problem of trying to establish the relationship between significance of objects in the systemic context (as implied by the textual and pictorial evidence) versus their representation in the archaeological record. Thus, the Early Colonial coin is a genre of material culture that remains largely invisible, partly for disciplinary reasons but also partly because of a specific kind of object biography that often leaves the archaeologist with "decontextualized" coins. As objects whose value lay in their potential to circulate in endless chains of market exchanges, their appearance in the archaeological record tends to index certain intentional diversions from their "intended" pathways (e.g., into *huacas*) or the constant material breakdowns of a coinage economy (whether as casual loss in privies or as the loss of entire cargos at sea).

A few archaeologists, primarily European classicists and medievalists, have explored some of the factors affecting coin deposition and recovery (e.g., Casey 1986). Drawing on this work, we can outline several parameters that potentially affect the visibility of coins in archaeological contexts: the sizes of the coins, the value of the coins, the kinds of contexts excavated, and the volume of circulation. However, although the Andean excavations tend to be smaller than some the massive projects in the Dominican Republic and Florida, the presence of coins at much smaller excavations in the Caribbean and a crude estimation of recovery rates seem to suggest that the differences are not simply explained by excavation strategies.

The sizes of the coins, the first parameter, probably had a simple impact on frequencies of coin loss. Eight-*real* coins were about 40 millimeters in diameter and 27 grams in weight, while 1-*real* coins were about 20 millimeters and 3.4 grams, which would tend to work against casual loss of larger denomination coins (Asbun-Karmy 1977; Craig 2000).

The value of early colonial coins and the consequent "search-for factor" (Casey 1986) is a second, related parameter to consider. Given that a 4-*real* coin was worth more than a day's wages for late sixteenth-century *mitayo* miners at Potosí (Vilar 1976), most people would have been particularly careful about transport and curation. Furthermore, in his discussion of highly mixed early midden deposits at the edge of colonial Lima, Mogrovejo Rosales (1996) suggests that the nearly total lack of glass and metal is indicative of intensive recycling activities, a behavior that is certainly worth considering further.

The third parameter—the kinds of contexts that have been excavated—is probably quite significant in this case. Clearly, the sites considered here are not fully representative of the range of early colonial contexts: Ferro Ingenio, with its resident silver workers and its proximity to the massive mining, minting, and market center of Potosí; Torata Alta's place on key trade routes between the Moquegua Valley and the Atiplano markets; and San Pedro de Mórrope as the only well-documented early colonial burial context are not representative of a generalizable Andean landscape. They do, however, seem to hint at specific engagements—wage labor, early trade routes, and hybrid burial practices—with an emerging, uneven set of material flows.

As nodes connecting local, regional, and global communities of circulation, urban sites potentially have much to offer in understanding the role of coins during the Early Colonial period. Unfortunately, given the circumstances mentioned here, there is comparatively little information on the many excavations already carried out at a wide range of domestic, governmental, and public contexts in Lima, Cuzco, Trujillo, Arequipa, and other colonial centers (Mogrovejo Rosales 1996).

The role of the fourth parameter, the actual volume and extant of circulation in the internal colonial economy, while not particularly clear, is clearly of relevance to the broader question of monetary penetration. Textual sources certainly suggest, given the double pull from the state and from transatlantic merchants, there was often an overall shortage of coins in the early Spanish New World, which was compounded by the fact that mints tended to produce few coins with smaller denominations (Paoletti et al. 2006; TePaske 2010).

Helman (1980), working on the French and British occupations of Fort Michilimackinac in northern Michigan, and de la Rosa Graell and Arrazcaeta Delgado (2004), working on historical contexts in Cuba, are among the few archaeologists to have considered these questions of coin taphonomy in colonial contexts. Their work appears to bolster the notion that, although the other parameters were important, an uneven circulation of coins may be a factor in their apparently uneven presence in the Andean archaeological record.

Communities of Circulation

Given the inherent polysemy of objects in colonial spaces (Stahl 2002), what did coins say and do to people in indigenous and *criollo* communities? Although the trope of "the fatal attraction of European goods" to the "innocent but hopelessly greedy" locals (per Thomas 1991:85) abounds in the historical literature, careful readings of documents such as *visitas* (accounts of regional inspection tours), tribute lists, court records, and wills seems to suggest that indigenous individuals were often quickly aware of the opportunities and problems of coinage and the marketplace (Ramírez 1996; Stern 1981). Despite (or even because) of this awareness, some indigenous individuals and communities found themselves increasingly entangled and even entrapped within these new material circulations. Carefully juxtaposing these historical sources with ethnographic accounts of more recent instances of economic entanglement in the Andes and beyond (e.g., Keane 2001; LiPuma 1999; Strathern and Stewart 1999 on Indonesia and Papua New Guinea) provides further hints at some of the contested microdynamics of "monetization."

The loss of cultivable land due to encroaching landowners, increasing tribute demands for silver, the growth of migrant worker (*forestero*) populations, and the appearance of old comestibles in new commoditized forms (e.g., coca) all tended to drive certain indigenous individuals and communities into increased participation with coinage (Cummins 2002; Ramírez 1996; Wightman 1990; Zulawski 1995). In many cases, coins were first used primarily for tribute payments to the state, but gradually they seeped into other arenas as the links between being a subject of the state and being a commodity producer/consumer began to emerge. As standards of value (uniform, interchangeable objects), coins had the new ability to make radically different things commensurable, as shifting tribute lists soon demonstrated (Ramírez 1996).

Also, as a means of storing value, the inherent durability of coins (versus perishables like pigs, camelids, birds, fish, and eggs) enabled different forms of accumulation that altered, in turn, the tempo of relations of obligation and reciprocity (Ramírez 1996).

Tribute documents are a particularly interesting means of tracing this gradual process of entanglement with new regimes of value. On one level, as Ramírez shows in her study of the Peruvian north coast, there was a progression in the sixteenth century from tribute lists detailing demands for local goods, including metals, to the introduction of cash and the possibility to commute other demands into cash, to lists that only detail amounts of money (1996:118). Even at an early stage, some indigenous individuals found wage jobs in towns and cities to earn money to buy tribute goods (Assadourian 1995). Following the reforms of Lima judge Gregorio Gonzalez de Cuenca in 1566, labor (whether for Spanish masters or for indigenous neighbors) was legally required to be recompensed with wages (Ramírez 1996).

However, this does not appear to have been a coherent and inexorable process by which coins gradually took over the lives of all people in equal measure. Some of the earliest *visitas* in the central Andes document an initial indigenous disinterest in waged labor: coins were considered utterly useless for obtaining food and other necessities (Assadourian 1995:114). Indigenous people were not immediately ideal subjects who needed and desired coinage for productive and social reproductive purposes.

At the same time, contrary to the model of *lo andino*, it may be particularly important to recognize the ways in which "Andean society" was not homogenous and begin to reconsider the earlier social divisions that clearly persisted into the colonial period and that often permitted certain individuals to engage with the new opportunities of the market at a very early stage. Indigenous Andean societies were *never* in total equilibrium, and after conquest, there were underlying tensions that began to manifest in new ways. Allen (2002:213) has written ethnographically about the desire of some contemporary agro-pastoralists to escape reciprocal obligations (*ayni*) by turning to the cash economy. In many cases, the collection of tribute was left in the hands of the *kurakas*, placing them in a strategic position between the new Spanish administration and local communities. In her research on the Peruvian north coast, Ramírez suggests that monetization only really involved the *kurakas* and emergent urban indigenous communities, with rural exchange on the north coast often remained apparently unmonetized during the sixteenth century (1995).

The potential for entanglement in new practices of consumption and accumulation is readily apparent in the wills that soon appeared after conquest (Ramírez 1995; Ramos 2010; Stern 1981). While money often appeared as a *means* to other ends (e.g., paying tribute or buying new commodities), the drift toward reconceptualizing money as *wealth* itself seems to have gradually occurred in some cases. Such wills are also suggestive of the ways in which the concealable qualities of money may have subtly started to shift existing conceptions of wealth (for instance, prestations of cloth) and its particular forms of social visibility.

Roadside *tambo*s and urban markets seem to have been particularly important loci for new kinds of exchange relations. Remnants of the Inka imperial infrastructure, *tambos* were often maintained to support the vital arteries of mercantile and administrative networks; while the local supply of labor, food, and fodder was initially provided under duress, some *tambos* seem to have emerged as new—if still somewhat exploitative—proto-markets for agricultural produce and wage labor (whether as porters or as prostitutes) (Glave 1991). In larger settlements, indigenous immigrants were soon significantly involved in markets and craft workshops. Even smaller *reducciones* were often designed with central plazas for weekly markets, which may have been the case at Magdalena de Cao (Quilter 2010), Torata Alta (Van Buren 1993), and Yanque and Coporaque in the Colca Valley (Wernke 2007).

As Ødegaard's shows in her recent ethnographic work on the informal markets of Arequipa today (2008), local engagement with the cash economy often remains poised between the dynamics of trust and suspicion, cohesion and hierarchy. Other ethnographic cases further bolster the case for the use of coins in local strategic action: in their study of communities in the Cuzco valley, Van den Berghe and Primov (1977) note that by choosing cash transactions over barter, local people could more easily avoid being swindled in the marketplace. The reasons for using cash often extend beyond the economic: in modern-day Quinua (Ayacucho), townspeople often use hard currency as a sign distinguishing themselves from the peasant sphere of bartering (Mitchell 1991). Wills from urban indigenous inhabitants dating from the early colonial period reveal emerging networks of credit and lending relations among kin and acquaintances (Ramírez 1996). The combination of new asymmetries based on exploitation and overcharging with the new, shared European-indigenous language of credit relations highlights the fact that rather then being a simple instrument of "destructuration" (Wachtel 1977), the circulation of coins remained fraught with social ambiguities.

It is by tracing these mundane practices and the new emergent communities of circulation that we can begin to consider the actual *making* of "the social," "the many contradictory ways in which social aggregates are constantly evoked, erased, distributed, and reallocated" (Latour 2005:41). Of course, the group so frequently forgotten in historical anthropological and archaeological narratives in the Andes is the growing community of urban *criollos*. Often implicitly grouped as a relatively elite stratum of the new colonial social order, it is worth recalling that, as in Spain, the poorer elements of this group were themselves only gradually using money with any real frequency. Indeed, these "poorer social strata" accustomed to barter exchange (Paoletti et al. 2006:20) provide a destabilizing and unexplored counterpoint to the transforming indigenous communities and point towards the broader processes transforming the sociomaterial logics on both sides of the Atlantic.

The Spanish State, Its Subjects, and Its Material Slippages

Although coins clearly acted at the levels of the daily entrapments of the markets and diverse engagements with the spiritual, we can also take a step back to consider the broader ways in which the production and circulation of coins illustrate the contradictory forms and forces of the early colonial project. As the case of the Spanish "price revolution" shows, the material circulations of the new colonial project often had dramatic unintended consequences; in Peter Pels's memorable phrase, these were certainly cases when "matter strikes back" (1998:91). There are several ways in which the very materiality of money enables it to slip the grasp of its "makers" and act in an almost subversive manner. While money may be "in terms of its pure concept ... nothing but the pure form of exchangeability" (Simmel 1984:130), money as coinage has stubborn, irreducibly multiple qualities. Because coins were made of silver, rather than pure, universal equivalent forms controlled by the state, it was always possible to translate them into other spheres of circulation.

As well as being particularly translatable, coins are also especially reliant on attenuated, integrated networks (Hodder 2012) of production, transport, and surveillance. These unstable material networks are characteristic of what Braudel terms the "insurmountable obstacles" of the preindustrial world (1973, xiv). The frequent sinking of *flota* boats (Craig 2000) and the quantities of contraband slipping though the porous borders of the Latin American viceroyalties (Schavelzón 2000) are again reminders that far from being simple "powerful actors" in their own right, coins were constantly dependent on a vast array of other human and material actors.

As well as this extension through the landscape, the new project of New World silver extraction and coinage also involved the organization of activity around new temporalities: because of weather patterns and the need for security, the *flotas* circulated between Seville and the New World only twice a year (Pérez Herrero 1988). Moreover, this maritime cycle had to intersect with the seasonality of mining at Potosí: production halted during the bitterly cold winter months when crucial water supplies froze (Craig 2000). The numerous mule and llama trains were a further critical link in this project, traveling hundreds of kilometers across the Andes and bearing immense burdens of silver ingots, coins, and mercury between Lima, Huancavelica, Potosí, and Arica. Safely keeping the king's royal fifth (*quinto*) of all assayed silver at the state treasuries meant the further dependence on increasingly complex networks of things and people: officials eventually arrived at the rather Latourian solution

Figure 2.4 Rebellious Silver: An early sixteenth-century 8-*real* Coin from Potosí (Photo by the author; coin from private collection, Zaña Valley, Peru).

of devising special chests with three locks opened by three keys held by three different officials (Craig 2000).

Despite the value of a coin nominally laying in its purity and weight as guaranteed by the state, considerable importance was also placed on "the beauty and perfection of its minting" (Casa Nacional de la Moneda 2006; my translation), and the appearance of coins could differ dramatically. These heterogeneous objects were often interpreted in terms of the moral failures of yet-to-be disciplined subjects. What one might think were critical mistakes in the frequently replaced dies (even misspelling the king's name as, for instance, PPHILIIPVS) were common in coins from Lima and particularly Potosí (Asbun-Karmy 1977), and were frequently attributed to the employment of careless Indians and illiterate *criollos* (Craig 2000). Craig, however, suggests that the cracked edges, crude dies, and poor striking of many Potosí coins are all symptoms of a drive by mint officials to cut costs (by using less charcoal for smelting and by using cheap local labor) and maximize production (2000).

The different "reputations" of coins often led to merchants and others hoarding "good" coins, a phenomenon also spurred by the practices of minting fraud and coin clipping (Bethel 1987:359). When the coins were produced, there were nominally all equivalent; however, such practices of clipping and hoarding pushed the coins back towards the singular end of the spectrum, again subverting the intention of equivalent instruments of exchange (see Kopytoff 1986).

Through the late sixteenth and into the seventeenth centuries, an increasingly assertive Spanish state sought to tame the colonial world's "wild profusion of existing things" (Foucault 1973:xv) in what may be seen as one of the many beginnings of a modernist project to purify the problematic heterogeneity of the world (Law 1994:7). Before coins were officially minted (starting in 1568 in Lima and in 1574 in Potosí), a largely unregulated system of exchange dominated the early colonial economy in Peru based on money of account, coins from Spain and Mexico, gold and silver bars and discs, gold dust, and lumps of silver called *pesos corrientes* (ordinary pesos) whose values were based on estimations *a ojo* (by eye) or *al toque* (by touch) (Paoletti et al. 2006:37). This unruly mixture of heterogeneous materials was gradually and intentionally disciplined into a respectable economic form, beginning with the advent of locally minted coins (Luque Luque 2005) and culminating in the eighteenth century with the introduction of milled edges and greater uniformity of weight, innovations that broadly coincided with the Bourbon state's takeover of the mints themselves (TePaske 2010:217). Through this "purification," money gradually became something separate from the rest of the colonial object world.

These attempts to discipline the subjects and objects of the state hint at the wider instabilities of "the colonial project." While historians have traditionally emphasized the strongly top-down nature of the double repression of the Spanish state and the Roman Catholic Church, a growing number of scholars have questioned such a model, pointing to the existence of multiple, poorly connected institutional networks (e.g., Lockhart and Schwartz 1983). Andrien (2001) emphasizes the continued political instability in the Peruvian viceroyalty throughout the sixteenth century, with persistent enclaves of neo-Inca resistance in the highlands, the Taki Onqoy revolt in the 1560s, and repeated episodes of civil war between colonists. Although territorial maps of the Peruvian viceroyalty are usually entirely filled in, even taking the circulation of money as an unproblematic index of the penetration of the state inclines one towards a more reticulated perspective (see Smith 2005).

As Braudel has suggested, in many ways the early modern "state was as yet an unfinished entity, seeking to create its identity, unable to exercise all its rights or carry out all its tasks, obliged in fact to call on the aid of others as a disagreeable necessity" (1984b:549), and often faced with an array of actors often actively choosing alternatives to the state order. Rather than projecting the modern activist state into this past, it is vital to recognize that in many ways the early Spanish state was characterized by competing, autonomous institutions and continuous legal negotiation (Lockhart and Schwartz 1983): more often than not, it was constantly working to maintain its hold over its partial networks of control and circulation.

At the same time, we should not ignore the selective power of this nascent state, particularly when faced with the relationship between state coercion and the indigenous body. While the historiography of the *leyenda negra* (and the Potosí *mita* in particular) is a complex one (see Gibson 1984; Tandeter 1993), Luis Capoche's 1585 eyewitness account provides a vivid description of conditions at Potosí. Working eight-hour shifts, miners moved up and down shafts of up to 670 meters in depth while carrying 23 kilogram sacks of ore from the warmth of the mountain's interior up to the entrance and then down the frigid, windblown slopes of Cerro Rico (Vilar 1976). A bioanthropological study of lungs in sixteenth-century mummies from Pica in northern Chile (Munizaga et al. 1975) starkly demonstrates the physical impact of these regimes of labor on the worker' body: out of 22 examined, 12 showed clear signs of pneumoconiosis from mining, while at least one showed evidence of very high levels of mercury and lead.

Discussion

Spurred on by historians' quotes about radical colonial transformation and the destructive penetration of market logic, I genuinely expected to find evidence for rapid, wholesale change. However, the extant archaeological, historical, and ethnographic evidence instead suggests a much more uneven, gradual process of entanglement between coins, the Spanish state, and colonial subjects—what Thomas has called "the peculiar combinations of transformation and intransigence on the colonial periphery" (1991:8)—that nevertheless has had powerful and enduring legacies. Rather than starting an analysis of the period with a coherent colonial economy, fully fledged Spanish capitalists, and traditionalist Andean peoples, I take a critical approach that begins with coins as "things" and begins to move "from the inside out" (Beaudry et al. 1991:163), stressing the contingent processes of engagement and dependence that began to unfold during the first century of contact.

I initially turned to the archaeological record to get a better grasp on the mundane aspects of monetization that are so frequently omitted in historical sources. Unfortunately, due to a number of reasons, including low levels of research and poor publishing practices, the archaeological body of evidence is sparser than initially expected. Following a review of the available literature, the archaeological record seems to emphasize an unpredictable unevenness of monetization in the Andes during the sixteenth and seventeenth centuries (contrary to notions of the rapid destruction of Andean social fabric through marketization). Despite the tentative nature of this conclusion, it is consistent with Andean ethnographic accounts of twentieth-century rural communities, as well as with the wider historical contexts of early modern monetization in both Europe and the New World. Behind the apparently simple transition between the two Guaman Poma de Ayala illustrations at the beginning of this chapter, it is increasingly clear that the dynamics of the early colonial economy were both multiple and constantly contested.

By considering the multiple uses and "readings" of coins, and the situations of contestation and failure, not only is the Spanish actor versus indigenous patient model brought into question, but the also the locus of change itself. From a perspective emphasizing the entanglements of the colonial, change is clearly not simply a matter of new ideas (or new people or, indeed, new objects). While the approach of recentering the coin might raise the question of its "material agency," in many ways this may be the wrong way of addressing the issue. The introductions of coins without ideas of money, or of ideas of money without coins, are both obvious impossibilities. At the same, reconsidering the place of "things" continues to be a vital move when engaging with narratives that all to often slip into tropes of immaterial discourses or technological determinism:[2] indeed, there is a striking disjunction between the discourses of wealth, glory, and empire and the banality, even crudeness of the coins at the heart of the colonial project (compare with González-Ruibal 2010).

Instead, it is the changing, often asymmetrical relationships *between* these particular humans, objects, and discourses that provide the basis for telling this story of changing and staying the same (Knappett 2008; Latour 2005). By problematizing the "universal power of money," one starts to uncover the wide range of processes by which actors tend to become entangled in particular projects of production and consumption, circulation and deposition. Rather than the imposition of a final order, these were uneven processes of colonial/capitalist orderings that involved constantly renewed attempts to align persons and things in particular ways (Law 1994). As "immutable mobiles," coins served to translate these attempts at ordering through multiple scales: as the minimal wages of *mitayos*, as new means of making old social ties of debt, as a new way to acquire old comestibles such as *chicha*, as a new form of offering to old *huacas*, as one of several ways to pay tribute to the state, and as transnational actors linking Lima to Manila, Buenos Aires, and Antwerp. While some of these processes were within the emerging colonial pattern of ordering, they also represent the constant tendency for the material to resist, mutate, fail, and even subvert.

Coda

I began this chapter by noting both history's account of contact as "destructuration" and the tendency for anthropology's "unitary conceptions of indigenous economies ... [to] suppress the entanglement with other systems such as capitalist trade" (Thomas 1991:4). The underlying structure of the "rupture of modernity" in these accounts is reproduced in disciplinary divisions between historians and anthropologists, prehistoric archaeologists and historical archaeologists. The resultant perspective is characterized by what Haber has termed a "metaphysical gap in time" (2007:220) by which those from "before history" are separated from those "within history," a divide that continues to create both analytical and political problems for archaeologists.

Monetization, as a process that entangled indigenous and Spanish communities, has ties to both pre-contact pasts (Ramírez 1996; Sallnow 1989;

Stern 1981) and "postcolonial" futures (Bradby 1982; Harris 1989). By tracing the sociomaterial linkages and disjunctures through the colonial project, a historical anthropology of entanglement can potentially provide an important wider context for understanding the complex regional dependences and dependencies (Hodder 2012; Stern 1988) that continue to unfold. Recent new reports highlight one of these very material legacies of colonial entanglement: after more than 400 years of exploitation, the famed Cerro Rico in Potosí has finally begun to collapse in on itself. Honeycombed with mine shafts dating back to the 1540s, the mountain is still excavated for silver, tin, and tungsten ores despite the hazards of silicosis and an increasingly unstable geology: as Omar Garcia, a young miner from Potosí, states, "In the city [of Potosí] you can only get a job in the mining sector. So, I'd have to move to find other work. I have no choice" (Cabitza 2011).

Acknowledgments

Many thanks to John Rick, Barb Voss, Lynn Meskell, Ian Hodder, Tamara Herzog, Nanouschka Myrberg, Enrique Rodríguez-Alegría, Francesca Fernandini, Guido Pezzarossi, Adam Nazaroff and the entanglement discussion group, Mary Van Buren, Brendan Weaver, Ross Jamieson, Juan Domingo Mogrovejo Rosales, Gary Urton, and Parker van Valkenburgh.

Notes

1. Silver coins were minted in denominations of half, 1, 2, 4 and 8 *reales*, where each *real* was equal to 3.43 grams of silver (i.e., 1/67 of a Spanish *marco*). Although gold coins were minted in Santa Fé de Bogotá beginning in 1622, no gold was minted in the central Andes until 1696 (Deagan 2002).
2. Townsend (2003) has noted an overall tendency to ignore the role of things in historical narratives of the conquest of Mexico.

References

Allen, Catherine J., 2002. *The Hold Life Has: Coca and Cultural Identity in an Andean Community*. Smithsonian Institution Press, Washington, D.C.

Andrien, Kenneth J., 2001. *Andean Worlds: Indigenous History, Culture, and Consciousness under Spanish Rule, 1532–1825*. University of New Mexico Press, Albuquerque.

Asbun-Karmy, Luis Alberto, 1977. *Monedas, Medallas, Billetes, Acciones y Documentos Bancarios de Bolivia*. Banco de Crédito Oruro, Oruro, Bolivia.

Assadourian, Carlos Sempat, 1978. La producción de la mercancía dinero en la formacíon del mercado interno colonial. *Economia* [PUCP, Lima] 1(2):9–55.

Assadourian, Carlos Sempat, 1995. Exchange in the Ethnic Territories between 1530 and 1567: The *visitas* of Huánuco and Chucuito. In *Ethnicity, Markets, and*

Migration in the Andes: At the Crossroads of History and Anthropology, edited by Brooke Larson, Olivia Harris, and Enrique Tandeter, pp. 101–134. Duke University Press, Durham, NC.

Beaudry, Mary C., Lauren J. Cook, and Stephen Mrozowski, 1991. Artifacts and Active Voices: Material Culture as Social Discourse. In *The Archaeology of Inequality*, edited by Randall McGuire and Robert Paynter, pp. 150–191. Blackwell Press, Oxford, UK.

Beck, Colleen M., Eric E. Deeds, Sheila Pozorski, and Thomas Pozorski, 1983. Pajatambo: An 18th Century Roadside Structure in Peru. *Historical Archaeology* 17(1):54–68.

Bethell, Leslie, 1987. *Colonial Spanish America*. Cambridge University Press, Cambridge, UK.

Bhabha, H. K., 1990. *Nation and Narration*. Routledge, New York.

Bloch, Maurice, 1989. The Symbolism of Money in Imerina. In *Money and the Morality of Exchange*, edited by M. Bloch and J. Parry, pp. 165–190. Cambridge University Press, Cambridge, UK.

Bloch, Maurice, and Jonathan Parry, 1989. Introduction: Money and the Morality of Exchange. In *Money and the Morality of Exchange*, edited by M. Bloch and J. Parry, pp. 1–32. Cambridge University Press, Cambridge, UK.

Bradby, Barbara, 1982. 'Resistance to Capitalism' in the Peruvian Andes. In *Ecology and Exchange in the Andes*, edited by David Lehmann, pp. 97–122. Cambridge University Press, Cambridge, UK.

Braudel, Fernand, 1972. *The Mediterranean and the Mediterranean World in the Age of Philip II*. Translated by Siân Reynolds. Harper and Row, New York.

Braudel, Fernand, 1973. *Capitalism and Material Life, 1400–1800*. Translated by Miriam Kochan. Harper and Row, New York.

Braudel, Fernand, 1984a. *Civilization and Capitalism, 15th–18th Century. Vol. 1: The Structures of Everyday Life: The Limits of the Possible*. Translated by Siân Reynolds. Collins, London.

Braudel, Fernand, 1984b. *Civilization and Capitalism, 15th–18th Century. Vol. 2: The Wheels of Commerce*. Translated by Siân Reynolds. Collins, London.

Burzio, Humberto F., and Emilio Ravignani, 1945. *La ceca de la villa imperial de Potosí y la moneda colonial*. Peuser s. a., Buenos Aires, Argentina.

Cabitza, Mattia, 2011. Bolivia's Exhausted Cerro Rico Mountain Risks Collapse. BBC News. Electronic document, www.bbc.co.uk/news/world-latin-america-12822247, accessed February 4, 2011.

Carrier, James G., 1992. Occidentalism: The World Turned Upside-Down. *American Ethnologist* 19(2):195–212.

Casa Nacional de Moneda, 2006. *Catálogo de monedas coloniales*. Casa Nacional de Moneda, La Paz, Bolivia.

Casey, P. J., 1986. *Understanding Ancient Coins: An Introduction for Archaeologists and Historians*. University of Oklahoma Press, Norman.

Craig, Alan K., 2000. *Spanish Colonial Gold Coins in the Florida Collection*. Florida Bureau of Archaeological Research, Division of Historical Resources, Gainesville.

Cummins, Thomas B. F., 2002. *Toasts with the Inca: Andean Abstraction and Colonial Images on Quero Vessels*. University of Michigan Press, Ann Arbor.

Deagan, Kathleen, 1983. The Mestizo Minority: Archaeological Patterns of Intermarriage. In *Spanish St. Augustine: The Archaeology of a Colonial Creole Community*, edited by Kathleen Deagan, pp. 99–124. Academic Press, New York.
Deagan, Kathleen, 2002. *Artifacts of the Spanish Colonies of Florida and the Caribbean, 1500–1800. Vol. 2: Portable Personal Possessions.* Smithsonian Institution Press, Washington, D.C.
de la Rosa Graell, Carlos, and Roger Arrazcaeta Delgado, 2004. Evidencias numismáticas en sitios arqueológicos de La Habana Vieja. *Gabinete de Arqueología* [Cuba] 3:19–30.
Flores Espinoza, Isabel, Lorenzo Huertas V., and Rubén García Soto, 1981. *Investigación arqueológica-histórica de la casa Osambela (o de Oquendo), Lima.* Instituto Nacional de Cultura, Centro de Investigación y Restauración de Bienes Monumentales, Lima, Peru.
Foster, Robert J., 2002. *Materializing the Nation: Commodities, Consumption, and Media in Papua New Guinea*. Indiana University Press, Bloomington.
Foucault, Michel, 1973. *The Order of Things: An Archaeology of the Human Sciences.* Vintage Books, New York.
Gibson, Charles, 1984. Indian Societies under Spanish Rule. In *The Cambridge History of Latin America*, Vol. 2, edited by Leslie Bethell, pp. 381–421. Cambridge University Press, Cambridge, UK.
Glave, Luis Miguel, 1991. Tambos y caminos andinos en la formacion del Mercado interno colonial. In *Reproducción y transformación de la sociedades andinas siglos XVI-XX*, Vol. 1, edited by Segundo Moreno Y. and Frank Salomon, pp. 285–348. Ediciones Abya-Yala (Movimiento Laicos para América Latina), Quito, Ecuador.
González-Ruibal, Alfredo, 2010. Fascist Colonialism: The Archaeology of Italian Outposts in Western Ethiopia (1936–41). *International Journal of Historical Archaeology* 14(4):547–574.
Gosden, Chris, 2004. *Archaeology and Colonialism: Cultural Contact from 5000 BC to the Present.* Cambridge University Press, Cambridge, UK.
Haber, Alejandro F., 2007. This Is Not an Answer to the Question "Who is Indigenous?" *Journal of the World Archaeological Congress* 3(3):213–229.
Hall, Martin, and Stephen W. Silliman, 2006. Introduction: Archaeology of the Modern World. In *Historical Archaeology*, edited by Martin Hall and Stephen W. Silliman, pp. 1–19. Blackwell Publishing, Oxford, UK.
Harris, Olivia, 1989. The Earth and the State: The Sources and Meanings of Money in Northern Potosí, Bolivia. In *Money and the Morality of Exchange*, edited by M. Bloch and J. Parry, pp. 232–268. Cambridge University Press, Cambridge, UK.
Helman, Donald P., 1980. Coins at Michilimackinac. *Historical Archaeology* 14:82–107.
Hicks, Dan, and Mary C. Beaudry, 2006. Introduction: The Place of Historical Archaeology. In *The Cambridge Companion to Historical Archaeology*, edited by Dan Hicks and Mary C. Beaudry, pp. 1–9. Cambridge University Press, Cambridge, UK.
Hodder, Ian, 2012. *Entangled: An Archaeology of the Relationships Between Humans and Things.* Wiley-Blackwell, Malden, MA.
Jamieson, Ross W., 1999. *Domestic Architecture and Power: The Historical Archaeology of Colonial Ecuador.* Kluwer Academic/Plenum Publishers, New York.

Jamieson, Ross W., 2005. Colonialism, Social Archaeology and lo Andino: Historical Archaeology in the Andes. *World Archaeology* 37:352–372.

Jordan, Kurt A., 2009. Colonies, Colonialism, and Cultural Entanglement: The Archaeology of Postcolumbian Intercultural Relations. In *International Handbook of Historical Archaeology*, edited by Teresita Majewski and David Gaimster, pp. 31–59. Springer, New York.

Keane, Webb, 2001. Money Is No Object: Materiality, Desire and Modernity in an Indonesian Society. In *The Empire of things*, edited by Fred R. Myers, pp. 65–90. School of American Research Press, Santa Fe, NM.

Klaus, Haagen D., 2008. Out of Light Came Darkness: Bioarchaeology of Mortuary Ritual, Health, and Ethnogenesis in the Lambayeque Valley Complex, North Coast of Peru (AD 900–1750). Unpublished Ph.D. dissertation, Ohio State University, Columbus, OH.

Knappett, Carl, 2008. The Neglected Networks of Material Agency: Artefacts, Pictures and Texts. *In Material Agency: Towards a Non-anthropocentric Approach*, edited by Carl Knappett and Lambros Malafouris, pp. 139–156. Springer, Berlin, Germany.

Kopytoff, Igor, 1986. The Cultural Biography of Things: Commoditization as Process. In *The Social Life of Things: Commodities in Cultural Perspective*, edited by A. Appadurai, pp. 64–91. Cambridge University Press, Cambridge, UK.

La Lone, Daryl E., 1982. The Inca as a Nonmarket Economy: Supply on Command vs. Supply and Demand. In *Contexts for Prehistoric Exchange*, edited by J. E. Ericson and T. K. Earle, pp. 292–316. Academic Press, Ann Arbor, MI.

Larson, Brooke, 1995. Andean Communities, Political Cultures, and Markets: The Changing Contours of a Field. In *Ethnicity, Markets, and Migration in the Andes: At the Crossroads of History and Anthropology*, edited by Brooke Larson, Olivia Harris, and Enrique Tandeter, pp. 5–53. Duke University Press, Durham, NC.

Latour, Bruno, 1999. On recalling ANT. *The Sociological Review* 47(S1):15–25.

Latour, Bruno, 2005. *Reassembling the Social: An Introduction to Actor-Network-Theory*. Oxford University Press, Oxford, UK.

Law, John, 1994. *Organizing Modernity*. Blackwell, Oxford, UK.

LiPuma, Edward, 1999. The Meaning of Money in the Age of Modernity. In *Money and Modernity: State and Local Currencies in Melanesia*, edited by David Akin and Joel Robbins, pp. 192–213. University of Pittsburgh Press, Pittsburgh, PA.

Lockhart, James, and Stuart B. Schwartz, 1983. *Early Latin America: A History of Colonial Spanish America and Brazil*. Cambridge University Press, Cambridge, UK.

Luque Luque, Juvenal, 2005. Lima, su moneda y su ceca. In *Lima en siglo XVI*, edited by Laura Gutiérrez Arbulú, pp. 567–604. Instituto de Riva-Agüero, Lima, Peru.

Martindale, Andrew, 2009. Entanglement and Tinkering: Structural History in the Archaeology of the Northern Tsimshian. *Journal of Social Archaeology* 9(1):59–91.

Mignolo, Walter, 2000. *Local Histories/Global Designs: Coloniality, Subaltern Knowledges, and Border Thinking*. Princeton University Press, Princeton, NJ.

Mignolo, Walter, 2005. *The Idea of Latin America*. Blackwell, Malden, MA.

Mitchell, William P., 1991. *Peasants on the Edge: Crop, Cult, and Crisis in the Andes*. University of Texas Press, Austin, TX.

Mogrovejo Rosales, Juan D., 1996. *Arqueología urbana de evidencias coloniales en la ciudad de Lima*. Instituto Riva-Agüero, Lima, Peru.

Munizaga, J., Marvin J. Allison, Enrique Gerszten, and David M. Klurfeld, 1975. Pneumoconiosis in Chilean Miners of the 16th century. *Bulletin of the New York Academy of Medicine* 51(11):1281–1293.

Murra, John V., 1972. El "control vertical" en un maximo de pisos ecologicos en la economia de las sociedades Andinas. In *Visita de la provincia de Leon de Huanuco en 1562,* Vol. 2, edited by John V. Murra, pp. 427–476. Universidad Nacional Hermilio Valdizán, Huanuco, Peru.

Myrberg, Nanouschka, 2010. The Social Life of Coins and the "Dilemma of Specialization." Paper presented at the Stanford Archaeology Center, Stanford University, CA, October 3, 2010.

Ødegaard, Cecilie V., 2008. Informal Trade, Contrabando and Prosperous Socialities in Arequipa, Peru. *Ethnos* 73(2):241–266.

Paoletti, Emilio, Maria Alessandra Woolson, and Daniel Sedwick, 2006. *8 Reales cobs of Potosí,* 2nd ed. [s.n.], Buenos Aires, Argentina.

Pels, Peter, 1998. The Spirit of Matter: On Fetish, Rarity, Fact and Fancy. In *Border Fetishisms: Material Objects in Unstable Spaces*, edited by P. Spyer, pp. 91–121. Routledge, New York.

Pérez Herrero, Pedro, 1988. *Plata y Libranzas: La Articulación Comercial del México Borbónico.* Centro de Estudios Históricos, Colegio de México, México City, Mexico.

Preda, Alex, 1999. The Turn to Things: Arguments for a Sociological Theory of Things. *The Sociological Quarterly* 40(2):347–366.

Quilter, Jeffrey, 2010. Magdalena de Cao Viejo: Archaeology and History at an Early Colonial Peruvian Church and Town. Electronic document, http://140.247.102.177/mcv/, accessed February 14, 2011.

Ramírez, Susan E., 1995. Exchange and Markets in the Sixteenth Century: A View from the North. In *Ethnicity, Markets, and Migration in the Andes: At the Crossroads of History and Anthropology*, edited by Brooke Larson, Olivia Harris, and Enrique Tandeter, pp. 135–164. Duke University Press, Durham, NC.

Ramírez, Susan E., 1996. *The World Upside Down: Cross-cultural Contact and Conflict in Sixteenth-century Peru.* Stanford University Press, Stanford, CA.

Ramírez, Susan E., 1997. Un mercader ... es un pescador: reflexiones sobre las relaciones económicas y los multiples roles de los indios americanos en el Perú del siglo XVI. In *Arqueología, antropología e historia en los Andes: homenaje a María Rostworowski*, edited by Rafael Varón Gabai and Javier Flores Espinoza, pp. 729–736. Instituto de Estudios Peruanos, Lima, Peru.

Ramírez, Susan E., 1998. Rich Man, Poor Man, Beggar Man, or Chief: Material Wealth as a Basis of Power in Sixtenth-Century Peru. In *Dead Giveaways: Indigenous Testaments of Colonial Mesoamerica and the Andes*, edited by Susan Kellogg and Matthew Restall, pp. 215–248. University of Utah Press, Salt Lake City, UT.

Ramos, Gabriela, 2010. *Death and Conversion in the Andes: Lima and Cuzco, 1532–1670.* University of Notre Dame Press, South Bend, IN.

Sallnow, M. J., 1989. Precious Metals in the Andean Moral Economy. In *Money and the Morality of Exchange*, edited by M. Bloch and J. Parry, pp. 209–231. Cambridge University Press, Cambridge, UK.

Schávelzon, Daniel, 2000. *The Historical Archaeology of Buenos Aires: A City at the End of the World.* Kluwer Academic Press, New York.

Simmel, Georg, 1984. *The Philosophy of Money*, edited by D. Frisby. Routledge, New York.

Smith, Monica L., 2005. Networks, Territories, and the Cartography of Ancient States. *Annals of the Association of American Geographers* 95(4):832–849.

South, S., 1978. Pattern Recognition in Historical Archaeology. *American Antiquity* 43(2):223–230.

Spalding, Karen, 1984. *Huarochirí: An Andean Society under Inca and Spanish Rule.* Stanford University Press, Stanford, CA.

Stahl, Ann B., 2002. Colonial Entanglements and the Practices of Taste: An Alternative to Logocentric Approaches. *American Anthropologist* 104(3):827–845.

Stern, Steve J., 1981. The Rise and Fall of Indian-White Alliances: A Regional View of "Conquest" History. *Hispanic American Historical Review* 61(3):461–491.

Stern, Steve J., 1988. Feudalism, Capitalism, and the World-System in the Perspective of Latin America and the Caribbean. *The American Historical Review* 93(4):829–872.

Stern, Steve J., 1995. The Variety and Ambiguity of Native Andean Intervention in European Colonial Markets. In *Ethnicity, Markets, and Migration in the Andes: At the Crossroads of History and Anthropology*, edited by Brooke Larson, Olivia Harris, and Enrique Tandeter, pp. 73–100. Duke University Press, Durham, NC.

Strathern, Andrew, and Patrick J. Stewart, 1999. Objects, Relationships and Meanings: Historical Switches in Currencies in Mount Hagen, Papua New Guinea. In *Money and Modernity: State and Local Currencies in Melanesia*, edited by David Akin and Joel Robbins, pp. 164–191. University of Pittsburgh Press, Pittsburgh, PA.

Tandeter, Enrique, 1993. *Coercion and Market: Silver Mining in Colonial Potosí, 1692–1826*. University of New Mexico Press, Albuquerque.

TePaske, John J., 2010. *A New World of Gold and Silver*, edited by Kendall W. Brown. Brill, Boston.

Thomas, Nicholas, 1991. *Entangled Objects: Exchange, Material Culture, and Colonialism in the Pacific.* Harvard University Press, Cambridge, MA.

Townsend, Camilla, 2003. Burying the White Gods: New Perspectives on the Conquest of Mexico. *The American Historical Review* 108:659–687.

Van Buren, Mary, 1993. Community and Empire in Southern Peru: The Site of Torata Alta under Spanish Rule. Unpublished Ph.D. dissertation, University of Arizona, Tucson.

Van Buren, Mary, 1999. Tarapaya: An Elite Spanish Residence Near Colonial Potosí in Comparative Perspective. *Historical Archaeology* 33(2):108–122.

Van Buren, Mary, 2010. The Archaeological Study of Spanish Colonialism in the Americas. *Journal of Archaeological Research* 18:151–201.

Van Buren, Mary, and Barbara H. Mills, 2005. Huayrachinas and Tocochimbos: Traditional Smelting Technology of the Southern Andes. *Latin American Antiquity* 16(1):3–25.

Van den Berghe, Pierre L., and George P. Primov, 1977. *Inequality in the Peruvian Andes: Class and Ethnicity in Cuzco.* University of Missouri Press, Columbia, MO.

Vilar, Pierre, 1976. *A History of Gold and Money, 1450–1920*. Translated by Judith White. Humanities Press, Atlantic Highlands, NJ.

Voss, Barbara, L., 2008. Gender, Race, and Labor in the Archaeology of the Spanish Colonial Americas. *Current Anthropology* 49(5):861–893.

Wachtel, Nathan, 1977. *The Vision of the Vanquished: The Spanish Conquest of Peru through Indian Eyes.* Harper and Row Publishers, New York.

Wallerstein, I. M., 1974. *The Modern World-system: Capitalist Agriculture and the European World Economy in the Sixteenth Century.* Academic Press, New York.

Weaver, Brendan J. M., 2008. Ferro Ingenio: An Archaeological and Ethnohistorical View of Labor and Empire in Colonial Porco and Potosí. M.A. thesis, Western Michigan University, Kalamazoo, MI.

Wernke, Steven A., 2003. An Archaeo-history of Andean Community and Landscape in the Late Prehispanic and Early Colonial Colca Valley, Peru. Unpublished Ph.D. dissertation, University of Wisconsin–Madison, Madison, WI.

Wernke, Steven A., 2007. Analogy or Erasure? Dialectics of Religious Transformation in the Early Doctrinas of the Colca Valley, Peru. *International Journal of Historical Archaeology* 11(2):152–182.

Wernke, Steven A., and Ericka Guerra Santander, 2010. *Informe técnico: Proyecto arqueológico Tuti Antiguo, valle del Colca—fase II: excavacíon en el sitio de Malata.* INC, Lima, Peru.

Wightman, Ann M., 1990. *Indigenous Migration and Social Change: The Forasteros of Cuzco, 1570–1720.* Duke University Press, Durham, NC.

Zulawski, Ann, 1995. *They Eat from Their Labor: Work and Social Change in Colonial Bolivia.* University of Pittsburgh Press, Pittsburgh, PA.

Chapter 3

Entangled Objects and Disarticulated Bodies: Managing Social Upheaval in Middle Horizon Peru

Justin Jennings and Willy Yépez Álvarez

In the summer of 1995, a bulldozer operator extending a soccer field exposed two burial contexts in the village of La Real. Bystanders immediately rushed in to look for the mummy bundles commonly found in later period tombs on the arid coast of far southern Peru. Called *pelotas*—the Spanish term for balls—a bundle is typically composed of a tightly flexed individual wrapped in multiple layers of textiles. Offerings were usually placed within the textiles or on the ground beside the mummy. Instead of pelotas, the villagers of La Real were greeted with a surface scatter of bones, cloth, ceramics, wood, and other material. The La Real contexts were quickly secured, and the ensuing excavations of the site directed by Pablo de la Vera demonstrated that mummy bundles *had* been deposited at La Real. With its feathered textiles, face-necked jars, engraved gourds, exotic animals, and precious metals, La Real was actually one of the richest tombs ever discovered in the region. Yet these bundles had been intentionally opened, and their contents broken, scattered, and often burned.

The destruction of the mummies was surprising. There is a long tradition in the Andes of keeping the individual intact after death since visiting with the deceased was often an integral part of ancestor worship (e.g., Dillehay 1995; Isbell 1997; Kaulicke 2000; see Figure 3.1). Archaeologists and locals both were accustomed to finding intact bundles in undisturbed burials in this region (e.g., Disselhoff 1969; Duchesne 2005), and initially suspected that the mummies had been broken apart during colonial or modern looting. Yet there was strong evidence to suggest that both contexts had been untouched since they were sealed near the end of the Middle Horizon period (AD 600–1000; Yépez Álvarez 2012a). Moreover, the layering within the contexts suggested that the destruction was not a single act of desecration or rebellion, but rather

Archaeology of Entanglement edited by Lindsay Der and Francesca Fernandini, 77–102

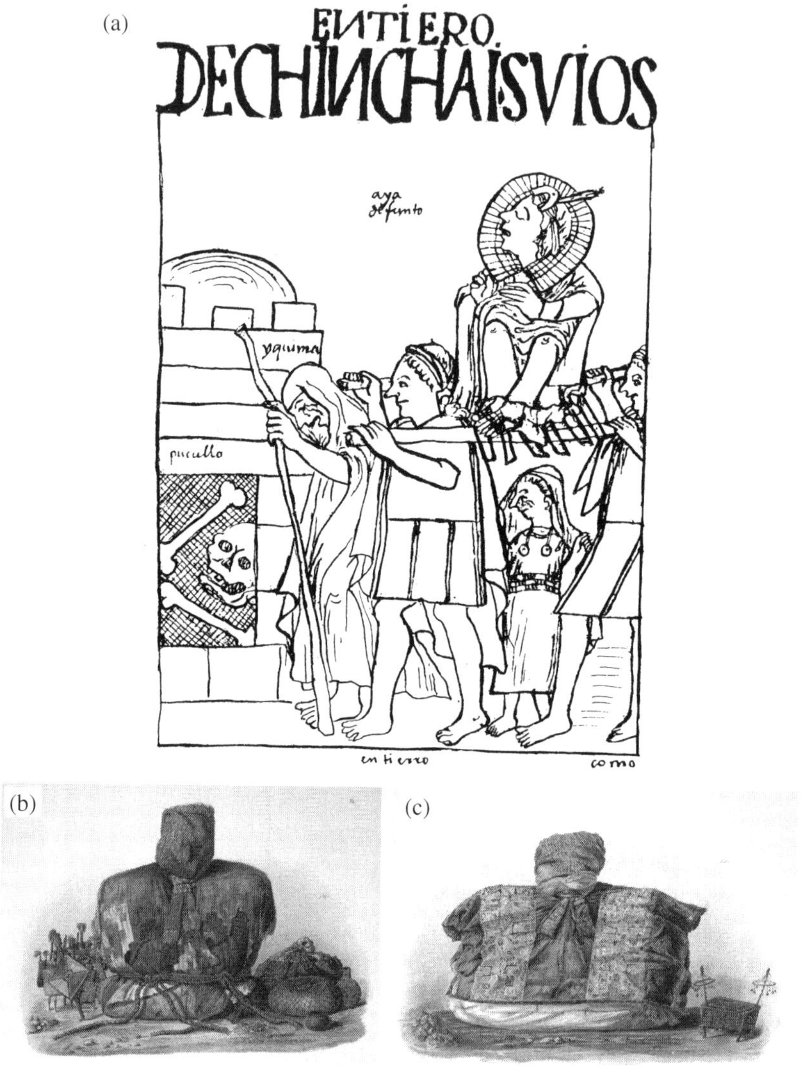

Figure 3.1 Typical Pre-Colombian Andean treatment of the dead: a) Guaman Poma de Ayala's depiction of a funerary procession is on the left (1980[1615], Folio 289), and b) and c)are two drawings by Reiss and Stübel of mummy bundles from the site of Ancón (1880–1887, Figures 15 and 16).

a routine procedure that followed the burial of an individual (Yépez Álvarez 2012a). It did not make sense: if the assemblage was destined to be destroyed, why would a group expend considerable effort to carefully prepare mummy bundles, as well as bring together a wide array of exotic and labor-intensive grave goods?

In this chapter we seek to provide a tentative answer to this question by tracing a few of the shifting sets of local, regional, and interregional relationships at the end of the Early Intermediate period (200 BC–AD 600) and throughout the Middle Horizon. Entanglement, as the editors note in their introduction to this volume, is perhaps best seen as a metaphor for how people are ensnared by their relations with other people, objects, and animals (also see Hodder 2012). The emphasis of this approach, seen from Latour's actor-network theory (2005) to Ingold's meshworks (2000), is often placed on incremental change and the construction of mutual dependencies: the creation of an often-taut web of interconnections that draws agents together. Our emphasis, however, is on disentanglement during the Middle Horizon. Once created, how are entanglements broken down?

We argue that the destruction of the La Real mummy bundles can be best explained as a reaction by some individuals to a surge in long-distant interactions that brought this part of Peru into contact with a variety of people, objects, and especially ideas that threatened the stability of centuries-old local traditions that celebrated relative equality. Newly won elite positions were initially legitimated through association with exotic and enchanted objects (e.g., Gell 1998; Helms 1988), but were replaced by the end of the period by objects that signaled ties to a burgeoning regional economy (Jennings et al. 2015a). The creation of status markers was part of an attempt to disentangle elites from village lifeways that tended to restrict such distinctions. Though these mechanisms proved instrumental in obtaining higher status positions among the living, they had a steep price: in death, elites were broken apart, scattered, and burned.

The Mortuary Contexts at La Real

La Real is located in the Majes Valley, a few kilometers below where the western flanks of the Andes give out to the coastal plain (Figure 3.2). The village today sits on top of the funerary portion of the archaeological site, while a series of deteriorating terraces above the village are all that remains of the site's domestic component. La Real has long been known for the occasional Middle Horizon artifact found by villagers (García Marquez and Buastamente Montoro 1990), and the quality of the objects unearthed at the site is higher that that found in other contemporary sites in the valley. The bulldozer that cut into the hillside in 1995 uncovered a variety of funerary contexts, the most important of which were a cave and adjoining semi-subterranean structure that were extensively excavated. The physical proximity of these locations, coupled with the seeming redundancy of their material, led the excavators to treat the two contexts as contemporaneous (Figure 3.3). Our analysis, however, reveals that the cave predates the outlying structure and was going out of use as a burial location by the time the structure was built (Jennings et al. 2015a).

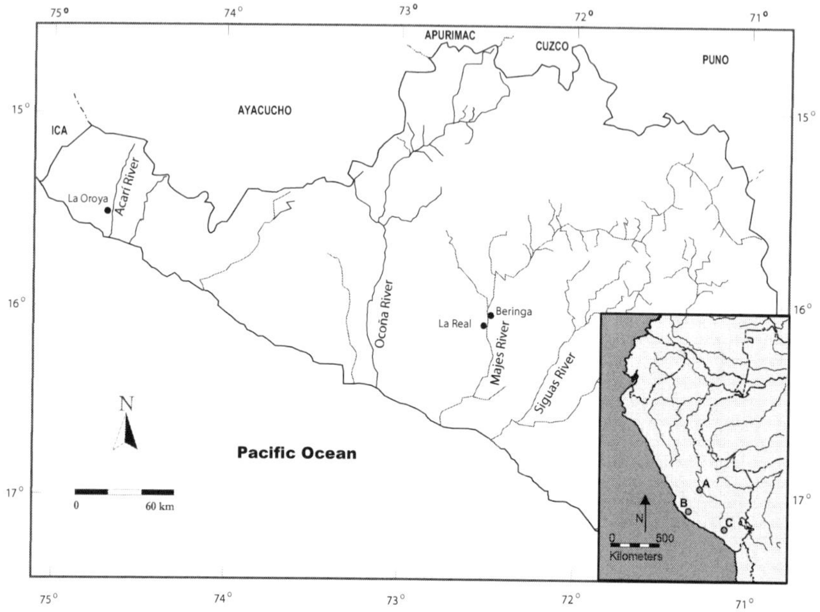

Figure 3.2 Location of La Real, Beringa, and La Oroya in the Department of Arequipa in southern Peru. Inset shows the relationship between a) the city of Huari in Ayacucho, b) the site of Pacheco in Nazca, and c) the funerary contexts of La Real (Map by Justin Jennings).

The cave was filled to a depth of almost 2 meters with the remains of mummy bundles and funerary offerings. We have all of the pieces that one would find in a bundle: the kinds of ropes used to bind an individual, for example, along with the plain-weave cloth with cactus spine pins to wrap around the flexed body and lots of the raw cotton batting that gave the bundle its egg shape (Jennings 2012a). Excavators also recovered likely funerary offerings such as ceramic vessels, snuff tablets, and other objects that were deposited around the individual (Huamán López 2012; Yépez Álvarez 2012a, 2012b), as well as the small bags filled with coca leaves, pigments, and other material that were likely placed inside the bundles (Jennings 2012a; Muñoz Rojas 2012). Among these offerings were at least seven trophy heads (Tung 2012a; see Figure 3.4).

Though everything that an archaeologist would expect in a later-period funerary context was there, the mummy bundles had been ripped open during the Middle Horizon. At the base of the cave, excavators found the bottoms of bundles that had been originally placed in upright positions. Many of the bundles had been partially burned, and there was a preponderance of foot bones excavated near the cave floor. The human remains, textiles, cotton batting,

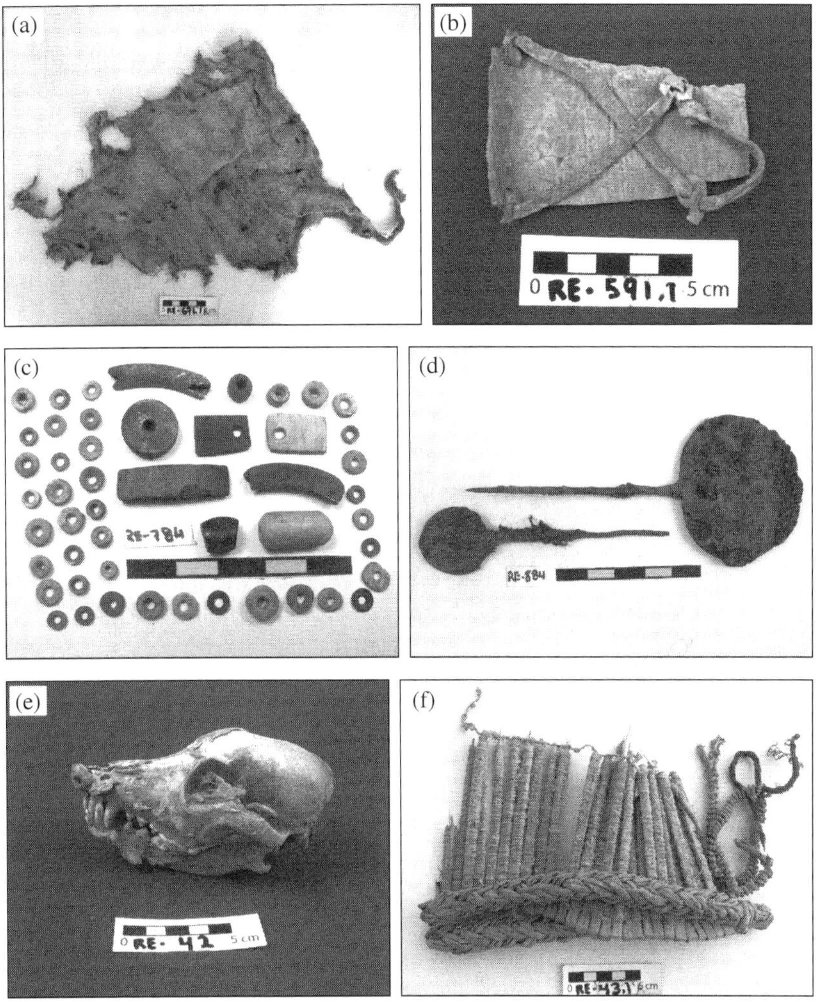

Figure 3.3 Examples of the material found in the funerary contexts at La Real: a) plain weave cotton cloth used as mummy bundle wrappings, b) a child's sandal, c) burnt shell and stone beads, d) two clothing pins, e) a dog's head, and f) a headdress that was originally decorated with tail feathers (Photos by Justin Jennings).

ceramics, and other artifacts above the floor were often fragmented, burned, dispersed, and then thoroughly mixed together (Yépez Álvarez 2012a). This sequence is perhaps best demonstrated by our reconstruction of vessels from the cave. A sherd blackened by burning from one part of the tomb could be joined with another sherd with no evidence of burning that was found a meter below on the opposite side of the tomb (Figure 3.5). The well-defined sublayers

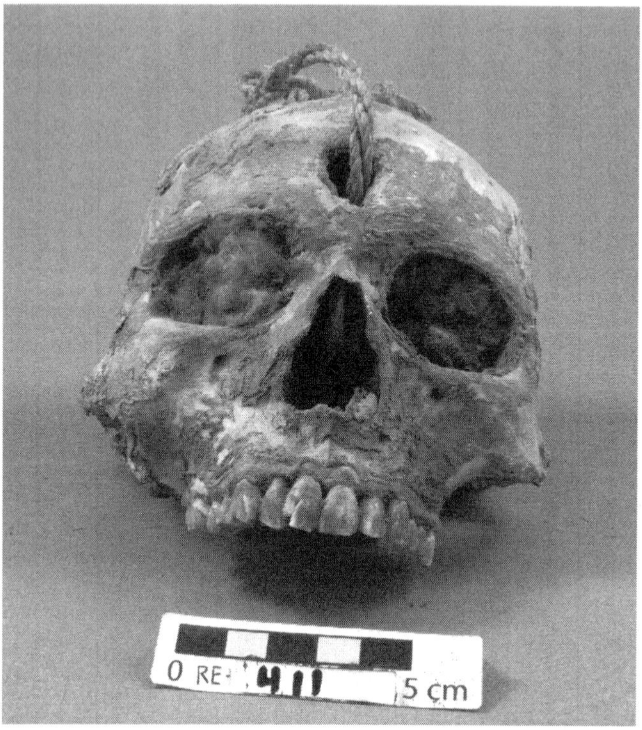

Figure 3.4 Trophy head from the cave at La Real (Photo by Justin Jennings).

Figure 3.5 A broken, burned, and refitted coastal-influenced vessel from the cave at La Real (Photo by Justin Jennings).

of mixed remains within the cave suggest a reoccurring mortuary process in which a group of mummy bundles was placed in the cave, destroyed, and then perhaps pushed deeper inside. This process would be repeated multiple times before the cave was sealed.

The semi-subterranean building also contains remains similar to those documented in the cave, but with two important distinctions. First, the floor of the building did not contain the base of mummy bundles, and instead it seems likely that the structure's funerary assemblages had been originally buried in another location(s). Second, there is no evidence for burning, even though the assemblage in the structure was as thoroughly mixed as that of the cave. Instead, brown stains running down the stucco walls hint at liquid offerings that may have been used to consecrate the structure, while cloth-wrapped bouquets of plants placed on top of assemblages suggest that ceremonies took place after the remains arrived. The existence of sublayers within the fill suggests an ongoing, likely ritually charged, process of moving material out of a tomb(s) and into the building. Insect casings, both in the cave and the structure, reveal that the tomb contents were exposed to the air.

A Bayesian analysis of the radiocarbon dates from the two contexts demonstrate that the cave's use dates primarily to the first part of the Middle Horizon (approximately AD 650–850), and that the structure dates primarily to the second part of the Middle Horizon (approximately AD 850–1050) (Figure 3.6; see Jennings [2012b:40] for additional information on radiocarbon dates). Our ceramics analysis supports this temporal distinction because the Wari-related material from the cave is largely Middle Horizon 1 in Menzel's sequence, while the ceramics from Middle Horizon 2 predominate in the structure (Huamán López 2012; Jennings et al. 2015a). The few Middle Horizon 2 sherds found in the cave are primarily associated with a final layer placed on top of the funerary assemblages that dates to the first half of the Middle Horizon. The notable remains in this layer were the heads of dogs (Jennings 2012a) and parrots (Ugarte-Lewis and Yépez Álvarez 2012), as well as disarticulated human bones that were tied together in bundles.

The temporal distinction between the cave and structure allows us to tentatively suggest the creation of a regional political economy by the second half of the Middle Horizon that linked coastal and highland Arequipa (Jennings et al. 2015a). This suggestion is based on a number of patterns in our data, including the decline in the percentage of foreign styles at La Real over time, and the replacement of these exotics by styles from highland Arequipa (Huamán López 2012); the disappearance of featherwork and the increasing standardization of textile production using locally available cottons (Coleman Goldstein and Yépez Álvarez 2012); and the shift from the use of a variety of obsidian sources to the exclusive exploitation of the closest source in the second half of the Middle Horizon (Glascock 2012).

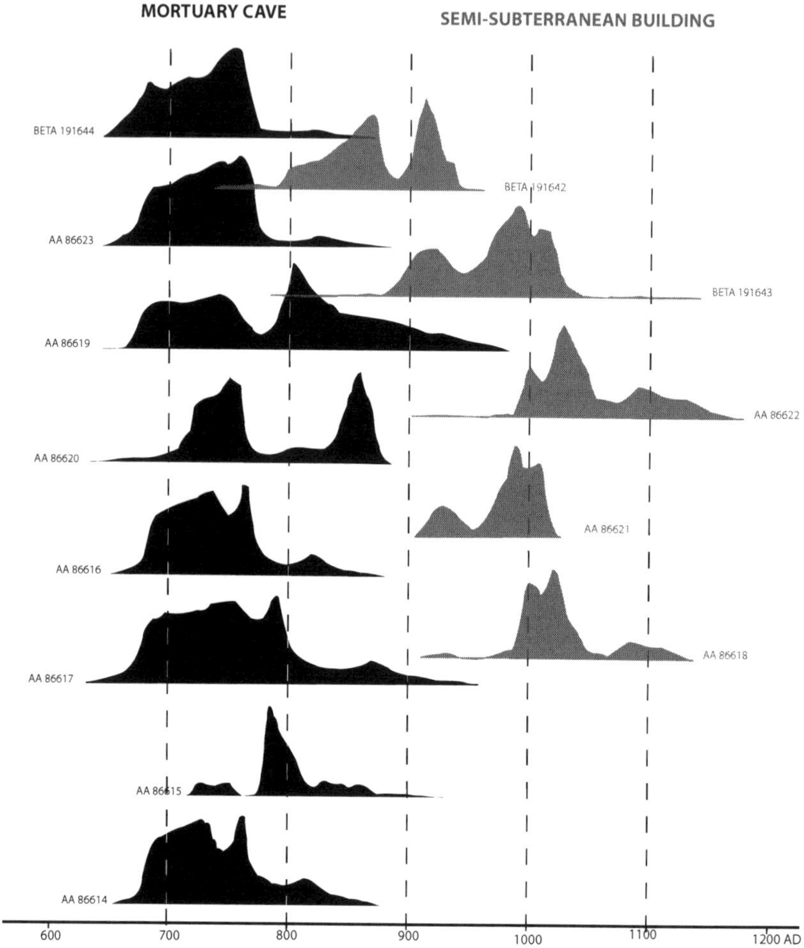

Figure 3.6 Bayesian calibration of radiocarbon assays from La Real (Figure by Justin Jennings).

Early Intermediate Period Entanglements and Middle Horizon Disruptions

To understand why the mummies at La Real were destroyed, we must first try to sketch the site's broader historical context. Although the cultural history of the Department of Arequipa before the Middle Horizon remains poorly understood, we know that hunter-gatherers arrived into the region by at least 9000 BC and that the first villages were likely settled sometime in the fourth millennium BC (Keefer et al. 1998; Perry et al. 2006; Sandweiss et al. 1998). A few scattered hints of emerging social complexity in Arequipa occur during the first millennium BC: a stone monolith recently discovered in a farmer's field, gold pectorals reportedly exhumed from coastal graves at the turn of the twentieth century, and a handful of exotic ceramics at highland sites all hint at both rising social inequality and connections to groups in the Lake Titicaca region (Chávez Chávez 1992; Jennings 2002; McEwan and Haeberli 2000; Neira Avendaño and Cardona Rosas 2001; Ziółkowski and Tunia 2005).

Although Lake Titicaca influence lingered on Arequipa textiles, the connections to this region seem to have disappeared before the beginning of the Early Intermediate period (200 BC–AD 600) (Haeberli 2002, 2006, 2009; also see Manrique Valdivia and Cornejo Zegarra 1990). The inchoate social complexity seen earlier in the first millennium BC also does not seem to have carried over into this period. The limited evidence we have suggests people lived in small, isolated, and largely egalitarian villages (e.g., Jennings 2002:178–181; Wernke 2010), and excavations of burials that show little to no status differences between them support this impression (Disselhoff 1969). The inhabitants of the region likely had contact with other regions in Peru since Arequipa's two obsidian sources were widely used throughout much of Peru during the period (Burger et al. 2000), yet local ceramic styles remained largely unchanged from the previous period (Santos Ramírez 1980). Conservatism thus seems to have been a cultural choice, and this conservatism was likely linked to village lifeways.

An Early Intermediate period village has yet to be excavated in Arequipa, but cross-cultural studies of villages have emphasized some of the myriad human and object entanglements that tend to limit change (Bandy and Fox 2010). If life in these earlier villages was broadly similar to that led by those living in isolated Andean communities today, then ancestor worship reinforced fealty to traditional practices, children spent a significant portion of their youth tending to animals far from home, and daughters inherited grinding stones and cooking pots from their mothers. Most "long-distance" relationships were economic and marriage ties to neighboring communities, while occasional llama caravans brought salt, seaweed, and gossip from further afield (Bolin 2006; Isbell 1978; Mayer 2002). Although details like these can only be revealed through future fieldwork, the scant evidence at our disposal suggests a profoundly local, tradition-bound existence for those living in the La Real region during the Early Intermediate period.

The same cannot be said for those living 300 kilometers to the north in the Nazca region, where village life was significantly less insular (Vaughn 2009). In the first centuries AD, the people of the region enjoyed long-distance ties to the sierra and other parts of the coast and were brought together into a shared religious system centered on the ceremonial center of Cahuachi (Silverman 2002). The region's population, however, was under considerable stress by the sixth century AD. The toll of deforestation and desertification in Nazca is evident in the archaeological record with mounting violence, lower life expectancy, and an increased reliance on imported foods (Beresford-Jones et al. 2009:325–327). This stress may have led to the collapse of Cahuachi and the aggregation of the drainage's population into larger settlements headed by warring chiefs (Isla and Reindel 2006; Schreiber and Lancho Rojas 2003; Silverman 2002).

While Nazca was fragmenting into a series of rival chiefdoms in the seventh century AD, the Wari state was beginning to coalesce in the central Peruvian highlands around a city named Huari. Settlers from this city entered the Nazca Valley and founded the site of Pacheco at the beginning of the Middle Horizon (Schreiber 1999). Although the site was likely built to provide more regular access to coastal products, the new outpost does not seem to have been welcomed by the Nasca people (Schreiber 2001:88). Instead, most groups fled the land around Pacheco; the only sites remaining were small villages perched in defensive locations (Conlee and Schreiber 2006:100).

Residents of the Nazca Valley may have resisted the encroachment of the Wari state, but they appear to have coveted and widely emulated Wari-style objects (Conlee 2010). They also embraced new varieties of crops during the Middle Horizon, and there is some tentative evidence of new terracing techniques being practiced in the upper reaches of the valley (Kellner and Schoeninger 2008:239; Schreiber 1999:169). Entanglements with the Wari state, as well as with other outsiders, created a more cosmopolitan environment even as population scattered. Many fled Pachecho's environs for Huaca del Loro, a site in the Las Trancas Valley of the Nazca drainage just to the south of Pachecho (Strong 1957). Others may have set off further south, setting off a wave of cultural change that would transform Arequipa society.

The elites of the Acarí Valley in the far north of the department had been using some Nasca objects and cultural practices to legitimize their rule in a valley beset with endemic warfare (Valdez 2009a, 2009c, 2009d). Wari influence arrived in Acarí soon after Pacheco was founded, and is perhaps best seen indirectly though the creation of the Chaviña style that is closely related to Loro, Nasca's *local* Middle Horizon style (Valdez 2009b:201–202). Ceramics and textiles in Wari styles from Ayacuhco were also introduced at this time, and Lidio Valdez describes a ritual smash of Middle Horizon ceramics from the site of La Oroya in Acarí (Valdez 2009b).

Smashing and then depositing richly decorated ceramics is often considered a Wari state practice (e.g., Schreiber 1992:111), and Valdez suggests that the La Oroya cache is evidence of imperial control over the region (2009c). The smash likely reflects the embracing of a persuasive Wari religious ideology linked not only to the smashing of pots, but also to an evolving set of practices that involved ritual violence, feasting, ancestor worship, and, a bit later, the reverence of a staffed deity (Isbell 2008:738–739). Yet this does not necessarily equate to a Wari conquest of the region. The La Oroya smash is in keeping with the pre-existing practices in Acarí of co-opting foreign objects and practices to legitimate elite positions. The burning associated with the smash seems to be a local addition to a Wari practice, and the mixing of Cajamarca and other non-Wari style wares into the cache might represent attempts by leaders to also signal links to other groups in the central Andes (Valdez 2009c:200–202).

When Wari ideological and stylistic influence arrived in the beginning of the Middle Horizon in the Siguas, Ocoña, and Majes valleys to the south, it had thus already been channeled through Nazca and Acarí's social environment of marked inequality and violence. The egalitarian ethos of Early Intermediate period coastal Arequipa appears to have eroded quickly as emerging elites vied against each other using a mixture of violence, feasting, exotica, and religion adopted from their northern neighbors (Jennings 2014). Village entanglements that had traditionally limited status gains, at least on the surface, were overwhelmed.

Tiffiny Tung's excavations at the nearby site of Beringa in the Majes Valley suggest that Middle Horizon villagers grew tolerant of a certain degree of social differences within a few generations. Slight wealth and status differences can be detected between households at the site, which were maintained in death (Tung 2003:46, 2007b:258–259). Most people at Beringa were buried in small, circular stone–lined cist tombs situated in domestic areas (Tung 2007b:258). However, more than 70 men, women, and children were buried in a unique, circular tomb that measured 4.5 meters in diameter. *Spondylus* shell, polychrome textiles, and other goods excavated from the larger tomb led Tung to tentatively suggest that the village's leading families may have chosen to be buried in this location together (Tung 2007b:259). The individuals buried in this tomb—and indeed across the entire site—were "enveloped in textiles and then wrapped with vegetal cord" to create mummy bundles (Tung 2007b:259). Unlike at the nearby site of La Real, the bundles were left intact.

The objects interred with the destroyed mummies at La Real were more ostentatious than those found at Beringa. The trophy heads, outlandish headgear, drug-taking paraphernalia, and other offerings were thus likely used to reinforce a claim of social difference that was more radical that that offered within villages (Tung 2007a:944). The individuals buried at La Real may have premised their positions on extralocal connections and the largesse that such connections could bring. Yet handing out beer, raiding villages—33% of the recovered crania at Beringa had at least one head wound (Tung 2007a:947)—and dressing up in costumes may have not been enough to overcome a lack of resonance with earlier beliefs (i.e., Hodder 2012:123–132).

No matter how it was packaged, aggrandizing strategies may not have felt right within a context of a longstanding egalitarian ethos. Despite status gains, the pre-existing entanglements that fostered conservatism were not so easily broken. The Wari-Nasca-Acarí connections offered a blueprint for a new society that many villagers seemed hesitant to embrace. Majes Valley elites would ultimately use this blueprint to entrench a stratified position in life, but the webs of village entanglements were ultimately too taut to allow for radical social differences in death (i.e., Hodder 2012:103–105): La Real's mummies were ripped apart, broken, and burned in a ritual cleansing.

Entangled Objects, Disarticulated Bodies, and Animal Farm

In George Orwell's *Animal Farm* (1945), the animals take over a farm and attempt to create a society premised on the guiding principle that "all animals are created equal." The pigs take on leadership roles and slowly begin to live in an ostentatious manner and assert their power over the other animals. When the other animals question them, the pigs say that their actions are selfless ones that benefit the entire community. When they finally manage to change the farm's principle to "all animals are created equal, but some are more equal than others," it is too late for protestations: the pigs are firmly in control.

Those buried at La Real also sought to create a stratified society without alienating its members. They would have faced similar obstacles to those of Orwell's pigs, but the book actually gives short shrift to the myriad struggles attendant to this transition (Vaughn et al. 2010). Leveling social differences is a central, ongoing struggle within egalitarian societies (Wiessner 1996), and egalitarianism has its own suites of entanglements: people would have used a variety of mechanisms from taunting to food sharing to limit individual aggrandizing. An ethos of relative equality likely ran deeply through the conservative relationships that bound together the people, animals, and objects of the Majes Valley. Considerably invested in maintaining the status quo, villagers would have been highly suspicious of any actions that ran counter to centuries-long traditions.

The sudden arrival of objects, ideas, and perhaps even people via the new Wari-Nasca-Acarí connections nonetheless managed to break and stretch some of the longstanding entanglements that fostered conservatism and egalitarianism in the Majes Valley. The swirl of new sights, sounds, and tastes in the period could not be ignored, and a few enterprising individuals sought to capitalize on these interregional interactions. One of the ways they did this was by shifting the relationships villagers had with exotic goods.

Entangled Objects

Many of the objects found at La Real can be seen in part as the emerging elite's attempt to signal connections to a distant world. A puma's foot, for example, was found in the cave, as was a condor's head (Jennings 2012a; Ugarte-Lewis and Yépez Álvarez 2012). Both animals were unlikely to have been available locally, and their internment alongside an array of exotic ceramics, textiles, metals, and woodwork was likely used to signal the magical qualities often associated with those that have access to unseen realms (Helms 1988). Most of these objects offered tangible proof of connections to expanding exchange networks that brought material to the site from across the central Andes (Jennings et al. 2015a). The hallucinogenic drugs likely inhaled from the site's snuff trays, however, did more than this: they propelled La Real's elites into the sky (Yépez Álvarez 2012b; see Torres and Repke 2006).

Only some of La Real's "exotic" material was actually made elsewhere. Three-quarters of the vessels in the two contexts share the valley's chemical signature (Bedregal et al. 2015), for instance, and the spindle whorls, shuttles, and other weaving equipment at La Real suggest a robust textile industry. In *Art and Agency* (1998), Alfred Gell talks about a group's corpus of art as a "distributed" object, within which "each piece, each motif, each line or groove, speaks to every other one" (1998:221). Many of the locally made objects found at La Real incorporated and often transformed foreign iconography. By interweaving (sometimes literally) local and introduced motifs and manufacturing techniques, artists sought to do more than just signal their long-distance connections; they also sought to make the exotic more coherent to the people of the Majes Valley by creating a hybrid artistic canon (e.g., Gell 1998:215).

Elite desires to connect their prestige items to distant groups *without* alienating local communities led to the creation of unique pieces. One example from the cave is a tunic that bore a tapestry weave on one face and a feathered panel on the other. The tunic's side panels were made with what is likely fox fur, and the bottom is fringed with braids of human hair (Figure 3.7). The tapestry

Figure 3.7 Portion of a tunic decorated with feathers, strips of fur, and braids of human hair

weave panel on the front of the tunic was in an iconic Wari style that was exceedingly difficult to make (Bergh 1999), while the feathered panel is likely derived from Nasca antecedents (Quequezana Lucano et al. 2012). At least some of the featherwork at La Real was probably made in the Majes Valley because of the use of a reoccurring motif—an anthropomorphic being with splayed arms and legs—that occurs locally across a range of artifact types. The foxes were likely found locally, and the hair may have been obtained in the valley as well.

Tunics like this one were pastiches that entangled the local and the foreign by their very production. Local artists used a Nasca-invented technique to attach rows of Amazonian feathers (though the parrots may have been raised in the valley) into motifs of local importance. They attached fur from locally acquired animals to imported textile, and may have even added a family member's hair to the ensemble. Pastiches like this were repeated throughout much of the assemblage. *Spondylus* shell from the warm waters off Ecuador was worked into a pendant and then strung together into bracelets with Amazonian beans (Jennings 2012a); metal clothing pins (*tupus*) often had Wari silhouettes, but were manufactured differently and sometimes featured elaborate punctate designs that have been found only on the far southern Peruvian coast (Velarde et al. 2012; Jennings et al. 2015b). The reoccurring creation of these hybrid objects was a persuasive argument for a new status quo that made external connections to the exotic foundational to local life.

Since most of the La Real assemblage shows signs of use, it is likely that the objects were routinely used prior to their burial and subsequent destruction. The people buried at La Real thus could have worn the hybrid tunics, drank from the imported vessels, and displayed their exotic animals (the foot of a black-chested buzzard-eagle from the cave has its claws clipped, suggesting that it was likely kept as a pet [Ugarte-Lewis and Yépez Álvarez 2012]). The new entanglements were inscribed repeatedly and very visibly on an array of garments and personal paraphernalia that would have almost certainly been used in highly charged ritual events. Emerging elites could thus hope to embody this local-exotic pastiche over time. They could argue for innate difference without sacrificing the community ties that were also integral to maintaining their position.

The blending of foreign and local elements did not take place overnight. In an alcove in the La Real cave, there were a number of largely intact objects that appear to date to around the earliest use of the context. Among these objects were a heavily mended bowl, spoon, and a figurative bottle with a bulbous face and protruding ears (Figure 3.8). The heavily mended bowl is in the Loro style of early Middle Horizon Nasca, the spoon is made in the Okros style of the Wari heartland, and the figurative bottle is a product of the local La Ramada style. These vessels may have been involved in feasts

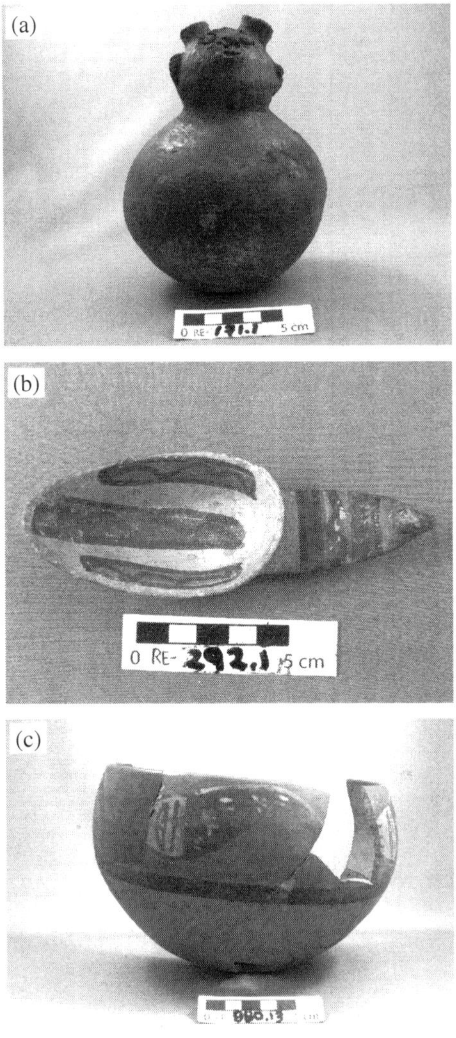

Figure 3.8 a) La Ramada style bottle, b) Okros style spoon, and c) Loro style bowl from the cave at La Real (Photos by Justin Jennings).

to reinforce incipient elite positions during the initial decades of the Middle Horizon (Coleman Goldstein 2010).

One might imagine a host signaling connections to other worlds by slurping soup out of a Nasca bowl with a Wari spoon. Yet, the host might have also clutched the La Ramada bottle. Two similar La Ramada–style bottles at

La Real had been filled with *molle* drupes. Molle is used to make beer in the Andes today, and is quite common at southern Peruvian sites in the Middle Horizon: 24% of the total potential food resources recovered by weight at Beringa consisted of molle drupes (Goldstein et al. 2009; Tung 2007b:260). The La Ramada bottle found in the alcove at La Real may have served as a decanter for molle beer, and thus our host may have signaled exterior relationships in one hand while offering refreshment in the other hand via a locally made vessel in a well-recognized, traditional style.

However the vessels may have been used prior to their placement in the cave, they were the products of three distinct art styles. Places like Nazca, the Amazon, and the central highlands remained far-off locales in the first decades of the Middle Horizon, a handful of loose, secondary entanglements that were captivating but of little importance to most people in the valley. As time went on, however, these global entanglements were repositioned, bleeding together into novel pastiches that circulated widely within the valley (e.g., Jennings 2011). As a regional economy grew, a more established elite would grow less dependent on signaling these broad, if likely quite shallow, relationships. Their legitimacy was now supported by a new emphasis on importing and incorporating styles from other valleys in Arequipa (Jennings et al. 2015b)

Disarticulated Bodies

Villagers in the Majes Valley incorporated the introduced iconographies into their domestically produced ceramics (Owen 2010), and they participated in the feasts, rituals, and other activities that created a more stratified society during the first centuries of the Middle Horizon. Those living in Majes were therefore at least somewhat receptive to the underlying ideologies of these imported styles that often, among other things, stressed the existence of a sacred covenant between the gods and a privileged few (Cook 2012; Knobloch 2011, 2012). They seemed willing to suffer through some level of social stratification in return for elite access to other realms (both spiritual and secular).

They did not reject the ethos of the previous era, however. Elites still found themselves entrapped in webs of local interactions based on equality and the priority of the community over the individual. Majes was not like Nazca or Acarí, where elite positions had become entrenched in the preceding Early Intermediate period. Aspiring elites could not legitimize their positions through the force of tradition: they could not depend on a web of taut, often-unquestioned entanglements that had built up slowly over generations. Instead, they needed to painstakingly create more tentative positions of power by finding a way to signal at the same time that they were both *of* and *above* the people. The creation of a hybrid artistic canon was one method elites used to broadcast this mixed message. Another method may have been by allowing themselves and their funerary goods to be destroyed in secondary mortuary rituals performed at La Real.

The cultural anthropologist Victor Turner studied the Ndembu of Africa during a period of surging long-distance interaction and culture change that is reminiscent of what was occurring in the Middle Horizon Majes Valley (1969). He suggested that Ndembu villagers dealt with tensions in part by engaging in rituals designed to create *communitas*, an intense feeling of social togetherness and belonging that exists when people find themselves standing momentarily together "outside" of society. Standing outside of society allows one to transgress social norms (e.g., Lincoln 1989), making violent, destructive, and painful acts prohibited at other times permissible, if not necessary, during ritual events (e.g., Bloch 1986). With the gulf between elites and non-elites widening in the Majes Valley, the ritual destruction of the most visible symbols of stratification could have been required to restore cosmic balance, a necessary corrective after death exacted by the community for status positions in life.

The La Real mummy bundles may thus have been a sacrifice. Buried together in a discrete location, richly attired, and surrounded by both prestigious imports and the masterworks of local artists, the bundles at the site were set apart from other deceased. The prayers, dances, drinking, and other activities that likely occurred during the mortuary ceremonies may have further stressed the differences between elite and non-elite. Yet showcasing elite status may have also ultimately highlighted the universalities of death *despite* earthly differences. Ian Kuijt argues that secondary mortuary practices are often used to reaffirm community identity and egalitarian beliefs during periods of mounting social inequality and shifting food regimes (1996; also see Kujit 2001). He suggests that the disarticulation and movement of skeletal remains from one context to the next transformed the deceased from an individual into a part of the community. The dismantling of the La Real mummies may have similarly served to erase an individual's identity. Initially placed in the cave as elite individuals, the mummies were then literally and figuratively broken down in subsequent ceremonies.

Yet it is important to stress that the destruction of the La Real mummies is not an example of a valley-wide ritual to break down all individuals and erase all status differences. If this were the case, we would expect to see similar kinds of destruction at Beringa and other sites. Reminiscent of La Real, Beringa's leading families were buried with prestige goods in a separate location. Yet Beringa bundles were all left intact (Tung 2012b:88–90). By destroying *only* the La Real mummies, participants tacitly allowed for limited status difference while also reaffirming the long-standing entanglements that encouraged egalitarianism. Some stratification was acceptable, but those who achieved the loftiest of positions in life were broken, scattered, and burned in death.

The breakup of the body, so anathema to many groups in the Andes (e.g., Isbell 1997), would have been a powerful symbol of *communitas*. When the mummy bundles were first placed in the cave, the clothing and objects that accompanied the dead clearly marked their elite status. Over time, these individuals and their status markers were effectively erased when the burial contexts were disassembled. Kuijt suggests that the mortuary and ritual practices in the Late Natufian Levant (10,800–10,100 BC) were reinforced over hundreds of years "as a system of codes for limiting the development and centralization of power and authority within early agricultural communities" (1996:332). Compared with that of the Levant, social differences in the Majes Valley arose more quickly, perhaps signaling the community's need for a more violent, purgative, ritual of status destruction to restore balance (e.g., Bloch 1986).

Rituals serve in part as safety valves that help release the social tensions that inevitably build up within communities. The events allow people to act in ways that are often not socially acceptable at other times, and can occasionally be used by participants to challenge existing conditions (Dirks 1994). The carefully prepared mummy bundles at La Real were laid to rest with a rich array of funerary offerings. The violence and thoroughness with which the mummy bundles were destroyed suggests zealous participation in the dismantling of these symbols of elite authority. Those that prepared the deceased for burial were likely unhappy with the destruction, but this was the price high elites paid for their positions. The ripping apart of bundles was likely a visceral reminder of the still quite precarious nature of status hierarchies in the Majes Valley.

Societal Disruptions and the "Prehistory of the Mass"

Ian Hodder's approach to entanglements is derived primarily from his work at Çatalhöyük, a town in Turkey that was occupied for almost 1,500 years. His careful work there over the last three decades has shown how societies can be transformed through "small changes in the daily practices of large groups of people" (Hodder 2006:63). A shift in the pottery temper used or the location chosen for an oven often had broad and lasting reverberations throughout the site's entanglements. Over time, the "little micro-details of life" built up enough "mass" to reshape society in the region (Hodder 2006:258).

Like other approaches to entanglement, Hodder's "prehistory of the mass" (2006:63) at Çatalhöyük deals little with the kinds of disruptive events that have the potential to shatter existing entanglements. William Sewell (2005) recognizes that catastrophic or unexpected occurrences can sometimes produce a cascade of societal disconnections that are often repaired in novel ways. These repairs can result in broad shifts in a society's social, economic, and political structures (also see Beck et al. 2007; Bolender 2010). Hodder also recognizes that such events can occur (2012:159–160), but they generally remain underdeveloped in entanglement approaches.

Our work in the Majes Valley provides a case study for how "eventful" archaeology can be incorporated into entanglement theory. Although we still lack the data necessary to track in detail the gossamer web of pre-Columbian interactions that bound people, objects, and animals together in the valley, the information that we have on hand suggests that the Middle Horizon was a period of sweeping social transformations triggered by Wari state encroachment into the Nazca Valley. The sudden influx of foreign influence into the Majes Valley created a rupture of the region's longstanding local entanglements that had celebrated conservatism and limited social stratification. Aspiring elite took advantage of this breach by using a combination of prestige goods, violence, feasting, and other mechanisms to tear and recast the entanglements that had previously bound together Majes society.

Elites, however, were not the only ones attempting to refashion the region's social webs at the beginning of the Middle Horizon. Most people had a vested interest in limiting elite control, and they would have also sought to create new entanglements that curtailed elite authority and amplified their responsibilities to the community. The entangled objects and disarticulated bodies of La Real were likely products of these competing efforts to stabilize a society that had been untethered during the first decades of the seventh century AD.

The valley-wide elite in Majes found themselves uncomfortably straddling two opposing worldviews. Like Orwell's pigs, they needed to maintain that everyone was equal while also arguing that some were more equal than others. This position was sustained in part by La Real's articulated objects that brought together the local and the global first separately, then as a pastiche. By incorporating global connections into the valley's artistic canon and then making these objects essential to local affairs, elites could more easily argue that they were public servants who maintained long-distance interactions for the benefit of all members of the community. They *were* different, but they suggested that these differences were necessary for the proper functioning of society.

The secondary mortuary rituals at La Real suggest, however, that a powerful counter-narrative was also being offered in the valley. Villagers seemed willing to accept certain status differences in life, but only if they were erased in death. Yet they demanded more than just an erasure: the thoroughness of the violent destruction at La Real might even be suggestive of a community's barely controlled wrath. The egalitarian ethos had frayed in the Middle Horizon, but was not broken. Under the aegis of ritual, people tore apart their former leaders, broke their belongings, and left their remains burned and scattered long after elite positions had been well established throughout the valley.

Acknowledgments

Analysis of the La Real artifact collection was supported by the Royal Ontario Museum's Kircheis Family Endowment and the Louise Hawley Stone Trust. We thank Lindsay Der and Francesca Giulietta Fernandini for the invitation to contribute to this volume, as well as two anonymous reviewers for comments on an earlier draft of this chapter.

References

Bandy, Matthew S., and Jake R. Fox, eds., 2010. *Becoming Villagers: Comparing Early Village Societies*. University of Arizona Press, Tuscon.

Beck, Robin A. Jr., Douglas J. Bolender, James A. Brown, and Timothy K. Earle, 2007. Eventful Archaeology: The Place of Space in Structural Transformation. *Current Anthropology* 48(6):833–860.

Bedregal, Patricia, Pablo A. Mendoza, Marco S. Ubillús, Willy Yépez Álvarez, Justin Jennings, and Eduardo H. Montoya, 2015. Wari Influence in Southern Peru: Provenance Study of Middle Horizon Pottery from the Archaeological Site of La Real. *Journal of Radioanalytical and Nuclear Chemistry*. Prepublished ahead of print May 8, 2015, as doi:10.1007/s10967-015-4128-z.

Beresford-Jones, David G., Susana Acre T., Olivier Q. Whaley, and Alex J. Chepstow-Lusty, 2009. The Role of Prosopis in Ecological and Landscape Change in the Samaca Basin, Lower Ica Valley, South Coast Peru from the Early Horizon to the Late Intermediate Period. *Latin American Antiquity* 20(2):303–332.

Bergh, Susan E., 1999. Pattern and Paradigm in Middle Horizon Tapestry Tunics. Unpublished Ph.D. dissertation, Columbia University, New York.

Bloch, Maurice, 1986. *From Blessing to Violence: History and Ideology in the Circumcision Ritual of the Merina*. Cambridge University Press, Cambridge, UK.

Bolender, Douglas J., ed., 2010. *Eventful Archaeologies: New Approaches to Social Transformation in the Archaeological Record*. State University of New York Press, Albany.

Bolin, Inge, 2006. *Growing up in a Culture of Respect: Child Rearing in Highland Peru*. University of Texas Press, Austin, TX.

Burger, Richard L., Karen L. Mohr Chávez, and Sergio J. Chávez, 2000. Through the Glass Darkly: Prehispanic Obsidian Procurement and Exchange in Southern Peru and Northern Bolivia. *Journal of World Prehistory* 14:267–362.

Chávez Chávez, José Antonio, 1992. El Formativo de la cultura Peruana. Unpublished master's thesis, Universidad Católica Santa María, Arequipa, Peru.

Coleman Goldstein, Robin, 2010. Negotiating Power in the Wari Empire: A Comparative Study of Local-Imperial Interactions in the Moquegua and Majes Regions during the Middle Horizon (550–1050 CE). Unpublished Ph.D. dissertation, Northwestern University, Evanston, IL.

Coleman Goldstein, Robin, and Willy Yépez Álvarez, 2012. Instrumentos textiles: Ruecas. In *Wari en Arequipa: Análisis de los contextos funerarios de La Real*, edited by Willy Yépez Álvarez and Justin Jennings, pp. 128–144. Museo Arqueológica José María Morante, Universidad Nacional de San Agustín, Arequipa, Peru.

Cook, Anita G., 2012. The Coming of the Staff Deity. In *Wari: Lords of the Ancient Andes*, edited by Susan E. Bergh, pp. 103–121. Cleveland Museum of Art, Cleveland, OH.

Conlee, Christina A., 2010. Nasca and Wari: Local Opportunism and Colonial Ties during the Middle Horizon. In *Beyond Wari Walls: Regional Perspectives on Middle Horizon Peru*, edited by Justin Jennings, pp. 96–112. University of New Mexico Press, Albuquerque, NM.

Conlee, Christina A., and Katharina Schreiber, 2006. The Role of Intermediate Elites in the Balkanization and Reformation of Post-Wari Society in Nasca, Peru. In *Intermediate Elites in Pre-Columbian States and Empires*, edited by Christina Elson and Alan Covey, pp. 94–111. University of Arizona Press, Tucson, AZ.

Dillehay, Tom D., ed., 1995. *Tombs for the Living: Andean Mortuary Practices*. Dumbarton Oaks, Washington, DC.

Dirks, Nicholas B., 1994. Ritual and Resistance: Subversion as a Social Fact. In *Culture/Power/History: A Reader in Contemporary Social Theory*, edited by Nicholas B. Dirks, Geoff Eley, and Sherry B. Ortner, pp. 483–499. Princeton University Press, Princeton, NJ.

Disselhoff, Hans D., 1969. Fruh-Nazca in Suden Perus, Provincia de Camana (Dep. Arequipa). *Verhandlungen des XXXVIII Internationalen Amerikanisten Kongress* 1:385–391.

Duchesne, Frédéric, 2005. Tumbas de Coporaque. Approximaciones a concepciones funerarias Collaguas. *Bulletin de L'Institut Français d'Études Andines* 34(3):411–429.

García Marquez, Manuel, and Rosa Bustamente Montoro, 1990. Arqueología del valle de Majes. *Gaceta Arqueológica Andina* 18/19:25–40.

Gell, Alfred, 1998. *Art and Agency: An Anthropological Theory*. Clarendon Press, Oxford, UK.

Glascock, Michael, 2012. Obsidiana: Síntesis de movilidad giratoria en el sitio. In *Wari en Arequipa: Análisis de los contextos funerarios de La Real*, edited by Willy Yépez Álvarez and Justin Jennings, pp. 174–181. Museo Arqueológica José María Morante, Universidad Nacional de San Agustín, Arequipa, Peru.

Goldstein, David, Robin Coleman Goldstein, and Patrick Ryan Williams, 2009. You Are What You Drink: A Sociocultural Reconstruction of Pre-Hispanic Fermented Beverage Use at Cerro Baúl, Moquegua, Peru. In *Drink, Power, and Society in the Andes,* edited by Justin Jennings and Brenda Bowser, pp. 133–166. University Press of Florida, Gainesville.

Guáman Poma de Ayala, Felipe, 1980 (1615). *Nueva corónica y buen gobierno*, edited by John V. Murra and Rolena Adorna. Translated by Jorge L. Urioste. Siglo XXI, Mexico City, Mexico.

Haeberli, Joerg, 2002. Tiempo y tradición en Arequipa, Perú, y el surgimiento de la cronología del tema de la deidad central. *Boletín de Arqueología PUCP* 5:89–137.

Haeberli, Joerg, 2006. When and Where Did the Nasca Proliferous Style Emerge? In *Andean Archaeology III: North and South*, edited by William H. Isbell and Helaine Silverman, pp. 410–434. Kluwer Academic/Plenum, New York.

Haeberli, Joerg, 2009. Tradiciones del Horizonte Temprano y del Período Intermedio Temprano en los valles de Sihuas, Vitor, y Majes, Departamento de Arequipa, Perú.

In *Arqueología del área centro sur Andina: Actas del simposio internacional 30 de junio–2 de julio de 2005, Arequipa, Perú*, edited by Mariusz S. Ziółkowski, Justin Jennings, Luis Augusto Belen Franco, and Andrea Drusini, pp. 205–227. Centro de Estudios Precolombinos, Universidad Warsaw, Warsaw, Poland.

Helms, Mary, 1988. *Ulysses' Sail: An Ethnographic Odyssey of Power, Knowledge, and Geographical Distance*. Princeton University Press, Princeton, NJ.

Hodder, Ian, 2006. *The Leopard's Tale: Revealing the Mysteries of Çatalhöyük*. Thames and Hudson, New York.

Hodder, Ian, 2012. *Entangled: An Archaeology of the Relationships between Humans and Things*. Wiley-Blackwell, Malden, MA.

Huamán López, Oscar, 2012. Presencia–ausencia y recurrencia: La cerámica. In *Wari en Arequipa: Análisis de los contextos funerarios de La Real*, edited by Willy Yépez Álvarez and Justin Jennings, pp. 54–97. Museo Arqueológica José María Morante, Universidad Nacional de San Agustín, Arequipa, Peru.

Ingold, Tim, 2000. *The Perception of the Environment: Essays on Livelihood, Dwelling and Skill*. Routledge, London, UK.

Isbell, Billie Jean, 1978. *To Defend Ourselves: Ecology and Ritual in an Andean village*. Waveland Press, Prospect Heights, IL.

Isbell, William H., 1997. *Mummies and Mortuary Monuments: A Postprocessual Prehistory of Central Andean Social Organization*. University of Texas Press, Austin, TX.

Isbell, William H., 2008. Wari and Tiwanaku: International Identities in the Central Andean Middle Horizon. In *Handbook of South American Archaeology*, edited by Helaine Silverman and William H. Isbell, pp. 731–759. Springer, New York.

Isla, John, and Markus Reindel, 2006. Burial Patterns and Sociopolitical Organization in Nasca 5 Society. In *Andean Archaeology III: North and South*, edited by William H. Isbell and Helaine Silverman, pp. 274–400. Kluwer Academic/Plenum, New York.

Jennings, Justin, 2002. Prehistoric Imperialism and Cultural Development in the Cotahuasi Valley, Peru. Unpublished Ph.D. dissertation, University of California, Santa Barbara.

Jennings, Justin, 2011. *Globalizations and the Ancient World*. Cambridge University Press, Cambridge, UK.

Jennings, Justin, 2012a. Otra Material. In *Wari en Arequipa: Análisis de los contextos funerarios de La Real*, edited by Willy Yépez Álvarez and Justin Jennings, pp. 219–232. Museo Arqueológica José María Morante, Universidad Nacional de San Agustín, Arequipa, Peru.

Jennings, Justin, 2012b. La Real y el horizonte medio en el Perú. In *Los rostros de Wari: Perspectivas interregionales sobre el horizonte medio*, edited by Justin Jennings and Luis Jaime Castillo, pp. 32–47. Boletín de Arqueología PUCP 16. Fondo Editorial de la Pontificia Universidad Católica del Perú, Lima, Peru.

Jennings, Justin, 2014. Una reevaluación del horizonte medio en Arequipa. In *Los rostros de Wari: perspectivas interregionales sobre el horizonte medio*, edited by Justin Jennings and Luis Jaime Castillo, pp. 165–188. Boletín de Arqueología PUCP 16. Fondo Editorial de la Pontificia Universidad Católica del Perú, Lima, Peru.

Jennings, Justin, Tiffiny A. Tung, Willy Yépez Álvarez, Cecilia Quequezana Lucano, and Marko López Hurtado, 2015a. Shifting Local, Regional, and Interregional Relations in Middle Horizon, Peru: Evidence from La Real. *Latin American Antiquity*, 26(3):382–400.

Jennings, Justin, María Inés Velarde, Franco Mora, and Willy Yépez Álvarez, 2015b. Wari Imperialism, Bronze Production, and the Formation of the Middle Horizon: Complicating the Picture. *Journal of Anthropological Archaeology* 39:63–75.

Kaulicke, Peter, 2000. *Memoria y muerte en el Perú Antiguo*. Fondo Editorial de la Pontificia Universidad Católica del Perú, Lima, Peru.

Keefer, David K., Susan D. deFrance, Michael E. Moseley, James B. Richardson III, Dennis R. Saterlee, and Amy Day-Lewis, 1998. Early Maritime Economy and El Niño Events at Quebrada Tacahuay, Peru. *Science* 281:1833–1835.

Kellner, Corina M., and Margaret J. Schoeninger, 2008. Wari's Imperial Influence on Local Nasca Diet: The Stable Isotope Evidence. *Journal of Anthropological Archaeology* 27(2):226–243.

Knobloch, Patricia J., 2011. La imagen de los Señores de Huari y la recuperación de una identidad antigua. In *Señores de los Imperios del Sol*, edited by Krzysztof Makowski, pp. 197–210. Banco de Crédito, Lima, Peru.

Knobloch, Patricia J., 2012. Archives in Clay: The Styles and Stories of Wari Ceramic Artists. In *Wari: Lords of the Ancient Andes*, edited by Susan E. Bergh, pp. 122–143. Cleveland Museum of Art, Cleveland, OH.

Kuijt, Ian,1996. Negotiating Equality Through Ritual: A Consideration of Late Natufian and Prepottery Neolithic A Period Mortuary Practices. *Journal of Anthropological Archaeology* 15(4):313–336.

Kuijt, Ian, 2001. Place, Death, and the Transmission of Social Memory in Early Agricultural Communities of the Near Eastern Pre-Pottery Neolithic. In *Social Memory, Identity, and Death: Anthropological Perspectives on Mortuary Rituals*, edited by Meredith S. Chesson, pp. 80–99. Archaeological Publications of the AAA, Vol. 10. American Anthropological Association, Washington, DC.

Latour, Bruno, 2005. *Reassembling the Social an Introduction to Actor-Network-Theory.* Oxford University Press, Oxford, UK; New York.

Lincoln, Bruce, 1989. *Discourse and the Construction of Society: Comparative Studies of Myth, Ritual, and Classification*. Oxford University Press, New York.

Manrique Valdivia, Julio, and Manuel Cornejo Zegarra, 1990. Vision sobre la arqueologia del valle de Camana. *Gaceta Arqueologica Andina* 5(18/19):21–24.

Mayer, Enrique, 2002. *The Articulated Peasant: Household Economies in the Andes*. Westview, Boulder, CO.

McEwan, Colin, and Joerg Haeberli, 2000. Ancestors Past but Present: Gold Diadems from the Far South Coast of Peru. In *Precolumbian Gold: Technology, Style, and Iconography*, edited by Colin McEwan, pp. 16–27. British Museum Press, London.

Muñoz Rojas, Lizette, 2012. Estudios paleobotánicos: Pauta de crecimiento e intercambio. In *Wari en Arequipa: Análisis de los contextos funerarios de La Real*, edited by Willy Yépez Álvarez and Justin Jennings, pp. 182–199. Museo Arqueológico José María Morante, Universidad Nacional de San Agustín, Arequipa, Peru.

Neira Avendaño, Máximo, and Augusto Cardonas Rosas, 2001. El Periodo Formativo en el área de Arequipa. *Andes: Boletín de la Misión Arqueológica Andina* 3:27–60.

Orwell, George, 1944. *Animal Farm*. Secker and Warburg, London, UK.

Owen, Bruce, 2010. Wari in the Majes-Camaná Valley: A Different Kind of Horizon. In *Beyond Wari Walls: Regional Perspectives on Middle Horizon Peru*, edited by Justin Jennings, pp. 57–78. University of New Mexico Press, Albuquerque, NM.

Perry, Linda, Daniel H. Sandweiss, Dolores R. Piperno, Kurt Rademaker, Michael A. Malpass, Adán Umire, and Pablo de la Vera, 2006. Early Maize Agriculture and Interzonal Interaction in Southern Peru. *Nature* 440(2):76–79.

Quequezana Lucano, Cecilia, Willy Yépez Álvarez, and Marko López Hurtado, 2012. Técnicas textiles: Vestidos e identidad colectiva. In *Wari en Arequipa: Análisis de los contextos funerarios de La Real*, edited by Willy Yépez Álvarez and Justin Jennings, pp. 98–127. Museo Arqueológica José María Morante, Universidad Nacional de San Agustín, Arequipa, Peru.

Reiss, Wilhelm, and Alphons Stübel, 1887. *Das todtenfeld von Ancon in Peru. Ein betrag zur kenntnisund industrie des Inca-Reiches*. A. Asher, Berlin, Germany.

Sandweiss, Daniel H., Heather McInnis, Richard L. Burger, Asunción Cano, Bernardio Ojeda, Rolando Paredes, María del Carmen Sandweiss, and Michael D. Glascock, 1998. Quebrada Jaguay: Early South American Maritime Adaptations. *Science* 281(5384):1830–1832.

Santos Ramírez, Rene, 1980. *Cerámica temprana, estilo la ramada*. Arqueos Perú, No. 1, Arequipa, Peru.

Schreiber, Katharina J., 1992. *Wari Imperialism in Middle Horizon Peru*. Museum of Anthropology, University of Michigan, Ann Arbor, MI.

Schreiber, Katharina J., 1999. Regional Approaches to the Study of Prehistoric Empires: Examples from Ayacucho and Nasca, Peru. In *Settlement Pattern Studies in the Americas: Fifty Years since Viru*, edited by Brian Billman and Gary Feinman, pp. 160–171. Smithsonian Institution Press, Washington, DC.

Schreiber, Katharina J., 2001. The Wari Empire of Middle Horizon Peru: The Epistemological Challenge of Documenting an Empire Without Documentary Evidence. In *Empires: Perspectives from Archaeology and History*, edited by Susan E. Alcock, Terrence N. D'Altroy, Kathleen D. Morrison, and Carla M. Sinopoli, pp. 70–92. Cambridge University Press, New York.

Schreiber, Katharina J., and Josué Lancho Rojas, 2003. *Irrigation and Society in the Peruvian Desert: The Puquios of Nasca*. Lexington Books, Lanham, MD.

Sewell Jr., William H., 2005. *Logics of History: Social Theory and Social Transformation*. University of Chicago Press, Chicago, IL.

Silverman, Helaine, 2002. *Ancient Nasca Settlement and Society*. University of Iowa Press, Iowa City, IA.

Strong, William Duncan, 1957. Paracas, Nazca and Tiahuanacoid Cultural Relationships in South Coastal Peru. *Memoirs of the Society for American Archaeology* 13:1–48.

Torres, Constantino, and David Repke, 2006. *Anadenanthera: Visionary Plant of Ancient South America*. Routledge, New York.

Tung, Tiffiny A., 2003. A Bioarchaeological Perspective on Wari Imperialism in the Andes of Peru: A View from Highland and Hinterland Skeletal Populations. Unpublished Ph.D. dissertation, University of North Carolina, Chapel Hill.

Tung, Tiffiny A., 2007a. Trauma and Violence in the Wari Empire of the Peruvian Andes: Warfare, Raids, and Ritual Fights. *American Journal of Physical Anthropology* 133(3):941–956.

Tung, Tiffiny A., 2007b. The Village of Beringa at the Periphery of the Wari Empire: A Site Overview and new Radiocarbon Dates. *Andean Past* 8:253–286.

Tung, Tiffiny A., 2012a. *Violence, Ritual and the Wari Empire: A Social Bioarchaeology of Imperialism in the Ancient Andes*. University Press of Florida, Gainesville, FL.

Tung, Tiffiny A., 2012b. Bio-antropología y condiciones de vida. In *Wari en Arequipa: Análisis de los contextos funerarios de La Real*, edited by Willy Yépez Álvarez and Justin Jennings, pp. 233–259. Museo Arqueológica José María Morante, Universidad Nacional de San Agustín, Arequipa, Peru.

Turner, Victor W., 1969. *The Ritual Process: Structure and Anti-structure*. Aldine, Chicago, IL.

Ugarte-Lewis Mauricio, and Willy Yépez Álvarez, 2012. Aves: Bienes suntuarios y viajes de intercambio. In *Wari en Arequipa: Análisis de los contextos funerarios de La Real*, edited by Willy Yépez Álvarez and Justin Jennings, pp. 145–173. Museo Arqueológica José María Morante, Universidad Nacional de San Agustín, Arequipa, Peru.

Valdez, Lidio M., 2009a. La investigación arqueológica en el valle de Acarí y la contribución de Francis A. Riddell. In *Arqueología del área centro sur Andina: Actas del simposio internacional 30 de junio–2 de julio de 2005, Arequipa, Perú*, edited by Mariusz S. Ziółkowski, Justin Jennings, Luis Augusto Belen Franco, and Andrea Drusini, pp. 255–279. Centro de Estudios Precolombinos, Universidad Warsaw, Warsaw, Poland.

Valdez, Lidio M., 2009b. Una ofrenda de cerámica ceremonial Wari en La Oroya, Valle de Acarí, Perú. *Revista de Antropología* 20(7–8):189–204.

Valdez, Lidio M., 2009c. Significado social de la cerámica Nasca Temprana en Valle de Acarí, Peru. *Revista de Antropología* 20(7–8):15–35.

Valdez, Lidio M., 2009d. Walled Settlements, Buffer Zones, and Human Decapitation in the Acarí Valley, Peru. *Journal of Anthropological Research* 65:389–416.

Vaughn, Kevin, 2009. *The Ancient Andean Village: Marcaya in Prehispanic Nasca*. University of Arizona Press, Tucson, AZ.

Vaughn, Kevin, Jelmer Eerkens, and John Kantner, eds., 2010. *The Evolution of Leadership: Transitions in Decision Making from Small-scale to Middle-range Societies*. School of American Research Press, Albuquerque, NM.

Velarde, María Inés, Franco Mora, and Justin Jennings, 2012. Tupus y placas de metal: Expresión creativa e imagen de prestigio. In *Wari en Arequipa: Análisis de los contextos funerarios de La Real*, edited by Willy Yépez Álvarez and Justin Jennings, pp. 215–218. Museo Arqueológica José María Morante, Universidad Nacional de San Agustín, Arequipa, Peru.

Wiessner, Polly, 1996. Leveling the Hunter: Constraints on the Status Quest in Foraging Societies. In *Food and the Status Quest: An Interdisciplinary Perspective*, edited by Polly Wiessner and Wolf Schiefenhéovel, pp. 171–191. Berghahn Books, Providence, RI.

Wernke, Steven, 2010. Asentamiento, agricultura y pastoralismo durante el periodo Formativo en el valle del Colca, Perú. *Chungara* 43(2):203–220.

Yépez Álvarez, Willy, 2012a. Recuperación del dato empírico: Descripción del sitio y excavación. In *Wari en Arequipa: Análisis de los contextos funerarios de La Real*, edited by Willy Yépez Álvarez and Justin Jennings, pp. 14–31. Museo Arqueológica José María Morante, Universidad Nacional de San Agustín, Arequipa, Peru.

Yépez Álvarez, Willy, 2012b. Componentes Psicotrópicos y parafernalia inhalatoria en el sitio La Real. In *Wari en Arequipa: Análisis de los contextos funerarios de La Real*, edited by Willy Yépez Álvarez and Justin Jennings, pp. 200–214. Museo Arqueológica José María Morante, Universidad Nacional de San Agustín, Arequipa, Peru.

Ziółkowski, Mariusz, and Kzysztof Tunia, 2005. La escultura lítica de Unchuy, Distrito de Pampacolca, provincia de Castilla. *Boletín de la Misión Arqueológica Andina* 5:421–434.

Chapter 4

From Enchantment to Entrapment: Following the Threads of Foreign Artifacts in San José de Moro

Francesca Fernandini

Introduction

Entanglement in archaeology entails following the entwinements and entrapments of the past not as an attempt to disentangle the relationships between people and things, but as a way to bring forward a flexible framework of study (Hodder 2011). This framework looks at the past as a complex meshwork of relations and interactions (Ingold 2010) and bridges several archaeological approaches into understanding the irreducible nature of life.

The focus moves away from the outcome of events onto the processes before, during, and after these events occur. In this sense, past events are observed and analyzed through the everyday practices and contingencies that develop through the interactions between things and people, things and things, and people and people (Hodder 2011). This flexible frame allows scholars to observe the trails left by these interactions and the way people develop dependences and dependencies on different things and become entrapped by their own histories.

Furthermore, history is observed as the gathering of relations and interactions where things and people depend on other things and people. In this scenario, the focus is on the situated responses that develop from these interactions and the further implications these responses entail (Martindale 2009). Historic events do not simply affect each other at the social level, but are a tangle of interactions of elements, forces, agents, spatial scales, and temporalities that shape one another (Mitchell 2002); it is the heterogeneity of these interactions that resists explanation and avoids bounded definitions.

Temporality is key to our understanding the dependences and dependencies that people-thing relations create. Time is not only understood in its absolute perception but also in terms of moments, periods such as Achille Membe's "time of entanglement" (in Nuttal 2009) in which internal relations become

Archaeology of Entanglement edited by Lindsay Der and Francesca Fernandini, 103–124

flexible and social and physical boundaries are permeated in general. Time in this sense encloses multiple durées made up of discontinuities, reversals, inertias, and swings that overlay one another and that define which traits persist, evolve, or fade.

In this chapter I attempt to understand the tangled and complex set of interactions and negotiations that characterized a heterogeneous and dynamic moment in Andean prehistory. I focus on the entanglements that led to the introduction of a set of foreign artifacts into a Moche ceremonial and elite cemetery between AD 600 and 850 and the entrapments it generated at the start of Middle Horizon period.

The Moches comprised a series of independent interactive polities that shared a flexible set of common ritual, social, and political practices (Castillo 2009; Castillo and Donnan 1994; Castillo et al. 2012; Quilter 2011; Quilter and Castillo 2010; Swenson 2011; Uceda 2000, 2001). These polities occupied the north coast of Peru between AD 200 and 900 (Koons and Alex 2014), and their physical presence has been associated with an elaborated and highly standardized ceramic tradition as well as a series of monumental ceremonial centers.

In this analysis I follow the interactions developed between the San José de Moro local leaders and the imported artifacts they included in their funerary arrangements. I argue that the technology and social background of these artifacts produced an enchantment that lured the San José de Moro people into establishing a dependence that, once faced with the political and physical constraints of import, led to a dependency. In turn, this dependency developed new types of interactions that further entrapped the San José de Moro ruling elite both in reference to long-distance transport and trade and, most important, in terms of their political and social position within their own society.

People and Things

As I note earlier in this chapter, understanding prehistory through entanglement entails following and analyzing human-thing relations. Humans during this time period were well spread along the Andean highlands and coastlands, establishing different political organizations that shared a flexible and unstable supra-community level of unity. For more than 10,000 years the Andean setting was home to a large-scale network of connections where routes and roads formed part of people's spatial constructions and things, whether manmade or natural, traveled thousands of kilometers, creating new nodes of relations.

Things, on the other hand, require a more complex definition. As Knappett points out, the tendency to use things, objects, and artifacts interchangeably often does not allow us to glimpse a more nuanced vision of their subtle differentiations (Knappett 2010). For instance, the inalienable, ambiguous, and unquantifiable character of things can be contrasted with the alienable, named, and quantifiable character of objects (Gosden 2004). According to Meskell (2004), the relation between these concepts can be seen through the practices of transformation that embed objects into the world and turn them into things.

One way to solve the problems raised by these issues is to shift our attention from the sphere of isolated and fixed categories (objects, artifacts, etc.) to the sphere of the fluid and relational transactions, or relations between people and things (Renfrew 2010). To achieve this, we must first avoid the distinctions and dichotomies that separate mind from thing and understand them as continuous and interdefinable processes that define human-thing relations based on situated practices. What these redefinitions imply is that past ways of thought need not just be *expressed in* material culture, but should also be seen as partly *constituted by* material culture (Knappett 2010).

Things then, whether one is referring to valuable ceramics, obsidian, or shells, etc., must be observed through the processes and relations they generated from their manufacturing or acquisition, distribution, and redistribution to their transformation and hybridization. In this manner, things in the Andean context can constitute their inhabitants and their entanglements as the threads that configure its history.

San José de Moro: Where the Things Were Found

San José de Moro was an elite cemetery and ceremonial center located on the right bank of the Jequetepeque Valley, on the north coast of Peru (Figure 4.1a, 4.1b). The site was occupied during the Early Intermediate period (AD 200) and Middle Horizon period (AD 600–1000) until the mid-Late Intermediate period (AD 1200) by Moche, Transitional, Lambayeque and Chimu populations (Castillo 2012a, 2012b; see Figure 4.2) During its long span of occupation, the site has been the location for a varied array of cultural and social events that are materially expressed in the archaeological record. The most recurrent seem to have been its use as a funerary site and as one of the main principal gathering and feasting areas for the population in the valley (Castillo 2000; Castillo et al. 2008; Muro 2008, Swenson 2006; Swenson and Warner 2012).

To provide a detailed focus, I limit my discussion of the temporal period of analysis to the Late Moche and Transitional period occupation of the site between AD 650 and 1100. This period covers the crucial moment that preceded the Moche demise in San José de Moro, which was characterized by an unstable political and social situation. Following the demise of the Moche elite at the site, the archaeological record shows a conspicuous absence of Moche-related material culture within tombs, while funerary arrangements such as funerary structure and orientation were reminiscent of Late Moche times.

The Late Moche period (AD 650–850) was a moment characterized by recurrent cultural shifts, such as the unprecedented appearance of a series of

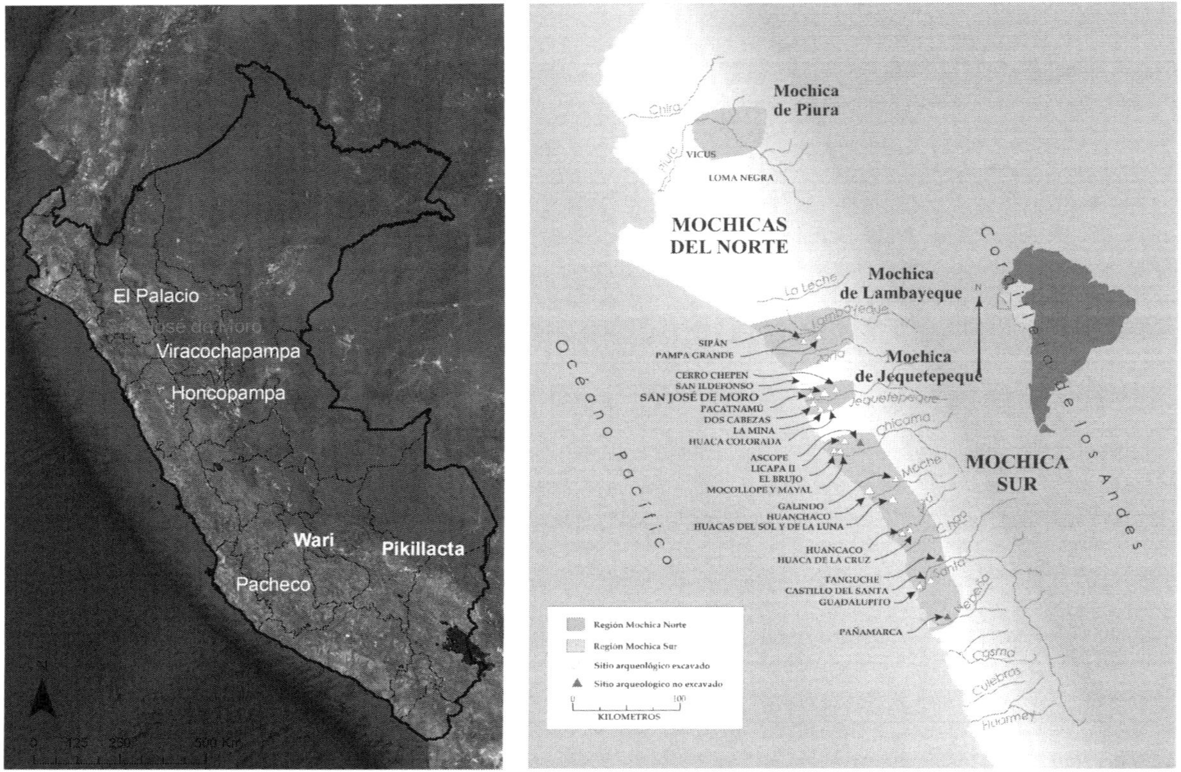

Figure 4.1 Site locations. a) Main Wari sites and San José de Moro. b) Peruvian north coast and the main Mochica sites

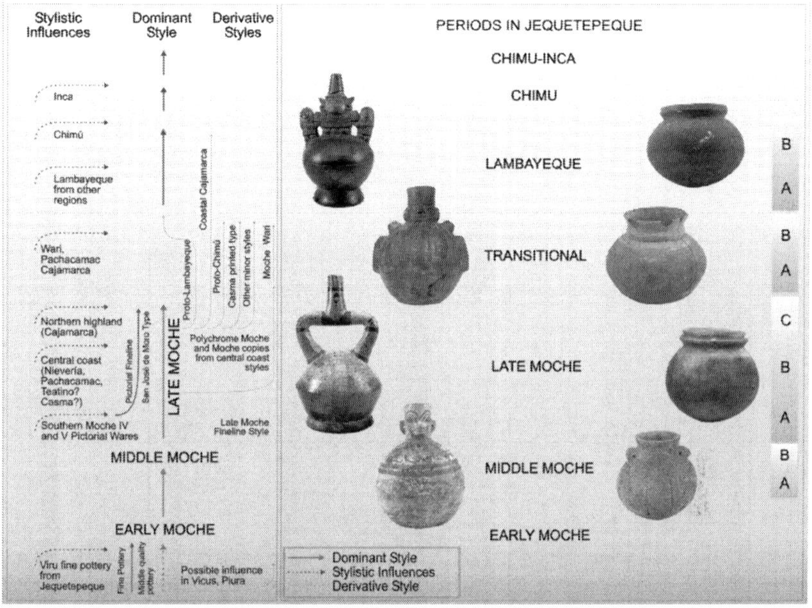

Figure 4.2 Chronological sequence for the Jequetepeque Valley with representative examples of ceramics related to the periods and phases of the occupational history of San José de Moro (Courtesy of the San José de Moro Archaeological Program).

foreign ceramics placed among the tombs of the Moche's deceased rulers at San José de Moro (Figure 4.3a–4.3c). These foreign introductions start during Late Moche A, which initially showed the exclusive presence of Moche Fineline (Figure 4.3a); during Late Moche B, a series of vessels from distinct areas of the Andes were recorded along with a hybrid Moche-Wari style of vessel (see Figure 4.3b) and the Moche Fineline style.

On the other hand, ceramics from the Transitional period present a clear absence of Moche-related styles through an inclusive record of material culture that presents a varied display of local non-Moche and foreign styles (Figure 4.3c, 4.3d). This Transitional period reveals a political change in the controlling elite, whether by a complete replacement of it or a redefinition of its cultural allegiance.

The Wari: The Origin of the Things

The Wari emerged in the central highlands of Peru around AD 550 to 600, establishing its capital, Huari,[1] in modern Ayacucho (Isbell 2001; Jennings 2010; Tung 2012). Based on the ubiquitous appearance of Wari-related material culture in the form of architecture, ceramics, lithics, and textiles from the

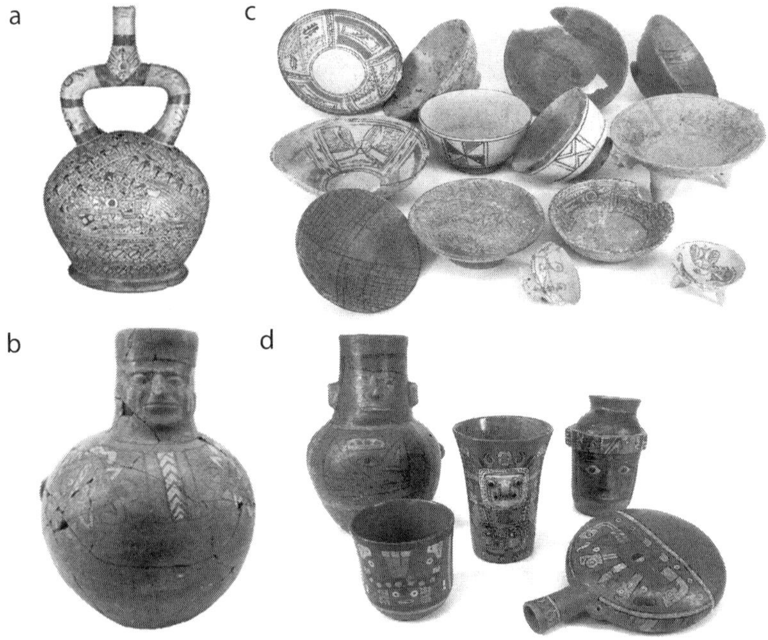

Figure 4.3 Ceramic examples. a) Moche vessel showing Fineline painting style from San José de Moro. b) Moche-Wari vessel from San José de Moro. c) Cajamarca plates from San José de Moro. d) Wari vessels from San José de Moro (Courtesy of the San José de Moro Archaeological Program).

central, south, and north highlands and coast, scholars argue that the Wari established a large and varied network of relations and colonies throughout the Andes (Isbell 2010; Lumbreras 2012; Schreiber 2012). The political and social nature of the Wari has been intrinsically related to this material culture and to its relation with Huari and its main provincial capitals (Schreiber 1992, 2004, 2012). In this sense, the archaeological definition of the Wari has relied mainly on its associated material culture, particularly on the ubiquitous presence of its ceramics and textiles.

Moche-Wari Interactions

The period between AD 600 and 1000 in the Andes is known as the Middle Horizon (Table 4.1), and has been characterized as a dynamic moment when new and old routes of social and political interaction were redrawn and reconfigured. Within this interactive scenario Wari society, with its capital in the southern highlands approximately 1,200 km from San José de Moro, seems to have played a pivotal role in the formation of new spheres of negotiation. Physical evidence of Wari or Wari-related material culture was widespread

Table 4.1 Andean Chronological Sequence

Years	*Period*	*Coast*	*Sierra*
AD 1532	Late Horizon	Inca	Inca
AD 1440			
AD 1400		Chimú	Cajamarca
	Late Intermediate period	Chancay	Huanca
AD 1000		Pachacamac	Chanca
AD 1000	Middle Horizon (1A–1B, 2A–B, 3, 4)	Lambayeque	
		Pachacamac-Nievería	Wari
AD 600		Moche V	
AD 600		Moche (I–IV)	Huaraz
	Early Intermediate period (1–8)	Lima (Maranga)	
		Vicús	Huarpa
200 BC		Paracas Necrópolis	Chanapata
300 BC		Chavín	Chavín
		Garagay	Pacopampa
900 BC	Formative (Early Horizon) period	Cupisnique	
		Huaca Lucía	Kotosh
		Paracas Cavernas	
800 BC		Guañape	Pacopampa
		La Florida	Huaricoto
1800 BC	Initial period	Chira-Villa	Kotosh
1800 BC		Las Aldas	La Galgada
		Caral	
	Late Preceramic period	Huaca Prieta	Kotosh-Mito
		El Paraiso	
3000 BC		Chilca	
3500 BC		Chinchorro	Telarmachay
	Early Preceramic Period	Paijan	Lauricocha
11,000 BC			Toquepala

along the Andes and appears to be a common denominator in both highlands and coastland within this time period. Although the locations of Wari colonies or provincial administrative sites have been established, the prevalence of Wari diagnostic material culture, principally recognized in ceramics and textiles, goes beyond the Wari political organization.

Recently, scholars have published nuanced perspectives on the nature of the Wari (Castillo et al. 2012; Edwards 2010; Fernandini and Alexandrino 2015; Isbell 2010; Jennings 2010; McEwan and Williams 2012; Nash 2012; Owen 2010; Schreiber 2012; Segura and Shimada 2010; Tung 2012, among others), recognizing it as a multilayered society. These multiple layers are expressed in the physical evidence, which obeys a varied set of direct mechanisms such as negotiation, co-option of local elites, and repatriation of Wari bureaucrats as well as indirect effects such as "fissioning or stepped budding" (Owen 2010:72) and emulation and globalization (Jennings 2010) among a series of circumstantial responses. The multifaceted nature of this society instilled Wari material culture with a particular allure that went beyond the economics of production or the political ideology that inspired it.

In contrast with this scenario, most of the north coast of Peru seems to have remained impermeable to Wari's allure (Castillo 2001; Castillo et al. 2012; Chapdelaine 2010). The absence of Wari or Wari-related material culture in most Moche contexts in those locations points to a purposeful strategy not to engage in any kind of material exchange or emulation of these artifacts or the complex set of relations associated with them. Conversely, in San José de Moro, unlike any other Moche site in the north coast, hundreds of Wari ceramics (Figure 4.3b, 4.3d) identical to those found in Wari sites (Castillo 2001; Castillo et al. 2012; Isbell 2000) have been recorded both in elite funerary contexts and in the fill associated with Late Moche and Transitional layers. Ceramic artifacts correspond to the two large stylistic divisions of Wari wares (Menzel 1964): Chakipampa, corresponding to the Middle Horizon Phase 1, associated with the Late Moche period; and Viñaque, which corresponds to the Middle Horizon Phase 2, associated with Transitional period contexts. The earliest examples of Wari artifacts date to the very beginning of the Late Moche period, and thus are contemporaneous with the appearance of Late Moche Fineline art, which presumably emerged from a migration of artists from the Chicama Valley 150 km to the south (Castillo 2009, 2012b; Rohfritsch 2010; Shimada 1994).

In this sense, the appearance of Chakipampa, Late Moche Fineline, and Polychrome Moche ceramic styles seem to be a part of the same process, hinting at the complex and intricate scenario of negotiations behind their acquisition. Local versions of several abstract figures typical of the Chakipampa style in Moche-Wari vessels point to a strong relationship between these styles and the possible origination of this Moche hybrid as a repercussion of Chakipampa's influence at San José de Moro. Furthermore, archaeometric analysis of these artifacts has shown that Moche Polychrome vessels were made locally using local clays and local manufacture techniques with Wari pigments and firing techniques (Castillo et al. 2012; Muro and Del Solar 2015). Other foreign-style artifacts found in association with Late Moche burials are Nieveria ceramics found in the Rimac Valley located in the central coast, around 700 km from San José de Moro (Figure 4.1a), and Cajamarca ceramics from the Cajamarca region located in the highlands 200 km east of the Jequetepeque Valley.

In general, it seems that once the Moche tradition is permeated at the start of the Late Moche period in the San José de Moro region, a varied set of Wari and Wari-related artifacts found their way into the elaborated elite burials at the site, particularly of the highest elite, represented by the Priestesses of San José de Moro[2] (Castillo 2005; Figure 4.4). In this sense, the association of foreign elements in the funerary setting of one of the most powerful actors in the San José de Moro ruling elite might be considered a strategic intentionality on behalf of the Moro political elite.

Figure 4.4 Chamber Tomb of the First Priestess of San José de Moro (Courtesy of the San José de Moro Archaeological Program).

On the other hand, speaking of intentionality by observing just the final stage of configuration and negotiation that leads to the construction of the funerary context might obscure the processes and contingencies that allowed its construction. The San José de Moro context must be observed both diachronically in terms of the settlements chronological sequence and synchronically based on the interactions and events taking place in both the Moche and Wari realms.

As I note earlier in this chapter, San José de Moro was an elite cemetery where different elite members along the Jequetepeque Valley interred their dead. The site also functioned as a gathering and ceremonial center where large quantities of *chicha* (fermented beer) was prepared and consumed. Although these ceremonies might have been celebrated following a particular ceremonial calendar (Hocquenghem 2008), scholars assume, judging from the archaeological remains, that several of these gatherings included the burial of important elite members as a central event (Castillo 2005, 2009, 2012b; Muro 2008).

It is nearly impossible to point to a particular moment when the collapse of a society begins. Nevertheless, for the Moches of San José de Moro, it seems that a radical change in pottery production that led to larger investment in elite tomb preparation may be taken as a break point in the site's cultural trajectory. It seems that between AD 550 and 600, Moche artisans from the southern valley of Chicama migrated to San José de Moro and started producing Moche Fineline vessels. These vessels were not only more technically complex than previous ceramics from the site, but entailed a very specific religious and ideological knowledge reflected in the themes and narratives depicted. At the same time, San José de Moro elite burial records also present a set of foreign ceramics from different distant and not-so-distant areas (Rucabado and Castillo 2003, 2006). Furthermore, this period was crucial in Moche history: along the north coast of Peru, people were abandoning smaller Moche settlements and centering in newly founded settlements located in the middle and upper zones of valleys (Bawden 1996, 2001 Shimada 1994, 2010).

During this time of movement, resettlement, and crisis San José de Moro tombs record the unprecedented presence of foreign material in their funerary contexts. These moments of turmoil and environmental stress might have pushed the San José de Moro elite to introduce both the new Moche ceramics from the south as well as the foreign Wari and Cajamarca elements.

When faced with the assumption that the introduction of these elements was part of an intentional choice at San José de Moro, one might argue that it was a situated response, based first on the rationale that the acquisition of these artifacts was not only an advantageous choice intended to cement their waning power by associating themselves with a powerful foreign ideology, but also because of the wide availability of these artifacts during the Middle Horizon period.

Following this line of thought, it is then necessary to explain the relationships between San José de Moro and Wari, where the pottery, pigments, and skills were originating. Because Wari ceramics in the Moche realm have been found almost exclusively in San José de Moro, and very little Moche or San José de Moro pottery has been found in Wari contexts, one might argue that the relationship was unidirectional, and that San José de Moro elites decided to establish an association between their local political power and the mighty Wari political organization due to internal and external stress.

While the archaeological record seems to emphasize this argument, it is necessary to keep in mind that neither the Moche nor the Wari were homogenous organizations existing as bounded entities (Castillo et al. 2012). Both belonged to a particular spatial and social context generated through years of interactions between their local people and things and neighboring people and things. Hence, when speaking of the situated responses the San José de Moro elite made, we have to understand them in relation with their interactions with Wari.

Things Being Things

I attempt to follow the behavior of artifacts—in this case, highly prestigious ceramics—and the way their interactions with people developed new social relations. For Knappett, there is a relational proximity that can be achieved cognitively (Amin and Cohendet 2004 in Knappett 2010) regardless of spatial distance. This proximity can be referred to as *virtual existence* and introduces the notion of "communities of artifacts" or "communities of practice." In artifact communities, the practice of imitation occurs across large geographical areas, and the occurrence of the same artifact produces a relationship of similarity. Furthermore, it seems to follow that these types of communities trigger a heterogeneity of interactions framed under a flexible network of relations redefined at every node. This redefinition implies a reformulation of meanings and symbols by the different people, artifacts, and things involved in it.

In terms of the Wari, this kind of relationship seems to have been created on a large scale through the mass distribution of Wari material culture among colonies, allies, and friends. As a result, local production of artifacts imitating originals, either distributed through Wari "agents"[3] (Knobloch 2005) or acquired indirectly, further cemented their relation or alliance with the powerful Wari center. Moreover, the Wari had several political and manufacturing centers along the Andes (Anders et al. 1994), which seems to have fostered a complex network of distribution of Wari emblematic material culture and the creation of communities of artifacts.

In this context, the multidimensionality of the Wari and, for that matter, that of the Moche (Castillo et al. 2012) introduces a flexibility and dynamism in the creation of these communities of politically controlled artifacts that most surely was affected by the different contingencies and circumstances that entail the manufacture and distribution on behalf of the Wari and acquisition, imitation, and hybridization on the part of the San José de Moro people.

Thus, while the Wari had developed a large-scale system of social interactions and the establishment of alliances through the distribution of artifacts by Wari "agents" (Knobloch 2005), the San José de Moro elite became entangled in this large-scale context and participated through the acquisition of artifacts. It seems that the Wari's foreign relations of negotiations and interactions created a flexible and dynamic context during the Middle Horizon that encouraged distant populations to become dependent on these artifacts. This new scenario was not planned and constructed directly by the Wari political system; more likely, it was formed through the engagement of Wari colonies and non-Wari neighbors in the acquisition and acceptance of these artifacts and the social implications associated with them. Regardless of the process, it seems as if their political relations tipped the power balance toward the Wari and helped aggrandize their political and ideological strength (Fernandini and Alexandrino 2015).

Following this line, the San José de Moro people's engagement in the entangled meshwork of relations that characterized the Middle Horizon establishes an indirect connection with the multidimensional facets of Wari power while at the same time reconfigures its own local political context. Hence, the Moche rulers from San José de Moro became part of this large-scale community of artifacts, while the artifacts themselves became hybridized by local politics.

But why were Wari ceramics so alluring? Gell explores how the power of certain artifacts rests partly on the fact that their origination is inexplicable and indecipherable (Gell 1992; Harrison 2006). In the case of San José de Moro, the indecipherability and awe not only resided in the technological innovations and different materials and pigments used in their creation, but also in their association with a large and novel society that was rapidly expanding along the Andean region. Hence, Wari ceramics in themselves represent an entanglement of forces that enchanted possible allies and neighbors and lured them into their network. Once inside the Wari network, societies such as San José de Moro, located more than a thousand kilometers away from the Wari center and with limited background in foreign relations, became dependent and apparently searched for alternative ways to satisfy this newly created dependency.

Once San José de Moro's people open their doors and particularly their elite tombs to foreign artifacts, they start depending on an outside source and so become entangled in the politics and negotiations of acquiring these artifacts. Once this dependence is created, their inability to maintain a fluid access to these objects, related both to the intricacies of foreign negotiations and to the difficulty posed by the means to transport vessels for thousands of kilometers to fulfill San José de Moro's growing demand, seems to have created a dependency on these things. To avoid these challenges, which inadvertently entangled themselves even further, San José de Moro's rulers decide to import raw materials, such as pigments, from the Wari area (Castillo et al. 2012) Also, either by bringing Wari artisans to train locals, sending local artisans to train in Wari, or another arrangement, San José de Moro started to produce local Moche Polychrome vessels and Moche-Wari vessels that used local clays and manufacture with Wari firing techniques and pigments. These vessels interchangeably presented Wari or Moche iconography and shapes (Muro and Del Solar 2015).

This scenario presents a shift in the strategies at San José de Moro that encourages the foreign introduction of technology and raw materials to fulfill the local demand for foreign vessels. While this practice may have entailed less investment and care in terms of transportation and foreign policy, the fact that local artisans were able to produce these artifacts locally and thus break their association with a powerful foreign ideology may have diminished the indecipherability and enchantment possessed by these artifacts.

Furthermore, the stratigraphic record reveals that this investment in producing Wari wares locally is immediately followed by the disappearance of Moche elements from the archaeological record. Thus, I propose that all of the processes and effort in acquiring these vessels and later investing in producing them locally were counterproductive. The entanglements behind the introduction of these artifacts in San José de Moro created a trap: while local elites continued to focus on associating themselves with foreign powerful entities either by importing ceramics or by teaching and allowing local artisans to produce them, the local population did not seem to internalize these practices. This failure to predict the outcome of political decisions is a clear example of the instability and lack of historical containment that one finds on the entanglements of people-thing relations (Thomas 1991), and helps us understand the processes hidden behind the demise of political organizations such as the Moche from San José de Moro.

Things Being More than Things

Now that I have analyzed the political and social background behind the production and acquisition of Wari artifacts, it is necessary to address the nature and allure created by these artifacts. Gell (1992) argues that the power of works of art or made objects does not reside in the object itself, but in the symbolic processes they provoke on the beholder. Hence, the object presents a resistance that lies not in the inability or difficulty to possess it, but in the incapacity to understand their coming into being as objects in the world through a technological process that transcends general understanding and forces its conception as magical (Gell 1992).

In this manner, introducing technologically enchanting and regionally inaccessible objects into the funerary context of a semidivine ruler created a magical setting that disappeared once the objects were produced locally and intermingled with local technologies. The fact that local elites decided to make locally available what was once unaffordable seems to have broken the enchantment and perhaps their own enchanted positions as semi-divine, all-powerful beings.

In this way, the public and ceremonial construction of a funerary setting with magical and enchanted works of technology is broken by the elimination of resistance through massive accessibility. The point Gell (1992) makes is that the attitude of the spectator towards an artwork or, in this case, a technologically complex ceramic vessel is fundamentally conditioned by the technical processes that created it and the fact that it was created by another person, an artist.

During the Middle Horizon, artisans seem to have held a relatively important position in society as beholders of intricate information and with the capacity to capture crucial elements of the idiosyncratic nature of a society in ceramics or textiles. Whether Moches or Waris, the information introduced into ceramic and textile iconography and the private knowledge and skills in the handling of raw materials and manufacturing placed artisans in a crucially important political and social position. This position entailed the capacity to create objects that had symbolic or magic powers, and in that sense exemplify a human-thing-human relationship in which these technologically enchanted objects seem to embody this power and knowledge.

Gell (1992) extrapolates the inability to grasp the processes behind the production of an object to the inability to understand how the leader with which the object is associated, such as the priestess in Moche society, holds power over her own people. In a sense, Gell argues that the object mediates between two beings (such as elite and non-elite members in a hierarchical society) and therefore creates a social relation. Hence, the artist or artisan who creates a technologically enchanted object for a king by means of his magical power over clay, pigments, and iconography enhances the king's authority and elevates it beyond the grasp of the spectators.

In this manner, Gell establishes an intrinsic asymmetry between the artists, the elite members who own the technologically enchanted objects, and the rest. In turn, during the Late Moche period the San José de Moro elite, whether intentionally or as a byproduct of different decisions and actions, introduced a series of technologically enchanting objects. The enchantment of these artifacts as a whole reflected the essence of San José de Moro religious and political ancestry and cosmogony through Late Moche Fineline vessels and the mystery and indecipherability of the unknown through Wari elements.

Judging from the limited number of themes, colors (bichromy), and shapes, ceramic production in Moche society seems to have been highly controlled. Whether people had seen foreign objects prior to their introduction in the San José de Moro cemetery context is questionable; nevertheless, if this contact had occurred, it must have been only fleeting because, judging from the archaeological context, they did not keep them. In this setting, the introduction of different sets of ceramic traditions altered the configuration of San José de Moro society not only because of its suddenness, but also because it was overwhelmingly varied. Between the Moche Fineline, the distinct Wari styles such as Chakipampa, Viñaque, and Huamanga, the Moche-Wari hybrids, the central coast Nieveria, and the Cajamarca specimens, both elite and non-elite members of the San José de Moro society were seeing their dead, semi-divine rulers buried with a non-Moche methodology. This type of funerary ceremony charged with Moche and non-Moche elements might have altered the already fragile asymmetric position between San José de Moro elites and non-elites and helped undermine their position as semi-divine and all-powerful beings.

One can argue that the start of the thread that leads to this entanglement are the things, both foreign and local, found in the tombs at San José de Moro. These things are mainly elaborately decorated ceramics[4] with Moche, Wari, and Moche-Wari iconography. Why were ceramics chosen to be a part of the tomb design and configuration? Moche elite burials in the San José de Moro site and elsewhere have always placed particular importance in the amount, quality, and position of the ceramics included. Although elaborate ceramics in highland Wari centers are not as ubiquitous in burials, it seems that once they arrived in San José de Moro they acquired the nature of Moche ceramics and were introduced into the local setting as such.

We know that these ceramics were important enough to accompany powerful leaders in their tombs and, judging from the archaeological and iconographic record, that these events were public so they became embedded in the collective memories of people in the community. Thus, to understand the importance and nature of these decorated ceramics inside tombs, we now turn to their place outside of them. Moche ceramics often present narrative iconographies associated with important moments in their lived or imagined (supernatural) history, such as battles and sacrificial and burial ceremonies as well as representations of people, animals, fruits, and vegetables. These types of vessels are largely ceremonial in nature; in terms of the archaeological record, the great majority has been found inside tombs.

The main narratives depicted in Late Moche Fineline vessels from San José de Moro can help us understand the rationality behind the elite of San José de Moro. The construction of a San José de Moro–Moche narrative is based on the depiction of a series of iconographic scenes that appear to portray some kind of supernatural event or mythic legend (Donnan 1977; Quilter 1990).

Moche iconography, particularly San José de Moro iconography, consists of a series of recurring scenes and narrations. One of the more common scenes depicts an important female character, or priestess, associated with the five "Priestesses of San José de Moro" excavated at the San José de Moro site based on their funerary offerings and contextual similarities (McClelland et al. 2007) This female character is continually shown in charge of sacrificing prisoners on islands close to the San José de Moro littoral. She appears to be acquiring the blood from these prisoners and providing it to the main Moche ruler ("Main Character"; see Figure 4.5a).

The narrative continues with the so-called Priestess of San José de Moro and her betrayal of the accepted world order. She starts a "rebellion of objects" in which clubs, vessels, and clothing among other objects develop legs and arms and help trap and kill male characters (Quilter 1990; Figure 4.5b). The rebellion ends when male characters capture the animated artifacts and take them to the main priest. The Priestess escapes in a vessel on the ocean, carrying with her sacrificial prisoners. She then proceeds to drink their blood from the same goblet used in official ceremonies where the Main Character is present, and returns into the mainland. In the end, the Priestess is captured, killed, and interred in the most magnificent of settings (Figure 4.5c).

This narrative presents revealing aspects of the nature of manmade objects in the Moche realm, were they acquire life and form part of a rebellion. These objects and their transformation into things are crucial in understanding the design of Moche burials, since all of the elements included in the funerary setting appear to exemplify the relationship between the person interred and its personhood. It is this relationship that was made public during burial

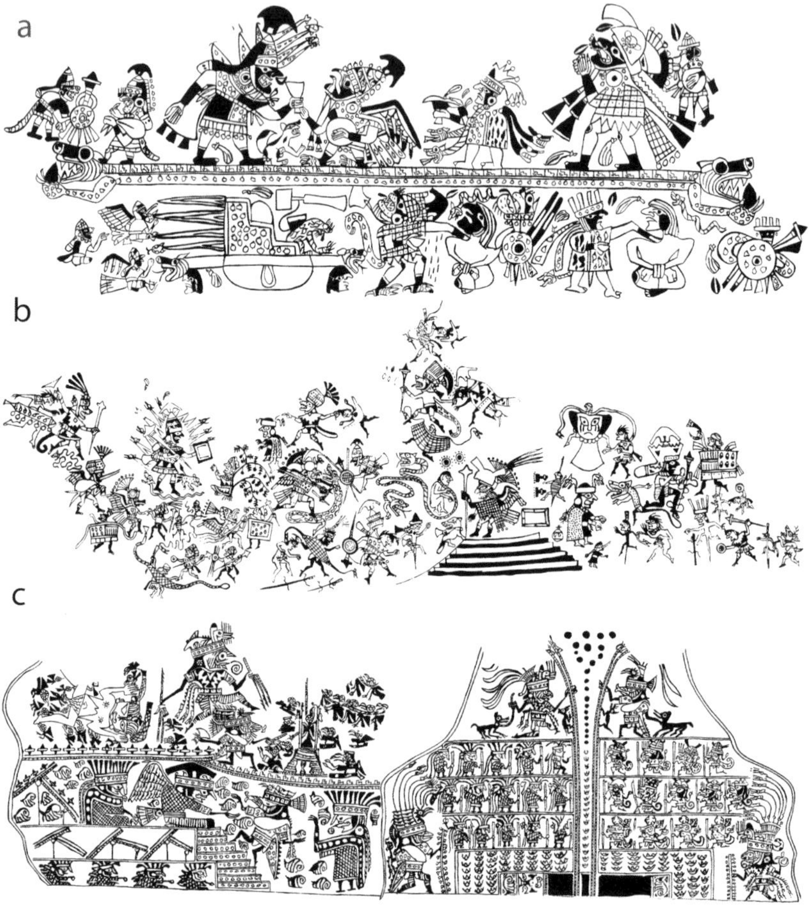

Figure 4.5 Fineline drawings of Moche vessels. a) Presentation Theme/Sacrifice ceremony from the Staatliches Museum für Völkerkunde, Munich, Germany [Museum Fünf Kontinente]. b) Scene of capture with animated implements from the Staatliches Museum für Völkerkunde, Munich, Germany [Museum Fünf Kontinente]. c) Burial Theme from the Museum of Art, Rhode Island School of Design, Providence, RI (All drawings by Donna McClelland from the Christopher B. Donnan and Donna McClelland Moche Archive).

ceremonies and configured the relationship among the spectators, the things, and the person interred.

In this sense, based on the iconography of Moche artifacts, the nature of foreign artifacts, and the fact that the great majority does not present any kind of use trace, it seems these objects were purposefully produced and acquired for the funerary design. Hence, they might be considered *objets chargées* (Spyer 1998) in the sense that they cannot be reduced to their materiality, but serve as a reference for some immaterial original (Pietz 1998), whether it be a mythical legend or a complex set of relations. Hence, the physicality of these things and their capacity to carry over certain forms of signification from one context of behavior to another, as well as to strain or transcend the human designs and constructions to which they are subject (Spyer 1998), created through ceremonial practices a particular place for these vessels in the Moche political, religious, and social spheres of interaction. In this manner, the negotiations and practices related to the controlled production, distribution, and use of these objects *charged* these things with a particular allure that does not emanate from the objects themselves, but rather from the issues these objects pose for subjects (Keane 1998); that is, the relationships that humans establish with things and the entanglements that arise as a result.

Conclusion

In this analysis of the enchantments and entrapments created by the acquisition and introduction of foreign artifacts into San José de Moro I point to the entanglements created between the practices of transforming objects into things through the situated responses, interactions, and engagements between people and things. In this context, things were used to enhance our understanding of people's intentions and practices as well as the contingencies and dependencies that weave their history.

The focus thus relies not in the outcome of the processes involved, but in the entanglements that develop through this process that in turn seem to lead to new processes. In this scenario, things and the material traces and trails they leave serve to describe, analyze, and understand the way people weaved and were woven by their relations with things and how the double-bind between these relations generates more people-things-people relations and thus further entangles the threads of life (Hodder 2011).

The case of the disappearance of Moche-related elements in San José de Moro and their relative contemporaneity with the Moche demise on the entire north coast seems to point to a moment of entanglement when regionally different Moche societies were recurring to differently situated responses. While people from the neighboring sites around San José de Moro did not relocate or come together into larger settlements, they opted for other type of responses that seemed more suitable and fitting to their context.

In this sense, it is the context where the threads of entanglement weave and are weaved, and the unexpected outcomes and processes involved, that define the nature of history. Following this line, the circumstances of particular moments provide a fitting context in which certain practices seem more suitable. Fittingness and suitability in this sense replace intention and allow us to follow situated practices where history and its threads are embedded in the instability and contingency of life.

In this way, San José de Moro rulers, influenced by environmental and social distress during the Late Moche period, decided to alter their traditional ritual practices by introducing foreign things with all of the threads they entailed. These threads in turn became more and more entangled until they ensnared local San José de Moro rulers into a social trap from which they were not able to escape.

Acknowledgments

Thanks are due to the San José de Moro Archaeological Program, directed by Dr. Luis Jaime Castillo, who allowed me to use their records and images, as well as to the Proyecto Arqueológico San José de Moro lab assistant Julio Saldaña, who guided me through the lab's database. Particular thanks go to Don McClelland and Shalimar White (Dumbarton Oaks) for allowing me to use their images. I would also like to thank Luis Muro and Sam Ghavami for their comments and suggestions on an earlier draft of this chapter.

Notes

1. Following Isbell and McEwan (1991), I use *Wari* for the cultural tradition and *Huari* for the archaeological site.
2. The Priestesses of San José de Moro are a series of women buried in the San José de Moro cemetery with a set of ornaments and artifacts that establish a direct correlation with the iconographic image of this character in numerous vessels and murals. Their importance as political and religious leaders in the San José de Moro community has been established based in the size, disposition, and wealth of their tomb's structure and associations.
3. Knobloch argues for the exact identification of a single individual or possible social group, through the term "agent" (Knobloch 2005).
4. Although tombs include many other material artifacts such as lithics, bone, textiles, etc., ceramics form 80 to 90% of the associated materials in a tomb.

References

Anders, Martha, Víctor Chang, Luis Tokuda, Sonia Quiroz, and Izumi Shimada, 1994. Producción cerámica del Horizonte Medio Temprano en Maymi, valle de Pisco, Perú. In *Tecnología y organización de la producción cerámica prehispánica en los Andes*, edited by Izumi Shimada, pp. 249–267. Pontificia Universidad Católica del Perú, Lima, Peru.

Bawden, Garth, 1996. *The Moche: The Peoples of the Americas*. Blackwell Press, Cambridge, UK.

Bawden, Garth, 2001. The Symbols of Late Moche Social Transformation. In *Moche Art and Archaeology in Ancient Peru*, edited by Joanne Pillsbury, pp. 285–305. National Gallery of Art, Washington, DC.

Castillo, Luis Jaime, 2000. Los rituales mochica de la muerte. In *Los dioses del antiguo Perú*, edited by Krzysztof Makowski, pp. 103–135. Banco de Crédito del Perú, Lima.

Castillo, Luis Jaime, 2001. La presencia Wari en San José de Moro. In *Huari y Tiwanaku: modelos vs. evidencias*, edited by Peter Kaulicke and William H. Isbell, pp. 143–179. Pontificia Universidad Católica del Perú, Lima.

Castillo, Luis Jaime, 2005. Las sacerdotisas de San José de Moro. In *Divina y humana, La mujer en los antiguos Perú y México*, pp. 18–29. Ministerio de Educación, Lima, Peru.

Castillo, Luis Jaime, 2009. Moche Politics in the Jequetepeque Valley: A Case for Political Opportunism. In *New Perspectives on Moche Political Organization*, edited by Jeffrey Quilter and Luis Jaime Castillo, pp. 81–107. Harvard University Press, Dumbarton Oaks Library and Collection, Washington, DC.

Castillo, Luis Jaime, 2012a. Looking at the Wari Empire from the Outside In. In *Wari: Lords of the Ancient Andes*, edited by Susan Bergh, pp. 47–64. Thames & Hudson, New York; The Cleveland Museum of Art, Cleveland, OH.

Castillo, Luis Jaime, 2012b. *San José de Moro y el fin de los Moches en el Valle de Jequetepeque, costa norte del Peru*. Unpublished Ph.D. dissertation, University of California, Los Angeles.

Castillo, Luis Jaime, and Christopher Donnan, 1994. Los Moches del norte y los Moches del sur, una perspectiva desde el valle de Jequetepeque. In *Vicús*, edited by Krzysztof Makowski, Christopher B. Donnan, and Ivan Amaro Bullon, pp. 143–181. Banco de Crédito del Perú, Lima.

Castillo, Luis Jaime, Francesca Fernandini, and Luis Muro, 2012. The Multidimensional Relations Between the Wari and the Moche States of Northern Peru. *Boletín de Arqueología PUCP* 16:53–77.

Castillo, Luis Jaime, Julio Rucabado Yong, Martín Del Carpio Perla, Katiuska Bernuy Quiroga, Karim Ruiz Rosell, Carlos Rengifo Chunga, Gabriel Prieto Burmester, and Carole Fraresso, 2008. Ideología y poder en la consolidación, colapso y reconstitución del estado Mochica del Jequetepeque: El Proyecto Arqueológico San José de Moro (1991–2006). *Ñawpa Paccha* 29:1–86.

Chapdelaine, Claude, 2010. Moche and Wari During the Middle Horizon on the North Coast of Peru. In *Beyond Wari Walls: Regional Perspectives on Middle Horizon Peru*, edited by Justin Jennings, pp. 213–232. University of New Mexico Press, Albuquerque.

Donnan, Christopher, 1977. The Thematic Approach to Iconography. In *Pre-Columbian Art History, Selected Readings*, edited by A. Cordy-Collins and J. Stern, pp. 407–420. Peek Publications, Palo Alto, CA.

Edwards, Mathew, 2010. Archaeological Investigations at Pataraya: A Wari Outpost in the Nasca Valley of Southern Peru. Unpublished Ph.D. dissertation, University of California, Santa Barbara.

Fernandini, Francesca, and Grace Alexandrino, 2015. Cerro de Oro: desarrollo local, cambio y continuidad durante el Período Intermedio Temprano y el Horizonte. In *Andes 9: Nuevas perspectivas en la organización política wari*, edited by Sociedad Polaca de Estudios. Latinoamericanos, Lima, Peru. In press.

Gell, Alfred, 1992. The Technology of Enchantment and the Enchantment of Technology. In *Anthropology, Art and Aesthetics*, edited by J. Coote and A. Shelton, pp. 40–66. Clarendon, Oxford, UK.

Gosden Chris, 2004. Archaeology and Colonialism. Cambridge University Press, Cambridge, UK.
Harrison, Rodney, 2006. An Artefact of Colonial Desire? Kimberley Points and the Technologies of Enchantment. *Current Anthropology* 47(1):63–88.
Hocquenghem, Anne Marie, 2008. Sacrifices and Ceremonial Calendars in Societies of the Central Andes. In *The Art and Archaeology of the Moche, An Ancient Andean Society of the Peruvian north coast*, edited by Steve Bourget and Kimberly Jones, pp. 153–178. University of Texas Press, Austin.
Hodder, Ian, 2011. Human-Thing Entanglement: Towards an Integrated Archaeological Perspective. *Journal of the Royal Anthropological Institute* 17(1):154–177.
Ingold, Tim, 2010. Bringing Things to Life: Creative Entanglements in a World of Materials. *ESRC National Centre for Research Methods, NCRM Working Paper Series*:1–15.
Isbell, William H., 2000. Repensando el Horizonte Medio. In *Huari y Tiwanaku: modelos vs. Evidencias. Boletín de Arqueología PUCP 4*, edited by Peter Kaulicke and William H. Isbell, pp. 9–68. Pontificia Universidad Católica del Perú, Lima.
Isbell, William H., 2010. Agency, Identity, and Control: Understanding Wari Space and Power. In *Beyond Wari Walls: Regional Perspectives on Middle Horizon Peru*, edited by Justin Jennings, pp. 233–254. University of New Mexico Press, Albuquerque.
Isbell, William H., and Gordon F. McEwan, 1991. *Huari Administrative Structure: Prehistoric Monumental Architecture and State Government.* Dumbarton Oaks, Washington, D.C.
Jennings, Justin, 2010. Beyond Wari Walls. In *Beyond Wari Walls: Regional Perspectives on Middle Horizon Peru*, edited by Justin Jennings, pp. 1–18. University of New Mexico Press, Albuquerque.
Keane, Webb, 1998. Calvin in the Tropics: Objects and Subjects at the Religious Frontier. In *Border Fetishisms: Material Objects in Unstable Spaces*, edited by Patricia Spyer, pp. 13–34. Routledge, New York.
Knappett, Carl, 2010. Communities of Things and Objects: A Spatial Perspective. In *The Cognitive Life of Things: Recasting the Boundaries of the Mind*, edited by Lambros Malafouris and Colin Renfrew, pp. 81–88. MacDonald Institute for Archaeological Research, Cambridge, UK.
Knobloch, Patricia J., 2005. Who Was Who? In the Middle Horizon Andean Prehistory. Electronic document, www-rohan.sdsu.edu/~bharley/WWWAgents.html, accessed October 11, 2013.
Koons, Michelle, and Bridget Alex, 2014. Revised Moche Chronology Based on Bayesian Models of Reliable Radiocarbon Dates. *Radiocarbo*n 56(3):1039–1055.
Lumbreras, Luis Guillermo, 2012. Introduction. In *Wari: Lords of the Ancient Andes,* edited by Susan Bergh, pp. 1–4. Thames & Hudson, New York.
Martindale, Andrew, 2009. Entanglement and Tinkering: Structural History in the Archaeology of the Northern Tsimshian. *Journal of Social Archaeology* 9(1):59–91.
McClelland, Donna, Donald McClelland, and Christopher B. Donnan, 2007. *Moche Fineline Painting from San José de Moro*. Cotsen Institute of Archaeology, Los Angeles.
McEwan, Gordon, and Ryan Patrick Williams, 2012. The Wari Built Environment: Landscape and Architecture of Empire. In *Wari: Lords of the Ancient Andes*, edited by Susan E. Bergh, pp. 65–81. Thames & Hudson, New York.

Menzel, Dorothy, 1964. Style and Time in Middle Horizon Peru. *Ñawpa Pacha* 2:1–105.
Meskell, Lynn, 2004. *Object Worlds in Ancient Egypt: Material Biographies Past and Present.* Berg Publishers, Oxford, UK; New York.
Mitchell, Timothy, 2002. *Rule of Experts: Egypt, Techno-politics, Modernity.* University of California Press, Berkeley, Los Angeles.
Muro, Luis, 2008. Reporte del análisis arqueométrico de piezas Wari provenientes del sitio San José de Moro. In *Programa prqueológico San José de Moro, temporada 2007*, edited by Luis Jaime Castillo, pp. 162–219. Pontificia Universidad Católica del Perú, Lima.
Muro, Luis, and Nino Del Solar, 2015. Characterizing the Relationship between Two Early States of the Moche, the Wari, and the Product of Their Contact: Archaeological and Archaeometric Perspectives. Paper presented at the 67th Annual Meeting of the Society for American Archaeology, San Francisco, CA, April 15–19, 2015.
Nash, Donna J., 2012. The art of feasting: building an empire with food and drink. In *Wari: Lords of the Ancient Andes*, edited by Susan E. Bergh, pp. 82–102. Thames & Hudson, New York.
Nuttal, Sarah, 2009. *Entanglement: Literary and Cultural Reflections on Post-apartheid.* Wits University Press, Johannesburg, South Africa.
Owen, Bruce, 2010. Wari in the Majes-Camanaì Valley: A Different Kind of Horizon. In *Beyond Wari Walls: Regional Perspectives on Middle Horizon Peru*, edited by Justin Jennings, pp. 57–78. University of New Mexico Press, Albuquerque.
Pietz, William, 1998. Afterword: How to Grow Oranges in Norway. In *Border Fetishisms: Material Objects in Unstable Spaces,* edited by Patricia Spyer, pp. 245–251. Routledge, London.
Quilter, Jeffrey, 1990. The Moche Revolt of the Objects. *Latin American Antiquity* 1(1):42–65.
Quilter, Jeffrey, 2011. *The Moche of Ancient Peru.* Peabody Museum Press, Cambridge, MA.
Quilter, Jeffrey, and Luis Jaime Castillo, eds., 2010. *New Perspectives on Moche Political Organization.* Harvard University Press, Cambridge, MA.
Renfrew, Colin, 2010. Introduction. In *The Cognitive Life of Things: Recasting the Boundaries of the Mind*, edited by Lambros Malafouris and Colin Renfrew, pp. 1–12. MacDonald Institute for Archaeological Research, Cambridge, UK.
Rohfritsch, Agnes, 2010. Contribución arqueométrica al estudio de las técnicas y de la organización de la producción de cerámica ritual en la sociedad Mochica (150–850 dc, costa norte del Perú). *Bulletin de l'Institut Français D'études Andines* 39(2):389–412.
Rucabado, Julio, and Luis Jaime Castillo, 2003. El periodo transicional en San José de Moro. In *Moche: Hacia el final del Milenio. Vol. I*, edited by Santiago Uceda and Elias Mujica, pp. 15–42. Pontificia Universidad Católica del Perú, Lima.
Rucabado, Julio, and Luis Jaime Castillo, 2006. Elite Mortuary Practices at San José de Moro During the Transitional Period: Rhe Case Study of Collective Burial M-U615. Unpublished Ph.D. dissertation, University of North Carolina, Chapel Hill.
Schreiber, Katharina, 1992. *Wari Imperialism in Middle Horizon Peru.* Museum of Anthropology, University of Michigan, Ann Arbor.

Schreiber, Katharina, 2004. Andean Empires. In *Andean Archaeology*, edited by H. Silverman, pp. 255–279. Blackwell, Malden, MA.

Schreiber, Katharina, 2012. Interpreting a Cosmopolitan Andean Society: The Rise of an Andean Empire. In *Wari: Lords of the Ancient Andes*. Thames & Hudson, New York.

Segura, Rafael, and Izumi Shimada, 2010. The Wari Footprint on the Central Coast: A Ciew from Cajamarquilla and Pachacamac. In *Beyond Wari Walls: Regional Perspectives on Middle Horizon, Peru*, edited by Justin Jennings, pp. 113–135. University of New Mexico Press, Albuquerque.

Shimada, Izumi, 1994. *Pampa Grande and the Moche Culture*. University of Texas Press, Austin.

Shimada, Izumi, 2010. Moche Sociopolitical Organization. In *New Perspectives on Moche Political Organization*, edited by J. Quilter and L. J. Castillo, pp. 70–82. Harvard University Press, Cambridge, MA.

Spyer, Patricia, 1998. Introduction. In *Border Fetishisms: Material Objects in Unstable Spaces,* edited by Patricia Spyer, pp. 1–11. Routledge, New York.

Swenson, Edward, 2006. Competitive Feasting, Religious Pluralism and Decentralized Power in the Late Moche Period. In *Andean Archaeology III: North and South*, Volume 3, edited by William H. Isbell and Helaine Silverman, pp. 112–142. Springer, New York.

Swenson, Edward, 2011. Feminine Powers, Ritual Warfare, and the Sacrificial Foundations of Contested Authority in Late Moche Jequetepeque, Peru. In *It's Good to be King: The Archaeology of Power and Authority,* edited by Shawn Morton and Don Butler, pp. 145–156. University of Calgary Press, Calgary, Canada.

Swenson, Edward, and John Warner, 2012. Crucibles of Power: Forging Copper and Forging Subjects at the Moche Ceremonial Center of Huaca Colorada, Peru. *Journal of Anthropological Archaeology* 31(3):314–333.

Thomas, Nicholas, 1991. *Entangled Objects: Exchange, Material Culture, and Colonialism in the Pacific.* Harvard University Press, Cambridge, MA.

Tung, Tiffiny A., 2012. *Violence, Ritual and the Wari Empire: A Social Bioarchaeology of Imperialism in the Ancient Andes*. University Press of Florida, Gainesville.

Uceda, Santiago, 2000. Los ceremoniales en la Huaca de la Luna: un análisis de los espacios arquitectónicos. In *Investigaciones en la Huaca de la Luna 1997*, edited by Santiago Uceda, Elías Mujica, and Ricardo Morales, pp. 205–214. Facultad de Ciencias Sociales de la Universidad Nacional de Trujillo, Trujillo, Peru.

Uceda, Santiago, 2001. Investigations at Huaca de la Luna, Moche Valley: An Example of Moche Religious Architecture. In *Moche Art and Archaeology in Ancient Peru*, edited by Joanne Pillsbury, pp. 47–67. National Gallery of Art, Washington, DC.

Watanabe, Shinya, 2001. Wari y Cajamarca. In *Huari y Tiwanaku: modelos vs. Evidencias. Boletín de Arqueología PUCP 4*, edited by Peter Kaulicke and William H. Isbell, pp. 531–541. Pontificia Universidad Católica del Perú, Lima.

Entanglements with the Natural World: Landscapes and Agriculture

Chapter 5

Entangled Banks and the Domestication of East African Pastoralist Landscapes

Paul J. Lane

Introduction

When the young Charles Darwin first encountered the Tierra del Fuego landscape in December 1832, he was clearly struck by its novelty, remarking that even a single glance had shown it to be "widely different ... from any thing" he "had ever beheld" (Darwin 1839:227). He also appears to have been bewildered, perhaps even taken aback, by certain aspects of this land, not least its human inhabitants, who he first observed "partly concealed by the entangled forest ... perched on a wild point overhanging the sea" (Darwin 1839:227). He seems, moreover, to have been somewhat disconcerted that this group of Fuegians responded to the *Beagle*'s passing by springing up, waving their "tattered cloaks" and uttering a "loud and sonorous shout" (Darwin 1839:227), although he does not record how he might have hoped for them to react. Subsequently, Darwin describes the Fuegians as "wild savages," with coarse, black, and entangled hair, and was clearly perplexed that these examples of the human species could be so unlike other humans in both appearance and behavior:

> These poor wretches were stunted in their growth, their hideous faces bedaubed with white paint, their skins filthy and greasy, their hair entangled, their voices discordant, their gestures violent and without dignity. Viewing such men, one can hardly make oneself believe they are fellow-creatures, and inhabitants of the same world (Darwin 1839:235; entry from December 1832).

Darwin's unease, moreover, was not restricted to his encounters with Tierra del Fuego's indigenous human inhabitants, as even the forests bordering the coast appeared to him as an "entangled mass" of vegetation that, although they reminded him of other forests he had visited, exhibited "a difference; for in these still solitudes Death, instead of Life, seemed the predominant spirit" (Darwin 1839:231).

Archaeology of Entanglement edited by Lindsay Der and Francesca Fernandini, 127–150

As Glendening (2007:1–6) has discussed, Darwin's use of "entanglement" as a descriptive adjective and as a metaphor with reference to Tierra del Fuego's vegetation and human occupants, both in diary entries[1] from his voyages on the *Beagle* and in their later published form as *The Journal of Researches* (Darwin 1839), differs from his use of entanglement in reference to other encounters during these voyages and, also, from his famous metaphorical use of entanglement in the concluding paragraph of his best-known book *On the Origin of Species*:

> It is interesting to contemplate an entangled bank, clothed with many plants of many kinds, with birds singing on the bushes, with various insects flitting about, and with worms crawling through the damp earth, and to reflect that these elaborately constructed forms, so different from each other, and dependent on each other in so complex a manner, have all been produced by laws acting around us (Darwin 1859:489).

Thus, for example, although he also describes the Brazilian rainforests he visited before reaching Tierra del Fuego as "entangled," his reactions were far more positive than those evoked by his later encounters at the "uttermost ends of the earth" (Gamble 1992). In his diary entry for 8 April 1832, for instance, Darwin describes himself as being "at an utter loss how sufficiently to admire" the scene presented by the "infinite numbers of lianas & parasitical plants & the contrast of the flourishing trees with the dead & rotten trunks" he observed in the hills behind Praia Grande, across the bay from Rio de Janeiro (Darwin 1839:137). Similarly, a few years later when visiting the country around All Saint's Bay (Bahía de Todos los Santos) on the Brazilian coast, it is the complexity and interconnections of the local vegetation that he admires most, commenting that:

> Learned naturalists describe these scenes of the Tropics by naming a multitude of objects & mentioning some characteristic feature of each. To a learned traveller, this possibly may communicate some definite ideas; but who else from seeing a plant in an herbarium can imagine its appearance when growing in its native soil? Who, from seeing choice plants in a hot house, can multiply some into the dimensions of forest trees, or crowd others into an entangled mass? (Darwin 1839:753; entry for 1–6 August 1836).

That Darwin used the metaphor of entanglement in such a contradictory manner is not entirely surprising in itself because the word has long carried these dual connotations. Derived from the word *tangle*, which seems to have entered into written English in the fourteenth century, *entanglement* as a concept first appears in the late seventeenth century, and in its earliest manifestations typically carried with it notions of entrapment rather than the more neutral notion of interconnectedness that Darwin stresses in the conclusion to *On the Origins of Species* (Glendening 2007:9). Yet, it was these more positive ideas of a network rather than a "tangled web," the former "connecting," the latter "disturbing and obscuring" (Williams 1970, cited in Glendening 2007:9), that eventually prevailed as Darwinian evolutionary theory became mainstream and biological scientists directed their energies toward reconstructing the individual lineages of different species and their various lines of association. In fact, the need to *disentangle* the contributions of different processes and genetic contributions to a specific complex form has often become the paramount concern of biological scientists. That this might be possible is because, as Darwin had intimated, despite the appearance of having been randomly created, the interconnections of biotic communities and their genetic ancestry are governed by specific natural laws. Thus, even though a specific ecological community, such as a hedgerow, may comprise a large number of elements that interact in a nonlinear manner, certain characteristics are predictable because of the existence of "general statistical regularities concerning the abundance and distribution of species," while "other features can be predicted on the basis of the geographic location of the respective community," the productivity of the specific environment, and the competitive abilities of the species that inhabit it (Storch and Gatson 2004:390).

Disentangling Drivers of Climate Change

In recent years, Darwin's likening of the natural world to an entangled bank that can nonetheless be deciphered through an understanding of evolutionary processes and the history of ecological relationships that connect different parts to one another has taken on fresh significance. Specifically, many scholars currently direct palaeoecological research toward differentiating anthropogenic and natural drivers of climate change, and widely use the trope of "disentanglement" to contextualise such studies and to demonstrate their applied relevance to ongoing debates about the future of the planet and the sustainability of different practices. Commenting on the current observable diversity in South American vegetation and environments, Fontana and colleagues (2012:1204), for example, emphasize the difficulties of trying to reconstruct the origins of this diversity, noting in particular that "it is not easy to disentangle forcing factors that operate on different timescales, especially when they operate continuously and interact in ways that are likely to be complex." In their recent discussion of climatic, vegetation, and cultural change in the eastern Mediterranean between ca. 9,000 and 2,500 calibrated years before present (years cal BP), Roberts and colleagues (2011:147) likewise note that it is "often hard to disentangle" the manner in which "climatic changes, coupled to increasing human impacts on the environment, transformed the region's landscapes." In addition, in a recent review of the state of research on East African palaeoenvironments and climate change, Gelorini and Verschuren (2012:8) comment that "the way in which past human societies have contributed to modification of the East African landscape remains highly controversial, as it needs to be disentangled from ... climate patterns on both short and longer time scales." Similar observations are found in a wide range of comparable studies conducted in these regions and elsewhere. They are also made with reference to particular aspects of environmental change, such as variations in atmospheric carbon dioxide concentration, changing herbivore densities, or the determinants of different fire regimes (Marchant and Lane 2014). Thus, for instance, for fire to ignite and spread requires a "suite of [different] biophysical conditions" with "the significant driving variables" changing across temporal and spatial scales (McWethy et al. 2013:2). The type of land use also affects the nature and spread of fires, whether deliberately set or a spontaneous ignition, because of variations in moisture content, fuel load composition, and vegetation structure (e.g., Mermoz et al. 2005). Once a fire regime is established, this too can initiate systemic feedbacks by changing soil processes and overall landscape dynamics (e.g., Lloret et al. 2002). Since humans have also long influenced and even altered fire regimes, efforts to "disentangle human versus climate drivers of past fire regimes" (McWethy et al. 2013:3) can be challenging and require a consideration of the relative effects of different drivers of fire activity at different temporal and spatial scales, along with such factors as the relative sensitivity of vegetation to anthropogenic intervention.

The ability to determine whether anthropogenic activities have been the primary drivers of recent landscape, ecological, and climatic change, and to be able to discriminate between these and certain "background" natural processes at global, regional, and local scales are undoubtedly critical in supporting arguments for changes in human behavior to secure an environmentally sustainable future for the planet. However, we can challenge the practice of constantly endeavoring to separate human from natural causes and processes on several grounds. In the first place, given that humans have either colonized or at least visited and influenced all ecological niches on the planet, including the deep oceans and high latitudes, and have as a species been shaping environments for more than 100,000 years (and much longer if we also include our hominin ancestors), it is questionable whether any locality on earth can be or should be considered "pristine" (e.g., Balée 2010; Denevan 1992; Ellis and Ramankutty 2008; Evans 2011; Willis et al. 2004). Humans, in other words, have long been a part of the ecological history of the earth, and much of the apparent "natural abundance" of many landscapes, including parts of the Amazonian rainforest that so inspired Darwin (e.g., Clement and Junqueira 2010; Heckenberger et al. 2007), as well as tracts of the Australian outback (e.g., Bird et al. 2005) and West African forest-savanna mosaics (e.g., Fairhead and Leach 1996), is now thought to have evolved through processes of ecological mutualism between humans and nonhuman species. In a related way, recent research on the spread of food production, whether farming or herding, highlights the close relationships that have emerged between humans and nonhuman animal and plant species as a direct consequence of a human presence in the landscape, with some scholars arguing that a food production system requires not just domestication of a narrow range of plant and animal species but also the domestication of entire landscapes (e.g., Arroyo-Kalin 2010; Terrell and Hart 2008; see also Fuller in this volume). Finally, as scholars extend the temporal depth of ecological studies of different landscape types through the incorporation of historical, archaeological, palaeoecological, and palaeobiological data (e.g., Rick and Lockwood 2013; Sandweiss and Kelley 2012; Willis and MacDonald 2011), it is apparent that many landscapes are far more resilient than previously believed (e.g., Bhagwat et al. 2012; Colombaroli et al. 2013; Sirami et al. 2010) and often exhibit alternating phases of high and reduced biodiversity as part of their "natural" dynamics. These cycles of "recovery" and "collapse" may only be observable over long time periods rarely captured by the available observational records (Dearing 2012), especially in settings where such documentation commenced only in the last two centuries.

The implication of these observations seems to be that instead of attempting to disentangle complex human-environment relationships, a more productive strategy might be to explore how different elements of the "natural" and "human" worlds have become increasingly entangled (Hodder 2011, 2012). In the following sections I explore this point further, referencing the domestication of East African pastoralist landscapes and particularly the role of animal dung in these processes.

Enduring Dung

Areas (typically 1.25–2.5 acres [0.5–1 ha] in size) of open, closely cropped grass within a wider mosaic of woody and/or bushy vegetation are a common feature of East African semiarid and arid environments. Often known as "glades," these have diverse origins and complex histories. Various natural processes including fires, long-term droughts, ungulate densities and grazing regimes, and the actions of large keystone species such as elephants and rhinos can all contribute to the creation of glades and the maintenance of grazing lawns (Archibald 2008). Once established, a series of feedback mechanisms can come into play that help maintain glades within the landscape by restricting tree recruitment. Researchers from several disciplines have sought to understand these processes and their shifting dynamics both from an ecological perspective and in relation to the implications for environmental management (Augustine, 2003; Augustine and McNaughton, 2004a; Blackmore et al. 1990; Reid and Ellis, 1995; Young et al. 1995).

This ecological research confirms that in some landscapes glades mark the location of abandoned pastoralist settlements where livestock are consistently penned overnight. The age of these abandoned settlements is variable, but longitudinal studies combined with interview data about the histories of these sites have shown that they can often be in excess of 50 to 100 years old (e.g., Augustine 2003; Muchiru et al. 2008; Young et al. 1995). Archaeologists familiar with these environments also note that glades often contain traces of previous settlement activity of variable date, including material dating to both the Pastoral Iron Age (ca. 1,200–800 years BP) and the Pastoral Neolithic (ca. 4,500–1,200 years BP), suggesting that some glades may survive in the landscape for considerable periods of time (for details on these archaeological periods, see Lane 2013). The lack of systematic investigation of the antiquity of specific glades, coupled with the well-documented evidence for frequent localized shifting of vegetation patches within these landscapes (Gillson 2004; Wiegand et al. 2005), makes it difficult to assess how long individual glades have been in existence. However, recent research on the Laikipia Plateau, in north-central Kenya, raises the possibility that some glades may remain open for up to approximately 750 years (Lane 2011). More research also needs to be conducted to establish the proportion of glades that are associated with former human settlement as opposed to those likely to have been created by nonhuman agents. Here again, however, research on the Laikipia Plateau has begun to shed light on this, with recent systematic surveys on Mugie Ranch suggesting (albeit from a small sample of groundtruthed examples) that between 25% and 30% of the glades here are centered on abandoned pastoralist settlements of variable antiquity (Causey 2008).

Far better known are the ecological processes that restrict tree and bush encroachment over recently abandoned settlements and the manner in which these promote positive ecological feedbacks that can enhance local biodiversity across several different trophic levels. Glades of this type represent nutrient-enriched patches derived from the accumulation of livestock dung and urine, and to a lesser degree the refuse scatters generated by human activity, during the occupation of pastoralist settlements. These can be occupied permanently (as in the Mara region in southwest Kenya), or may be reoccupied on a seasonal basis (such as in the Amboseli Basin in southeast Kenya) or peripatetically in truly nomadic systems such as among the Turkana in northern Kenya (Reid and Ellis 1995). After three to five years, the accumulated dung and its associated parasites make the settlements uninhabitable (Western and Dunne 1979), forcing a move to another location. Settlement and herd sizes can be highly variable both between different ethnic groups and over time within a single landscape such as in the Mara (Lamprey and Reid 2004). In the mid-twentieth century, for instance, some Rendille settlements in northern Kenya contained upwards of 60 houses and measured more than 150 meters in diameter, whereas Samburu settlements located marginally further south only contained four to six independent families and had house diameters of 30 to 40 meters and herd sizes averaging around 80 animals in total (Spencer 1973:19–21). In recent decades, Maasai settlements in southern Kenya and northern Tanzania contained between six to eight independent polygamous households averaging 50 to 80 people, and had houses measuring between 40 and 80 meters in diameter (Western and Dunne 1979), with the total number of small and large stock ranging between approximately 200 to 1,500 or more individual animals (Homewood and Rodgers 1991).

Regardless of the precise differences, in all such settlements the regular penning of livestock inside the settlement enclosure results in dense accumulations of dung, producing mounds up to 2 meters above ground surface in some circumstances. With the regular contributions of animal urine, these deposits result in heightened concentrations of a number of soil minerals, especially nitrogen (N) and phosphorous (P), but also minerals such as magnesium (Mg), calcium (Ca), carbon (C), and sodium (K) that are all beneficial to plant productivity. In the low-nutrient soils of southern Turkana (Kenya), for example, soils on abandoned pastoralist settlements typically contain "nine times more C, three times more N, and six times more P" than found at background levels, and even 20 years after abandonment nutrient levels are at least twice as high (Reid and Ellis 1995:984). Decomposition of the accumulated dung also enhances the water retention capacity of the soil, possibly by reducing evapotranspiration rates (Muchiru et al. 2008; Reid and Ellis 1995) and enhancing rainwater penetration.

Aside from its pivotal role in the creation of nutrient-rich hotspots within, animal dung, especially that of domestic animals, is an important resource for pastoralist communities that has both utilitarian and possibly symbolic value.[2] The region's pastoralists consider dung to have certain medical properties, among other uses. The Samburu, for example, make a purgative from sheep's dung and urine mixed with a solution produced from the root of the "toothbrush" tree (*Salvadora persica* L.) for abortions (Fratkin 1996:91). Maasai herbalists are also reported to use sheep dung mixed with water and parts of the shrub *Grewia tembensis* to form a salve to close skull fissures (Kiringe 2006:65). They also use elephant dung mixed with the boiled roots of *G. villosa* as a treatment for epilepsy (Ibrahim and Ibrahim 1998:143). Both cattle and elephant dung are also burned for more prosaic reasons such as a mosquito, tick, and/or biting fly repellent (Gifford 1978). More important, animal dung mixed with mud is a primary building material among some East African pastoralists, notably eastern Nilotic (e.g., Maasai, Samburu) and southern Nilotic (e.g., Datoga) speakers (for Maasai, see Mbae 1990; for Samburu, see Straight 1999; for Datoga, see Umesao 1969). It is used mainly for plastering external and internal walls and the house roof, although Maasai also line postholes with dung when erecting the house frame (Andersen 1977:176). In all these contexts, houses are built and maintained exclusively by women, and every married woman is expected to build her own dwelling, thereby establishing a close embodied relationship with it and the materials (including dung) used in its construction (Straight 1999).[3]

Sustained and repeated occupation of these settlements also results in the progressive removal of trees and bushes for use as building materials and fuel as well as intensive grazing of the surrounding sward. The choice of settlement location in these environments is partly constrained by the location of water points (which need to be sufficiently accessible to sustain both humans and livestock). As a result, the shape and size of the effective grazing (typically within an approximately 6.5 km radius around the settlement) and wood collection areas can be quite variable. Nonetheless, studies in a variety of locations and environments show that in broad terms these areas are characterized by two concentric and roughly elliptical zones, with that closest to the settlement being the most heavily used for fuel wood, building materials, and livestock grazing (Spencer 1973:15–18; see Figure 5.1a) and the greatest impact

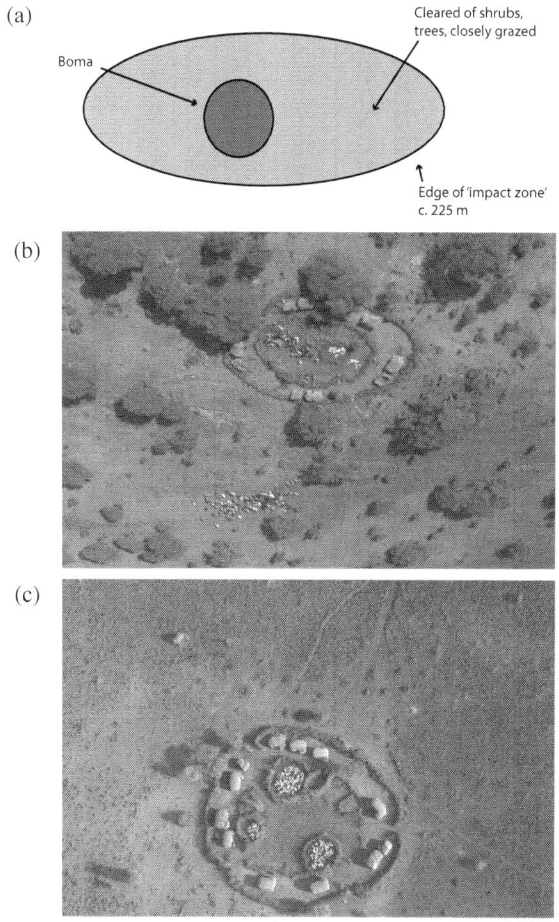

Figure 5.1 Visualizing ecological "impacts" around occupied East African pastoralist settlements: a) Generalized model of "impact" zone (adapted from Spencer 1973:15); b) Inhabited *boma* (Maasai pastoralist settlements) in savannah parkland; c) Inhabited *boma* in Amboseli lava field, showing immediately adjacent vegetation-free zone.

occurring within a radius of approximately 200 to 225 meters or so from the perimeter thorn fence surrounding the settlement (Western and Dunne 1979).

Naturalizing Settlement

Following abandonment, the high phosphorous and nitrogen content of the soil over former livestock pens, including the main cattle pen toward the center and more peripheral enclosures for penning calves and small stock (i.e., sheep and goats), restricts the sequence of plant recolonization to certain species that can tolerate these levels. The precise composition of these pioneer communities varies according to different bioclimatic conditions. In the Amboseli Basin, for example, the early colonizers include forbs such as *Amaranthus graecizans*, *Tribulus terrestris*, and *Zaley pentrandra* Burm. (Muchiru et al. 2009:329), along with *Cynodon plectostachyus*. Often referred to by its common name "manyatta grass," this is also ubiquitous on abandoned pastoralist settlements on the Laikipia Plateau alongside *T. terrestris* (Augustine and McNaughton, 2004b:831), although in the later stages of plant succession *Pennisetum stramineum* can dominate (Veblen 2012:123). On the Athi Plains in southern Kenya, *Cynodon nlemfuensis* is the dominant grass (Stelfox 1986) on such sites, while in the more arid context of Somalia *C. dactylon*, *Cleome tenella*, and *Gisekia pharnaceoides* predominate (Barker et al. 1990:294–295). Distance from the center of the settlement is another significant variable in the recolonization process, with grass species dominating within the first 50-meter radius from the settlement boundary, forbs up to 150 meters away, and small trees and shrubs beyond this zone (Muchiru et al. 2009:325).

Longitudinal study of abandoned pastoralist settlements (Figure 5.2) has indicated that within five years, overall herbaceous biomass and species richness typically exceeds that at the periphery of the "impact zone" and reaches a peak around 20 years after abandonment, steadily declining thereafter (Muchiru et al. 2009:325–327). There is also a distinct sequence of plant succession. Early colonizers include C. *plectostachyus* and various forbs; after 20 years these are supplanted by other species, including *B. ciliaris* and *S. pallida* (Muchiru et al. 2009:325–327). Overtime, woody biomass increases, and certain species, such as *Acacia tortilis* become particularly dominant. In southern Turkana, an interesting relationship of ecological mutualism between this species and domestic animal dung has evolved. Specifically, *A. tortilis* seedpods are rich in protein and are fed to young and milking livestock in the dry season when other forage sources are scare or of poor quality (Reid and Ellis 1995:979), and a system of usufruct rights governing access to different concentrations of *A. tortilis* has evolved (Barrow 1990). Ingestion of the seed helps stimulate germination and destroys seed-predating bruchid beetles, while the dung layers in which they are deposited provide a nutrient-rich seed

(a)

(b)

(c)

Figure 5.2 Occupied and abandoned Maasai pastoralist settlements (*bomas*) in the Amboseli Basin, Kenya, in February 2009: a) Inhabited *boma* and cattle pen in Amboseli lava field looking out to its adjacent high-intensity resource extraction zone; b) *Acacia tortilis* growing in a former goat pen; c) Sequence of occupied and abandoned *bomas* in Amboseli lava field (All photos by author).

bank (Lamprey et al. 1974). Although variations in rainfall and herbivory can further influence seedling establishment, the greater water retention properties of the dung layers across abandoned pastoralist settlements appears to play a critical role in enhancing survival rates during the first—and most critical—dry season (Reid and Ellis 1995). A further, possibly beneficial consequence is that since the genus Acacia is very effective at N_2 (nitrogen gas) symbiotic fixation in the soil (Cech et al. 2008:992), the presence of stands of *A. tortilis* on abandoned settlements may help offset the loss of N through leaching and ammonia volatization that otherwise occurs on such sites (Augustine 2003). The overall result is that southern Turkana is scattered with rings of *A. tortilis* marking the location of former livestock pens, which, because they stand out as distinctive green patches in the landscape during the dry season, effectively means that the history of human settlement becomes encoded within the prevailing vegetation. Indeed, learning to read such "natural" traces of human settlement is often a more effective means of locating archaeological settlement remains in these landscapes than relying on the detection of more conventional material traces such as ceramics and stone tools, especially as dung undergoes a series of entangled taphonomic processes (Figure 5.3) following its initial deposition, making it potentially more archaeologically visible than other forms of material culture (Shahack-Gross 2011 and references therein).

Recycled Dung

Once established, the glades that develop around abandoned pastoralist settlements are further perpetuated in the landscape by browsing and grazing activities on the part of both wild and domesticated animals, which act to suppress the invasion of tree and shrub seedlings, while their dung adds to the overall supply of nutrients. As with vegetation succession, a complex set of ecological relationships emerge over time, with the spatial patterning and densities of grazers and browsers varying in response to the changing vegetation mosaic. Thus, for instance, in Amboseli species such as zebra, wildebeest, Thomson's gazelle, Grant's gazelle, oryx, and gerenuk, all tend to concentrate preferentially around abandoned settlements, while all other species, including livestock, "peak at intermediate distance from [abandoned] settlements and then [decline] with distance away from settlements" (Muchiru et al. 2008: 946). While several factors may account for such behavior, including the protection offered against predators by the greater visibility in open areas, the higher nutrient content of the herbaceous and woody biomass around abandoned pastoralist settlements relative to the surrounding bushland (Augustine 2003; Muchiru et al. 2008) and the greater palatability of grasses such as *C. plectostachyus* and *C. dactylon* likely explain the phenomenon. The region's pastoralists, including the Maasai, Turkana, and Ariaal, certainly recognize the value of these and other species (e.g., *Digitaria abyssinica*, *Themeda triandra*) as good indicators of quality grazing (Mapinduzi et al. 2003; Oba et al. 2000;

Figure 5.3 Entangled dung: "natural" and "anthropogenic" taphonomic processes affecting dung deposits on East African pastoralist settlements, Amboseli, February 2009 (Figure 5.3a based on Shahack-Goss 2010: Figure 5; All photos by author).

Roba and Oba 2009); the Maasai in particular often single out C. *plectostachyus* as a high milk-producing grass.

Aside from increasing the overall density of wild ungulates and the species richness of the surrounding vegetation at the landscape scale,[4] additional research indicates that the localized concentration of nutrients in abandoned pastoralist settlements can have beneficial effects at other trophic levels. For example, Söderström and Reid (2010) note that invertebrate populations, specifically members of the insect orders Diptera and Coleoptera, show "significant positive correlations to [the] amount of dung deposited on abandoned settlements" (2010:187), and may be twice as numerous on such sites than in offsite locations. Other studies (on the Laikipia Plateau) indicate that glades may also host higher populations of arboreal geckos (which may partly be due to the increased densities of insects) (Donihue et al. 2013), and also heightened densities of both termites and rodents (Veblen 2008). In fact, as Weissbrod (2010:313) has noted, even when the settlements are occupied, insectivorous specialists such as the lesser elephant shrew may be preferentially drawn to these locations because cattle and sheep dung contain seeds and attract insects.

Higher populations of insects may also partly account for the higher densities and wider species diversity of birds near abandoned settlements. A recent study in Kajiado District, southern Kenya, focusing on game bird densities, for instance, found that "mean species richness of game birds was the highest in abandoned settlements" yet with significant intraspecies variation (Morris et al. 2009:51). Dove densities were especially high (as much as 10 to 20 times more than other species), whereas Francolin and Spurfowl only occurred at low densities on grazed habitats (including abandoned settlement sites). In their study in the Maasai Mara, Söderström and Reid (2010:187) also found that relative to control sites 1 km away, abandoned settlements typically support many more birds and species. Among the less common species (48 species in all), this figure is at times three times higher than at the control sites. As with studies of plant recolonization, they also noted some spatial variation in microhabitat preference among different bird species. For instance, Ring-Necked Dove and Grassland Pipit tend to be most abundant directly in the area of the abandoned settlement, whereas Crowned Lapwing and Red-Capped Lark "reached their highest abundances at 0.5 km distance from settlements" (Söderström and Reid 2010:187). This latter observation points to another significant feature of glades formed over abandoned pastoral settlements, namely their "edge effects," or the manner in which the existence of an ecological boundary between the open glades and the surrounding woody bushland shape local ecosystem function and structure. While these remain understudied, recent studies on the Laikipia Plateau demonstrate that the positive ecological feedbacks of abandoned pastoralists settlements extend beyond the actual boundary of the glades for up to 50 meters, resulting in a variety of responses including more large trees (taller than 4 meters), greater understory plant cover (albeit with reduced diversity), different soil properties, and greater usage of these areas by large herbivores (Donihue et al. 2013:4 and references therein). When taken together, it is evident that these diverse ecological relationships imply that East Africa's pastoralist landscapes, although often envisaged as wild spaces that have accommodated a human presence but only tenuously so, are in fact highly "domesticated" spaces in which the complex entanglements between dung, humans, and a wide range of nonhuman "things" have a critical role to play.

Entangled Nature

Like other human-thing entanglements, such as those that emerged during the occupation of the Neolithic settlement of Çatalhöyük (Hodder 2012), the relationship between East Africa's pastoralists and animal dung can have negative as well as positive consequences. Cattle, as the primary producers of the dung in their settlements (producing easily 30 times more dung than either sheep or goat per individual animal),[5] are an important measure of wealth and source of symbolic capital in most of these societies,[6] and probably have been socially valued since herders first entered the region around 4,500 years BP. Archaeological evidence from further north, where pastoral cultures and economies first emerged on the continent (Marshall et al. 2011), certainly lend support to such a suggestion. In these areas, examples of such symbolic elaboration include formal burials of articulated and disarticulated cattle under stone-covered tumuli, dated to around 6,900 years BP at Nabta Playa in the Eastern Sahara (Wendorf et al. 1997); the inclusion of cattle bucrania (frontal cranial bones) in the Ancient Kerma necropolis (ca. 4,500–4,050 years BP) in Sudanese Nubia (Chaix and Grant 1992); rock art in Somalia depicting elaborate scenes of cattle herding (Brandt and Carder 1987); and, in rather cruder form, its depiction as graffiti on C-group pottery from Faras in Nubia (where cattle skulls have also been recovered from burials; Adams 1977). DiLernia (2006) suggests that cumulatively, this evidence may even point to the origins of a "cattle cult" and the elevated social value of cattle among contemporary African pastoralists across northern, western, and northeastern Africa.

There is far less archaeological evidence for such overt material elaboration of the social importance of livestock in East Africa, with the exception of the Jarigole Pillar site in northern Kenya, where at least 12 cattle clay figurines and one possible clay model of a sheep have been recovered from an ossuary complex in which bundles of human remains, broken Pastoral Neolithic ceramics, beads and animal remains were interred (Nelson 1995). Another possible exception might be some of the simpler geometric painted and engraved rock art motifs found in parts of northern and central Kenya, given their apparent resemblance to the designs used more recently to brand cattle and camels (Gramly 1975; Lynch and Robbins 1977; for a critique, see Russell 2013). Nonetheless, both historically and ethnographically it is well documented that the more cattle a household owns, the more extensive are their exchange networks (e.g., Bollig 1998; de Vries et al. 2006), which in turn helps to spread and limit the economic risks posed by drought, disease, and warfare.[7] The size of the dung heap is thus often regarded as a sign of household wealth, as documented among the Borana in southern Ethiopia and northern Kenya, for example (Tache and Sjaastad 2010). However, larger herd sizes also means potentially greater rates of dung accumulation, larger settlements to accommodate the herds, and a larger residential kin group needed for their management. All such factors can deplete the supply of available grazing and fuel-wood that can be reached conveniently from the settlement at a faster rate than would be the case with smaller herd sizes, and so may in the longer term result in shorter periods of site occupancy as the available supplies of grazing and fuel-wood are depleted at a faster rate.

As long as sufficient rangeland exists elsewhere that can be used in the next cycle, the buildup of dung—and all that comes with it—does not pose a significant problem, and by stimulating periodic abandonment and settlement relocation, the dung heaps help initiate new cycles of recolonization by nonhuman things. However, although the presence of dense concentrations of dung in these landscapes may improve the overall quality of grazing and perhaps browsing and so favor an increase in wild herbivores, these eventually compete with domestic livestock for nutrients and may suppress livestock populations. Recent studies on Laikipia (Odadi et al. 2011) suggest the impacts on cattle are particularly acute during the dry season because of reduced forage, forcing cattle to expend more energy and forage less efficiently, resulting in reduced weight gain. Furthermore, where access to land becomes restricted, whether from expansion of neighboring communities, competition from other keystone species such as elephants, bush encroachment as a consequence of climate change, the spread of cattle diseases and their biological hosts such as the tsetse fly, or some combination of these, the ecological balance can become more precarious and may even reach a critical tipping point that initiates a complete or partial restructuring of human-thing relationships. An additional consequence of this can be more frequent reoccupation of abandoned pastoralist settlements,[8] which can interrupt or slow down the sequence of plant succession that would otherwise result in heightened biodiversity. There is also some evidence to suggest that where there is a relatively high concentration of glades created from abandoned settlements, the kind of ecologically beneficial edge effects noted above may also decline because of the increased proximity of their boundaries to one another (Porensky 2011).

Conclusion: Entangled Banks Revisited

The overarching conclusion I draw from the studies discussed here is that the ecological relationships initiated by the concentration of animal dung in distinct patches across East African savanna landscapes are as every bit entangled as those characterizing the hedgerows of the farmland around Down House in Kent that were a source of inspiration for Charles Darwin as he was completing *On the Origin of Species* (Keynes 2001). That these nutrient hotspots remain within East African landscapes minimally for 50 to 100 years and, in some cases much longer, as suggested by evidence from the Maasai Plains site on Mugie Ranch, Laikipia (Lane 2011), underscores arguments about the benefits to regional biodiversity that have arisen from the presence of pastoralists, as well as that understanding these entanglements requires an interrogation of evolving human-thing relationships over the long term. Similarly, like other ecological features of the English countryside, the hedgerows around Down House and their species composition also have their own entangled *human* histories, shaped most obviously by management practices but also a variety of locally, regionally, and nationally specific sociocultural and economic factors of the kind documented for nearby Otford from the medieval period onward (Hewlett 1973). Darwin was probably well aware of this. He certainly acknowledged, in an earlier passage in *On the Origin of Species*, that vegetation mosaics could be co-produced by humans and nature:

> When we look at the plants and bushes clothing an entangled bank, we are tempted to attribute their proportional numbers and kinds to what we call chance. But how false a view is this! Every one has heard that when an American forest is cut down, a very different vegetation springs up; but it has been observed that the trees now growing on the ancient Indian mounds, in the Southern United States, display the same beautiful diversity and proportion of kinds as in the surrounding virgin forests (Darwin 1859:74).

Surprisingly, even though Darwin noted some forests in the Americas give the illusion of being entirely pristine, when in fact more careful study often reveals them to contain abandoned human settlements, he did not draw a similar conclusion concerning the settlement remains of the Fuegians, although he recognized their close association with particular species:

> The Fuegians inhabit the same spot for many years; in one place I found 10 inches of fine vegetable mould over the layer of muscle [*sic*] & limpet shells, in consequence of this *these mounds may be told at a distance by the bright green of the vegetation*—amongst the concomitant plants are mostly the wild celery, scurvy grass, black-currant tree; these, although not used by the Fuegians, are the most useful plants in the country & seem placed to attract attention (Darwin 1839:133, entry for January and February 1833; my emphasis).

Whether such associations arise here as a result of human activity rather than in spite of a human presence, in a manner akin to that described in this chapter for East African savannas, is a matter for future research. Regardless of what such research might determine, as Darwin so presciently observed but has so often been overlooked since, humanity's entanglement with nature has always been a matter of co-production, rather than simply about either responding to more powerful forces or disturbing a pre-existing orderly universe. Understanding how these shared histories have both entrained and afforded possibilities and connections over the *longue durée* is a challenge that archaeology, by employing the precepts of historical ecology, is well placed to tackle. And, perhaps, if archaeology does indeed go in this direction, we may see the production of narratives that are far less anthropocentric than those that have characterized the discipline thus far.

Acknowledgments

Aspects of the archaeological research on Laikipia Plateau reported here, and the drafting and presentation of earlier iterations of this paper, were generously supported by the British Institute in Eastern Africa as part of its "Settlement and Land-Use Change in Semi-Arid Areas of Eastern and Southern Africa" project, generously funded by the British Academy, and the European Union under the auspices of the "Historical Ecologies of East African Landscapes" project at the University of York, through a Marie Curie Excellence grant (MEXT-CT-2004–517098) awarded to Paul Lane. Thanks are also due to the Ministry of Education, Kenya, and the National Museums of Kenya for permission to undertake this research. Earlier versions of this paper were presented under different guises as research seminars in the MacDonald Institute, University of Cambridge (2009); Department of Social Anthropology, University of Oslo (2011), at the 8th African Archaeology Research Day (Institute of Archaeology, University College London, 2011); and the 2nd International Landscape Archaeology Conference (Berlin, 2012). I would like to thank all the convenors of these meetings for their invitations and the participants for constructive comments. Particular thanks are also due to the editors of this volume for their own comments on an earlier draft (and their endless patience), and also David Western, Jeff Worden, Rob Marchant, Andrew Reid, Matthew Collins, Bilinda Straight, and anonymous external reviewers for sharing their own knowledge and insights. Thanks are also due to David Western and Jeff Worden for the opportunity to visit (and fly over) Amboseli with them in 2009. All remaining shortcomings and errors are my own responsibility.

Notes

1. These can be consulted online at Van Wyhe (2002).
2. The symbolic significance, if at all, of dung among East Africa's pastoralist communities remains an under-researched topic; in the light of Moore's (1986) findings concerning the gendered distinctions between goat dung and other forms of

household "refuse" made by the agro-pastoral Marakwet, the possibility that some of East Africa's pastoralists make comparable conceptual distinctions is certainly worth exploring.

3. The provision of a new house is an important part of marriage ceremonies in these societies, and among the Maasai, a newly married couple's house "is blessed during a communal firemaking ceremony . . . performed in the centre of the new homestead" (Ärhem 1991:62). In the Samburu case, elephant dung is burned on the internal fireplace and the smoke from this is thought to act as a good-luck blessing to the newlywed couple (Kuriyan 2004). More significantly, as Straight (1999:53) notes, the lighting "of the first house fire is a multivalent action [that propitiously inaugurates] the bride's nurturing and fecund role as caretaker who will ensure the health and vitality of her husband, livestock, and future children."
4. On the glades themselves, plant species diversity is lower than in the surrounding landscape precisely because of the specific histories of these spaces, but glades nonetheless often support more of the less common species.
5. A wide variety of factors can influence the quantities of manure cattle and small stock produce on a daily basis, especially the moisture content of their forage and overall dietary composition. Body mass is another critical variable, as are sex, breed, herd management regime, and stocking density. Direct comparison is thus difficult, and is compounded by the limited amount of relevant published data. Indicative figures are available, however, and for West African dwarf sheep (between approximately 0.38–0.44 kg per day for sheep with live body weights between 17.9–18.2 kg; Fasae et al. 2009) and commercially farmed cattle in Australia (which give ranges between 13.2 kg per day for a 220 kg animal to 36 kg for a 600 kg animal), among others. About half of this volume is likely to be voided while the animals are penned inside the settlement overnight (Burchard 1993:131).
6. In some, such as the Rendille, camels are more important.
7. While these stock associations are typically between men, women also develop exchange networks, often through the transfer of beads, other classes of artifacts (such as decorated calabashes), beer (and other alcohol), or milk products; these too can have similar benefits.
8. In the Amboseli Basin, for example, this resettlement, at least of prime sites, takes place roughly every 20 to 25 years (Western and Dunne 1979).

References

Adams, W. Y., 1977. *Nubia Corridor to Africa*. Allen Lane, London.

Andersen, K. B., 1977. *African Traditional Architecture: A Study of the Housing and Settlement Patterns of Rural Kenya*. Oxford University Press, London.

Archibald, S., 2008. African Grazing Lawns—How Fire, Rainfall, and Grazer Numbers Interact to Affect Grass Community Status. *Journal of Wildlife Management* 72(2):492–501.

Århem, K., 1991. The Symbolic World of the Maasai Homestead. In *Body and Space: Symbolic Models of Unity and Division in African Cosmology and Experience*, edited by A. Jacbson-Widding, pp. 51–79. Acta Universitatis Upsaliensis (Uppsala Studies in Cultural Anthropology 16), Uppsala, Sweden.

Arroyo-Kalin, M., 2010. The Amazonian Formative: Crop Domestication and Anthropogenic Soils. *Diversity* 2(4):473–504.

Augustine, D. J., 2003. Long-term, Livestock Mediated Redistribution of Nitrogen and Phosphorus in an East African Savanna. *Journal of Applied Ecology* 40(1):137–149.

Augustine, D. J., and S. J. McNaughton, 2004a. Regulation of Shrub Dynamics by Native Browsing Ungulates on East African Rangeland. *Journal of Applied Ecology* 41(1):45–58.

Augustine, D. J., and S. J. McNaughton, 2004b. Temporal Asynchrony in Soil Nutrient Dynamics and Plant Production in a Semiarid Ecosystem. *Ecosystems* 7(8):829–884.

Balée, W., 2010. Contingent Diversity on Anthropic Landscapes. *Diversity* 2(2):163–181.

Barker, J. R., T. L. Thurow, and D. J. Herlocker, 1990. Vegetation of Pastoralist Campsites Within the Coastal Grassland of Central Somalia. *African Journal of Ecology* 28(4):291–297.

Barrow, E. C. G., 1990. Usufruct Rights to Trees: The Role of *Ekwar* in Dryland Central Turkana, Kenya. *Human Ecology* 18(2):163–176.

Bhagwat, S. A., S. Nogué, and K. J. Willis, 2012. Resilience of an Ancient Tropical Forest Landscape to 7500 Years of Environmental Change. *Biological Conservation* 153:108–117.

Bird, D. W., R. B. Bird, and C. H. Parker, 2005. Aboriginal Burning Regimes and Hunting Strategies in Australia's Western Desert. *Human Ecology* 33(4):443–464.

Blackmore, A. C., M. T. Mentis, and R. J. Scholes, 1990. The Origin and Extent of Nutrient-enriched Patches Within a Nutrient-poor Savanna in South Africa. *Journal of Biogeography* 17:463–470.

Brandt, S. A., and N. Carder, 1987. Pastoral Rock Art in the Horn of Africa: Making Sense of Udder Chaos. *World Archaeology* 19(2):194–213.

Bollig, M., 1998. Moral Economy and Self-interest: Kinship, Friendship, and Exchange Among the Pokot (N.W. Kenya). In *Kinship, Networks, and Exchange*, edited by T. Schweizer and D. R. White, pp. 137–157. Cambridge University Press, Cambridge, UK.

Burchard, I., 1993. Pastoralists and African Ecology: Questions for Archaeologists on the Effects of Burning and Dung Deposition. *Azania* 28:130–133.

Causey, M., 2008. Delineating Pastoralist Behaviour and Long-Term Environmental Change: A GIS Landscape Approach on the Laikipia Plateau, Kenya. Unpublished Ph.D. dissertation, University of Oxford, Oxford, UK.

Cech, P. G., T. Kuster, P. J. Edwards, and H. O. Venterink, 2008. Effects of Herbivory, Fire and N_2-fixation on Nutrient Limitation in a Humid African Savannah. *Ecosystems* 11(6):991–1004.

Chaix, L., and A. Grant, 1992. Cattle in Ancient Nubia. *Anthropozoologica* 16:61–66.

Clement, C. R., and A. B. Junqueira, 2010. Between a Pristine Myth and an Impoverished Future. *Biotropica* 42(5):534–536.

Colombaroli, D., M. Beckmann, W. O. van der Knaap, P. Curdy, and W. Tinner, 2013. Changes in Biodiversity and Vegetation Composition in the Central Swiss Alps During the Transition from Pristine Forest to First Farming. *Diversity and Distributions* 19(2):157–170.

Darwin, C. R., 1839. *Narrative of the Surveying Voyages of His Majesty's Ships Adventure and Beagle Between the Years 1826 and 1836, Describing their Examination of the Southern Shores of South America, and the Beagle's Circumnavigation of the Globe. Journal and Remarks. 1832–1836*. Henry Colburn, London.

Darwin, C. R., 1859. *On the Origin of Species by Means of Natural Selection, or the Preservation of Favoured Races in the Struggle for Life*. John Murray, London.

Dearing, J., 2012. Approaches to Understanding Long-term Human-Environment Interactions: Past, Present and Future. In *The SAGE Handbook of Environmental Change: Volume 1: Approaches, Evidences and Causes*, edited by J. A. Matthews, P. J. Bartlein, K. R. Briffa, A. G. Dawson, A. De Vernal, T. Denham, S. C. Fritz, and F. Oldfield, pp. 134–162. SAGE Publications, London.

Denevan, W. M., 1992. The Pristine Myth—the Landscape of the Americas in 1492. *Annals of the Association of American Geographers* 82(3):369–385.

de Vries, D., P. Leslie, and J. McCabe, 2006. Livestock Acquisitions Dynamics in Nomadic Pastoralist Herd Demography: A Case Study Among Ngisonyoka Herders of South Turkana, Kenya. *Human Ecology* 34(1):1–25.

DiLernia, S., 2006. Building Monuments, Creating Identity: Cattle Cult as a Social Response to Rapid Environmental Changes in the Holocene Sahara. *Quaternary International* 151(1):50–62.

Donihue, C. M., L. M. Porensky, J. Foufopoulos, C. Riginos, and R. M. Pringle, 2013. Glade Cascades: Indirect Legacy Effects of Pastoralism Enhance the Abundance and Spatial Structuring of Arboreal Fauna. *Ecology* 94(4):827–837.

Ellis, E. C., and N. Ramankutty, 2008. Putting People in the Map: Anthropogenic Biomes of the World. *Frontiers in Ecology and the Environment* 6(8):439–447.

Evans, S., 2011. Icy Heritage—Managing Historic Sites in the Antarctic: Pristine Wilderness, Anthropogenic Degradation or Cultural Landscape? *The Polar Journal* 1(1):87–100.

Fairhead, J., and M. Leach, 1996. *Misreading the African Landscape: Society and Ecology in a Forest-savanna Mosaic*. Cambridge University Press, Cambridge, UK.

Fasae, O. A., O. S. Emiola, and I. F. Adu, 2009. Production of Manure from West African Dwarf Sheep. *Archivos de Zootecnia* 58(1):601–604.

Fontana, S. L., M. M. Bianchi, and K. D. Bennett, 2012. Palaeoenvironmental Changes since the Last Glacial Maximum: Patterns, Timing and Dynamics Throughout South America. *The Holocene* 22(11):1203–1206.

Fratkin, E., 1996. Traditional Medicine and Concepts of Healing among Samburu Pastoralists of Kenya. *Journal of Ethnobiology* 16:63–97.

Gamble, C., 1992. Uttermost Ends of the Earth. *Antiquity* 66(252):710–711.

Geloroni, V., and D. Vershuren, 2012. Historical Climate-human-ecosystem Interaction in East Africa: A Review. *African Journal of Ecology* 51(3):1–9.

Gifford, D. P., 1978. Ethnoarchaeological Observations of Natural Processes Affecting Cultural Materials. In *Explanation in Ethnoarchaeology*, edited by R. A. Gould, pp. 77–101. University of New Mexico Press, Albuquerque.

Gillson, L., 2004. Testing Non-Equilibrium Theories in Savannas: 1400 Years of Vegetation Change in Tsavo National Park, Kenya. *Ecological Complexity*, 1(4):281–298.

Glendening, J., 2007. *The Evolutionary Imagination in Late-Victorian Novels: An Entangled Bank*. Ashgate, Aldershot, UK.

Gramly, R. M., 1975. Meat-feasting Sites and Cattle-brands: Patterns of Rock-Shelter Utilization in East Africa. *Azania* 10(1):107–121.

Heckenberger, M. J., J. C. Russell, J. R. Toney, and M. J. Schmidt, 2007. The Legacy of Cultural Landscapes in the Brazilian Amazon: Implications for Biodiversity. *Philosophical Transactions of the Royal Society B–Biological Sciences* 362(1478):197–208.

Hewlett, G., 1973. Reconstructing a Historical Landscape from Field and Documentary Evidence: Otford in Kent. *Agricultural History Review* 21:94–110.

Hodder, I., 2011. Human-Thing Entanglement: Towards an Integrated Archaeological Perspective. *Journal of the Royal Anthropological Institute* 17(1):154–177.

Hodder, I., 2012. *Entangled: An Archaeology of the Relationships Between Humans and Things.* Wiley-Blackwell, Malden, MA.

Homewood, K., and W. Rodgers, 1991. *Maasailand Ecology: Pastoralist Development and Wildlife Conservation in Ngorongoro, Tanzania.* Cambridge University Press, Cambridge, UK.

Ibrahim, F., and B. Ibrahim, 1998. The Maasai Herbalists in Arusha Town, Tanzania. *GeoJournal* 46(2):141–154.

Keynes, R., 2001. *Annie's Box: Charles Darwin, his Daughter, and Human Evolution.* Fourth Estate, London.

Kiringe, J. W., 2006. A Survey of Traditional Health Remedies Used by the Maasai of Southern Kaijiado District, Kenya. *Ethnobotany Research & Applications* 4:61–73.

Kuriyan, R., 2004. *Linking Local Perceptions of Elephants and Conservation: Samburu Pastoralists in Northern Kenya.* Center for African Studies, University of California, Berkeley. Electronic document, www.escholarship.org/uc/item/1wf778kk, accessed December 2, 2013.

Lamprey, H. F., G. Halevy, and S. Makacha, 1974. Interactions Between Acacia Bruchid Seed Beetles and Large Herbivores. *East African Wildlife Journal* 12(1):81–85.

Lamprey, R. H., and R. S. Reid, 2004. Expansion of Human Settlement in Kenya's Maasai Mara: What Future for Pastoralism and Wildlife? *Journal of Biogeography* 31(6):997–1032.

Lane, P. J., 2011. An Outline of the Later Holocene Archaeology and Precolonial History of the Ewaso Basin, Kenya. *Smithsonian Contributions to Zoology* 632:11–30.

Lane, P. J., 2013. Trajectories of Pastoralism in Northern and Central Kenya: An Overview of the Archaeological and Environmental Evidence. In *Pastoralism in Africa: Past, Present and Future*, edited by M. Bollig and H. P. Wotzka, pp. 104–143. Berghahn Books, Oxford, UK.

Lloret, F., E. Calvo, X. Pons, and R. Díaz-Delgado, 2002. Wildfires and Landscape Patterns in the Eastern Iberian Peninsula. *Landscape Ecology* 17(8):745–759.

Lynch, B. M., and L. H. Robbins, 1977. Animal Brands and the Interpretation of Rock Art in East Africa. *Current Anthropology* 18(3):538–539.

Mapinduzi, A. L., G. Oba, R. B. Weadji, and J. E. Colman, 2003. Use of Indigenous Knowledge of the Maasai Pastoralists for Assessing Rangeland Biodiversity in Tanzania. *African Journal of Ecology* 41(4):329–336.

Marchant, R. A., and P. J. Lane, 2014. Past Perspectives for the Future: Foundations for Sustainable Development in East Africa. *Journal of Archaeological Science* 51:12–21.

Marshall, F., K. Grillo, and L. Arco, 2011. Prehistoric Pastoralists and Social Responses to Climatic Risk in East Africa. In *Sustainable Lifeways: Cultural Persistence in an Ever-changing Environment*, edited by N. F. Miller, K. M. Moore and K. Ryan, pp. 39–74. University of Pennsylvania Museum Publications, Philadelphia.

Mbae, N. B., 1990. The Ethnoarchaeology of Maasai Settlements and Refuse Disposal Patterns in the Lemek Area. In *Early Pastoralists of South-Western Kenya*, edited by P. T. Robertshaw, pp. 279–292. British Institute in Eastern Africa, Memoir 11, Nairobi, Kenya.

McWethy, D. B., P. E. Higuera, C. Whitlock, T. T. Veblen, D. M. J. S. Bowman, G. J. Cary, S. G. Haberle, R. E. Keane, B. D. Maxwell, M. S. McGlone, G. L. W. Perry, J. M. Wilmshurst, A. Holz, and A. J. Tepley, 2013. A Conceptual Framework for Predicting Temperate Ecosystem Sensitivity to Human Impacts on Fire Regimes. *Global Ecology and Biogeography* 22(8):900–912.

Mermoz, M., T. Kitzberger, and T. T., Veblen 2005. Landscape Influences on Occurrence and Spread of Wildfires in Patagonian Forests and Shrublands. *Ecology* 86(10):2705–2715.

Moore, H. L., 1986. *Space, Text and Gender: An Anthropological Study of the Marakwet of Kenya*. Cambridge University Press, Cambridge, UK.

Morris, D. L., D. Western, and D. Maitumo, 2009. Pastoralist's Livestock and Settlements Influence Game Bird Diversity and Abundance in a Savanna Ecosystem of Southern Kenya. *African Journal of Ecology* 47(1):48–55.

Muchiru, A. N., D. J. Western, and R. S. Reid, 2008. The Role of Abandoned Pastoral Settlements in the Dynamics of African Large Herbivore Communities. *Journal of Arid Environments* 72(6):940–952.

Muchiru, A. N., D. J. Western, and R. S. Reid, 2009. The Impact of Abandoned Pastoral Settlements on Plant and Nutrient Succession in an African Savannah Ecosystem. *Journal of Arid Environments* 73(3):322–331.

Nelson, C. M., 1995. The Work of the Koobi Fora Field School at the Jarigole Pillar Site. *Kenya Past and Present* 27:49–63.

Oba, G., E. Post, P. O. Syvertsen, and N. C. Stenseth, 2000. Bush Cover and Range Condition Assessments in Relation to Landscape and Grazing in Southern Ethiopia. *Landscape Ecology* 15(6):535–546.

Odadi, W. O., A. S. Abdulrazak, M. M. Karachi, and T. P. Young, 2011. African Wild Ungulates Compete with or Facilitate Cattle Depending on Season. *Science* 333(6050):1755–1757.

Porensky, L. M., 2011. When Edges Meet: Interacting Edge Effects in an African Savannah. *Journal of Ecology* 99(4):923–934.

Reid, R. S., and J. E. Ellis, 1995. Impacts of Pastoralists on Woodlands in South Turkana, Kenya: Livestock-mediated Tree Recruitment. *Ecological Applications* 5:978–992.

Rick, T. C., and R. Lockwood, 2013. Integrating Paleobiology, Archeology, and History to Inform Biological Conservation. *Conservation Biology* 27(1):45–54.

Roba, H. G., and G. Oba, 2009. Community Participatory Landscape Classification and Biodiversity Assessment and Monitoring of Grazing Lands in Northern Kenya. *Journal of Environmental Management* 90(2):673–682.

Roberts, N., W. J. Eastwood, C. Kuzucuoglu, G. Fiorento, and V. Caracuta, 2011. Climatic, Vegetation and Cultural Change in the Eastern Mediterranean During the Mid-Holocene Environmental Transition. *The Holocene* 21(1):147–162.

Russell, T., 2013. Through the Skin: Exploring Pastoralist Marks and their Meanings to Understand Parts of East African Rock Art. *Journal of Social Archaeology* 13(1):3–30.

Sandweiss, D. H., and A. R. Kelley, 2012. Archaeological Contributions to Climate Change Research: The Archaeological Record as a Paleoclimatic and Paleoenvironmental Archive. *Annual Review of Anthropology* 41(1):371–391.

Shahack-Gross, R., 2011. Herbivorous Livestock Dung: Formation, Taphonomy, Methods for Identification, and Archaeological Significance. *Journal of Archaeological Science* 38(2):205–218.

Sirami, C., A. Nespoulous, J. P. Cheylan, P. Marty, G. T. Hvenegaard, P. Geniez, B. Schatz, and J. L. Martin, 2010. Long-term Anthropogenic and Ecological Dynamics of a Mediterranean Landscape: Impacts on Multiple Taxa. *Landscape and Urban Planning* 96(4):214–223.

Söderström, B., and R. S. Reid, 2010. Abandoned Pastoral Settlements Provide Concentrations of Resources for Savannah Birds. *Acta Oecologica* 36(2):184–196.

Spencer, P., 1973. *Nomads in Alliance: Symbiosis and Growth among the Rendille and Samburu of Kenya*. Oxford University Press, London.

Stelfox, J. B., 1986. Effects of Livestock Enclosures (Bomas) on the Vegetation of the Athi Plains, Kenya. *African Journal of Ecology* 24(1):41–45.

Storch, D., and K. J. Gaston, 2004. Untangling Ecological Complexity on Different Scales of Space and Time. *Basic and Applied Ecology* 5(5):389–400.

Straight, B., 1999. House, Fire, Gender. *Material Religion* 3(1):48–61.

Tache, B., and E. Sjaastad, 2010. Pastoralists' Conceptions of Poverty: An Analysis of Traditional and Conventional Indicators from Borana, Ethiopia. *World Development* 38(8):1168–1178.

Terrell, J. E., and J. O. Hart, 2008. Domesticated Landscapes. In *Handbook of Landscape Archaeology*, edited by B. David and J. Thomas, pp. 328–332. Left Coast Press, Inc., Walnut Creek, CA.

Umesao, T., 1969. The Meaning and Structure of the Dwellings of the Datoga. *Kyoto University African Studies* 3:55–76.

Van Wyhe, J., ed., 2002. *The Complete Work of Charles Darwin Online*. Electronic document, http://darwin-online.org.uk/EditorialIntroductions/Freeman_JournalofResearches.html, accessed 12/1/2013.

Veblen, K. E., 2008. Season- and Herbivore-dependent Competition and Facilitation in a Semiarid Savanna. *Ecology* 89(6):1532–1540.

Veblen, K. E., 2012. Savanna Glade Hotspots: Plant Community Development and Synergy with Large Herbivores. *Journal of Arid Environments* 78:119–127.

Weissbrod, L., 2010. Biological Indicators of Occupation Intensity: An Environmental Ethnoarchaeology of Maasai Settlements. In *The Archaeology of Anthropogenic Environments*, edited by R. M. Dean, pp. 295–320. Southern Illinois University Press, Carbondale, IL.

Wendorf, F., R. Schild, A. Applegate, and A. Gautier, 1997. Tumuli, Cattle Burials and Society in the Eastern Sahara. In *Dynamics of Populations, Movements and Responses to Climatic Change in Africa*, edited by B. E. Barich and M. C. Gatto, pp. 90–104. Bonsignori, Rome, Italy.

Western, D., and T. Dunne, 1979. Environmental Aspects of Settlement Site Decisions among Pastoral Maasai. *Human Ecology* 7(1):75–98.

Wiegand, K., D. Ward, and D. Saltz, 2005. Multi-scale Patterns and Bush Encroachment in an Arid Savanna with a Shallow Soil Layer. *Journal of Vegetation Science* 16(3):311–320.

Young, T. P., N. Partridge, and A. Macrae, 1995. Long-term Glades in Acacia Bushland and their Edge Effects in Laikipia, Kenya. *Ecological Applications* 5(1):97–108.

Williams, R., 1970. *The English Novel from Dickens to Lawrence*. Oxford University Press, London.

Willis, K. J., L. Gillson, and T. M. Brncic, 2004. How "Virgin" is Virgin Rainforest? *Science* 304(5669):402–403.

Willis, K. J., and G. M. MacDonald, 2011. Long-term Ecological Records and Their Relevance to Climate Change Predictions for a Warmer World. *Annual Review of Ecology, Evolution, and Systematics* 42:267–287.

Chapter 6

Entanglements and Entrapment on the Pathway toward Domestication

Dorian Q. Fuller, Chris Stevens, Leilani Lucas, Charlene Murphy, and Ling Qin

Introduction

The domestication of wild species that sustained hunter-gatherers, as happened with cereals, is a prime example of cultural and ecological entanglement. As humans relied more on a narrower range of species for calories, the changes associated with their processing required them to engage in different behavioral patterns. In turn, the species themselves evolved characteristics that is, domestication traits, which further transformed human behavior. Eventually these changes made plants reliant on human management and propagation for reproduction, and likewise humans became more dependent on plants to maintain subsistence and cultural trajectories.

The notion of domestication pathways as entanglement has recently gained ground as the complex mesh of interrelationships involved has become increasingly evident (e.g., Barton and Denham 2011; Fuller et al. 2010, 2012; Hodder 2012). In this chapter we explore different domestication pathways for four main regions, placing instances of crop domestication within their ecological and cultural contexts: (1) sedentary cereal cultivators of the Levant, (2) wetland rice cultivators of the Yangtze Basin, (3) millet cultivators of the northeast Asian steppe, and (4) millet-pulse cultivation and pastoralism in the southern India savannah.

These contrasting case studies provide a means by which each entanglement, comprising varying ecologies, aspects of plant physiology, and cultural traditions resulted in differing domestication pathways. While there are many commonalities to domestication in how plants adapted to cultural landscapes, these cases reveal important differences between the four regions that are a product of variations in lifestyles and their distinct cultural histories.

Archaeology of Entanglement edited by Lindsay Der and Francesca Fernandini, 151–172

Within the last decade, evidence for morphological changes of domestication supports a protracted process (Fuller et al. 2012, 2014; Tanno and Willcox 2012), particularly in the case of the Neolithic Near East, the most widely studied region for agricultural origins. In addition, there is growing recognition that the anthropogenic ecology of early agriculture created new plant communities, or weed floras (Willcox 2012). These lines of complementary evidence allow us to deduce early cultivation behaviors and the resulting changes from those behaviors, thus unravelling the complex feedback between human action and evolutionary change in crops and associated arable weeds (Fuller et al. 2010).

The expansion of archaeobotanical research in other regions, such as China, India, and sub-Saharan Africa, allows the study of parallel pathways to domestication (Fuller and Allaby 2009; Manning et al. 2011). This forces some reconsideration of the universality of Neolithic Near Eastern processes, which is often taken to represent the origins of agriculture on a global level. Evidence from these additional three regions provides informative contrasts between each other and the Near East. In this chapter, we sketch these alternative agricultural pathways and consider how the entanglements of plant species characteristics and pre-existing hunter-gatherer lifeways conditioned different pathways of subsistence change that ultimately converged on what we recognize as agriculture.

At a global level, the long-term impacts of agriculture have been sedentism, population increase, increased reliance on a more limited range of domesticated foodstuffs, and a diversification of material technologies, including ceramics, which in all but one region, the Neolithic Near East, preceded domestication. Despite many aspects of convergence in the broadest sense by which various regions domesticated plants, the timing of the domestication of animals, ceramics, and villages, and the sequence and timing by which this "Neolithization" occurred appears to have varied greatly (Figure 6.1).

As a basis for comparison, we outline our current understanding of five key aspects of the domestication entanglement using the presumed prototype, the Neolithic Near East, for comparison. First, we consider the environmental context of the wild progenitors of the following crops: wheat and barley in the Fertile Crescent; East Asian rice and millets; and the pulses and millet of southern India. We discuss how these species would have been incorporated into foraging practices in terms of spatial and seasonal availability, and how cultivation may have created new opportunities and costs in terms of other resources. Second, we consider the creation of fields, including clearance activities. Third, we consider the gathering and processing of crops from harvesting through dehusking and winnowing to storage. Fourth, we consider how site occupation—seasonal versus sedentary—appears to relate to foraging and early cultivation, and how convergent trends toward full sedentism are linked with the transition to full domestication. Fifth, we consider traditions of food preparation and cooking and how the selections of crops, wild

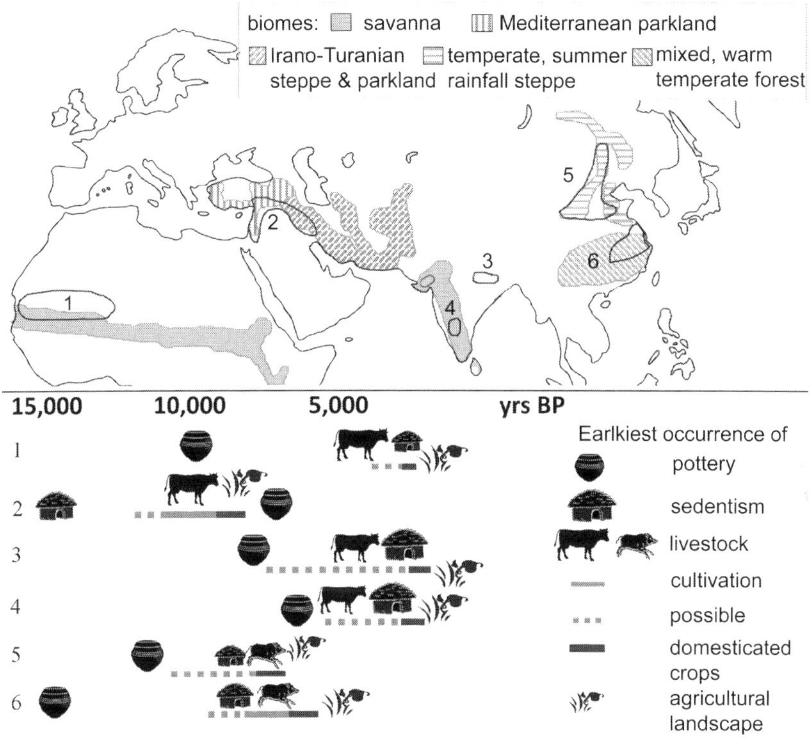

Figure 6.1 Map and schematic timelines for the emergence of Neolithic agricultural elements in selected Old World regions in relation to selected vegetational zones. For the cases of Gangetic India and western Africa, not discussed here, see Fuller (2011) and Manning et al. (2011).

foods, and development of technologies followed differing trajectories with or after the advent of cultivation. Under this heading we consider the practices of grinding, oven baking, and the use of ceramics. Ultimately, by the end of the Neolithic, ceramic technologies were used everywhere, but the nature of ceramic form and function and their centrality to food preparation systems differed markedly with geographic region and the crops processed and consumed (Fuller and Rowlands 2011).

Elements of Entanglement on the Pathway to Domestication for the Sedentary Cereal Cultivators of the Levant

Within the interrelationships that form the domestication entanglement, we can group the "things" that humans are dependent on (such as in Hodder 2012), and in turn are dependent on humans, under three categories: (1) plant physiology/morphology, (2) human behavior, and (3) resource environment.

The wild progenitors of the Neolithic Near Eastern crops are generally well known and well understood compared with those of other regions (Zohary et al. 2012). These wild cereals—wheats and barley—were generally distributed over the drier oak parkland steppe, lying between the Mediterranean woodland zone and the open-grassland steppe. The wild progenitors of the legumes, lentil, pea, chickpea, and vetches were also distributed within this general area in woodland clearings and margins.

Within plant physiology we find a number of factors possibly affected by human interaction, via conscious or unconscious selection (see Fuller and Allaby 2009; Harlan et al. 1973; Zohary 1969). Particularly significant are changes to plant reproduction cycles and therefore the survival of future generations (Figure 6.2). These include loss of dispersal mechanisms, such as awns (Elbaum et al. 2007; Fuller and Allaby 2009); changes in growth habit, such as the degree of side-branching (see Doust 2007); and the size (Fuller et al. 2013) and number of the seeds (Zohary et al. 2012). Of greater significance are changes resulting in the loss of dormancy in seeds (Fuller and Allaby 2009), causing seeds to germinate straight after seed-setting rather than forming a persistent seed bank; the loss of shattering, in which seeds remain on the plant in the ear rather than falling to the ground (Fuller and Allaby 2009;

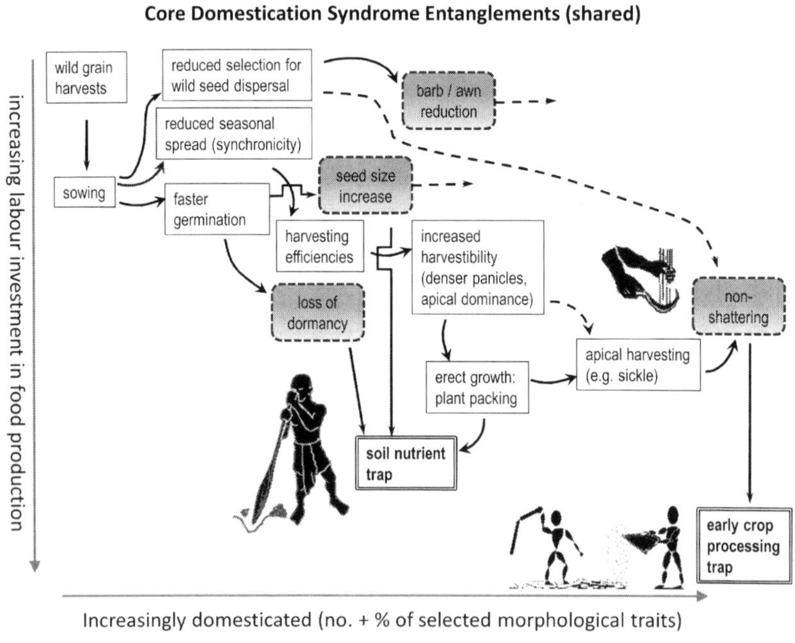

Figure 6.2 Core domestication syndrome entanglements (shared across regions and cereal taxa).

Fuller et al. 2014); and finally the synchronous ripening of grains upon the ear (Fuller 2007). Moreover, research has shown that many of these changes may be genetically tied; for example, seed dormancy, shattering, and color are all interrelated in rice (Gu et al. 2005). Therefore, conscious or unconscious selection by humans for one trait may inadvertently bring about changes within other traits, although such genetic linkage is still under-researched across most crops.

As an archaeologically detectable trait, the increase in seed size as a result of human-plant interaction provides a good scenario for the exploration of entanglements. This is documented across a wide number of species, including cereals, pulses, and oilseeds (Fuller et al. 2014). The act of bringing wild-type plants into the cultivated environment, in which soil is cleared and loosened for sowing, leads to an unintended evolutionary trend for greater seed size (see Fuller et al. 2010; Harlan et al. 1973). There is experimental evidence for some species that greater depth of seed burial may select for this change (Kluyver et al. 2013), although other aspects of the new soil conditions of cultivation were also probably important. On the most basic level larger seeds provide more energy reserves and hence provide a competitive advantage to larger-seeded plants in terms of establishing themselves in the field (Moles et al. 2007). As with all traits, there appears to be an optimum size over which this competitive advantage is lost. As such, investigations into changes in seed size for domesticates show a leveling off over time, more or less concomitant with full domestication (Fuller et al. 2014).

As these changes were brought about by human behaviors, over time, these changes came to modify human behavior on the pathway from collection, to cultivation, to domestication. First, the increase of grain size brought about gains in yield per harvest, making these increases better than those in wild stands of the same of species. Other human adjustments include those affecting material culture and technology, such as the development of tools, ceramics, and structures to modify the growing environment; for harvesting, storage, and processing; and finally to grind, cook, and consume the grain. In the Neolithic Near East, grinding tools have a long history; the earliest evidence dates to the later Palaeolithic, but there is a marked increase in the number of quernstones for flour preparation correlated with the Pre-Pottery Neolithic A (PPNA) and the first clear evidence for plant cultivation (Fuller and Rowlands 2011; Wright 1994). Sickles that enhanced harvesting predate this period, although some question whether these were developed specifically for wild cereals (Fuller 2007; Sherratt 1997:274), rather than, for example, basketry, it is nevertheless clear that these eventually were used for cereal harvests in later occupations.

These actions then modified the scheduling of labor, which in turn transformed social relationships embedded within the production and consumption of the Levantine cereals. A major example is that the processing sequence inevitably underwent changes with the evolution of nonshattering cereal forms. This fundamental transformation created labor demands for threshing activities to break apart the ear (Figure 6.2). However, nonshattering forms would have assured greater yields per harvest (Fuller et al. 2010; Hodder 2012:76), shifting the collection of cereals to later in the year and allowing the synchronized harvest of fully ripened stands.

We also must consider the soil environment, which is modified through clearance, effectively removing other plants competing with the cereals, and through tillage, in which the soil is aerated and prepared (see Fuller 2007). In turn, the act of removing vegetation can result in the depletion of soil nutrients, leading to further modification of human behavior with the need to manure. Recent inferences about early Neolithic Near Eastern agriculture and its Neolithic European derivatives suggest smaller-scale cultivation with intensive maintenance of soil fertility (Bogaard et al. 2013). This indicates further labor traps of the increasingly productive cultivation. These labor traps, as well as increased yields to store, contribute to reduced mobility, in which humans become tied to fields, threshing floors, cereal stores, and the house.

Thus, the aspects of human behavior that determine the shift from gathering of wild cereals to planting and harvesting became increasingly limited in space and in time. Hunter-gatherers might move through the landscape over a protracted time period, harvesting from wild stands as they ripen (Zohary 1969:57), in a time-effective system. By contrast, the domestication entanglement traps humans into harvesting cereals from a single set of fields (space-limited) in a limited time period. In addition, the limited space means that harvesting likely moved toward increasing efficacy of return from each unit of land through either multiple harvests or new techniques, such as sickles (Fuller 2007). Thus, the space-limited and time-constrained nature of cultivation forced a growing importance on permanent storage.

Plants compete with each other on many levels. In particular, given that many wild progenitors of crop species do not ripen synchronously and have seed dormancy, we can deduce that natural selection pressures favor plants that spread their seed over protracted time periods. The act of repeated annual clearance, followed by the sowing of seed, creates a level playing field in which there is a clear competitive advantage to those plants able to get their seeds into the next seedcorn to be sown. Thus, cultivation populations favor seeds without dormancy mechanisms that are capable of germinating immediately, as well as larger seeds producing larger, faster growing seedlings. These seedlings more effectively compete with each other, and other species, for space and sunlight or in emerging from soil depths (compare with Harlan et al. 1973). Re-sowing also favors seeds ripening when most other plants are ripening so they can be concentrated in the same harvest.

Changes in processing may also be seen in terms of space-limited returns. The grinding of grain favors increased edible calories from the same amount of grain, and hence the amount of harvested land or the same amount of time cultivating. This efficiency in returns from land, however, does come with the cost of food preparation, but likely was reinforced by a desire for more food, not just to feed more people, but to support more seasonal, social gathering and feasting among the seasonally and spatially concentrated cultivation populations (Asouti and Fuller 2013). Growing taste for the kinds of food produced, such as breads, also reinforced the agricultural and processing labor.

Plant Domestication by Wetland Collectors: The Case of East and South Asian Rice

The wild progenitor (*Oryza rufipogon*) of East Asian rice is a wetland perennial, which makes it distinct from the annual species of other regions. The perennial ancestor of early East Asian rice (*O. sativa* subsp. *japonica*) differed from the annual ancestor (*O. nivara*) of the early cultivars of India (*O. sativa* subsp. *indica*; see Fuller and Qin 2009; Fuller et al. 2010). The archaeological consensus is that in the Yangtze basin, broadly speaking the Middle or Lower Yangtze, possibly including northern tributaries, the ancestors of *japonica* rice were domesticated in the early to middle Holocene (Cohen 2011; Fuller et al. 2010; Qin 2012).

Ethnographic work in North America indicates how wild rice may have been used as a stable component of hunter and gathering economies in general. The staple of the Ojibwa people was American wild annual rice (*Zizania aquatica*), similar ecologically and a taxonomic cousin of East Asian rice, although as an annual it was more uniformly a high grain producer. Of particular relevance is the recording of the binding of individual rice panicles (the inflorescence, or ear) to prevent grain loss (Danziger 1979; Doolittle 2000). The slow ripening of the panicle provided the potential for two to three harvests a year (compare with Vennum 1988), and the Ojibwa harvested the rice by knocking the heads (Danziger 1979), presumably to prevent damage to the plant before the next harvest. Similar binding practices have also been reported from tribes in eastern India who gather wild rice (*O. rufiopogon/nivara*) as a supplement to their agricultural diets (e.g., Vaughan et al. 2008).

One of the many early genetic mutations in rice that differentiates domesticated *O. sativa* from its wild progenitors is the transition to a more tightly growing panicle (Ishii et al. 2013). In early wild-type populations, this tighter form led to spikelets that became entangled in the panicle and its branches when they separated from the rachis, making the harvest of wild grains more efficient, perhaps yielding 50% more grains per effort (Ishii et al. 2013). In essence, this mutation would have reduced the need for practices such as binding.

A key implication of poor grain production in wild perennial rice species is that drought stress increases seed productivity as the plants respond to possible demise (Fuller and Qin 2009). At first, cultivating populations may have simply cleared the shallow and seasonally dry margins of natural wetlands and sowed early wild rice crops there. However, later it may have become necessary to extend these drying wetland margins artificially, perhaps leading to experiments that increased grain production by simulating drought stress. Excavation of some of the earliest preserved field systems, dating to approximately 4000 BC (Late Majiabang period), supports these theories and clearly shows that they were well suited for control of water flow. Such systems comprise small dugout fields, just a few meters across, connected by channels and linked to deeper pits for water drainage (Fuller and Qin 2009). These small field systems were ideal for closely managing water, and potentially could be drained prior to flowering to bring out the drought response for higher grain production. The natural growth habit of wild rice is loose and spreading, and has the advantage under wild conditions of colonizing more soil space, resulting in greater access to soil nutrients and soil water. However, such growth habits are ill suited to these small field units for effective growing conditions or, indeed, production. Thus, the evolution of dense, erect-growth habit was likely selected in earlier cultivation (before 4000 BC) to make these small fields effective.

Higher grain production would have depleted the soil of nutrients; however, these small field units would have been relatively manageable in terms of artificial input of fertilizing material. In the absence of herds of dung-producing ungulates, archaeological evidence points to the usage of settlement midden material within manuring practices. Such behavioral practices can account for the quantities of typical midden components comprising charred plant remains and ceramic sherds recovered from these early paddy soils. The need to add nutrients to the soil can be called the "soil nutrient trap" (Fuller et al. 2010:19), as increased plant productivity entrapped people into adding nutrients into the soil.

The result of this entanglement of interrelationships between humans, rice, and fields made rice more productive, but reduced the time available for the gathering of wild plant foods such as water chestnuts (*Trapa* spp.) and foxnuts (*Euryale ferox*) (Fuller and Qin 2010). These nuts are available generally from late summer to autumn, when demand for labor for managing both crop and fields would be at its greatest. Further, managing the local landscape to grow rice pushed the deeper habitats of the aquatic nuts further away and potentially reduced the area of their availability.

The archaeological evidence bears testament to how this domestication entanglement played out, and we see how an increasingly complex relationship with just a single crop led to a decline in the archaeobotanical record for wild foods, in particular acorns and water chestnuts (Fuller and Qin 2010). Sickles, or harvesting knives for harvesting whole panicles, arrive within the Lower Yangtze relatively late, after domestication, perhaps around 3300 BC (Fuller et al. 2008). In contrast, sickles are present in the Neolithic Near East before domestication. Thus, we speculate that rice was harvested during the domestication process probably through uprooting, with denser closed panicles leading to less seed loss within shattering wild-type plants, but over time favoring nonshattering forms. The emergence of nonshattering spikelets in larger proportions would have, in turn, entrapped people into threshing and into adjusting harvest practices. Thus, physiological changes within the plant itself entrapped humans into performing additional labor (Figure 6.2) and developing subsequent technological innovations. The coincidence of the rice harvest season with that of wild forest resources means that further investment in rice, which had its own rewards of higher yields, pushed people to abandon many of their wild staples, such as acorns and *Trapa* (Fuller and Qin 2010). The particular problem of perenniality, in which wild rice was a poor producer, meant that the necessary labor inputs during the domestication process represented a greater level of entrapment than was true of early annual cultivars, such as wheat, barley, or millets (Figure 6.3).

Plant Domestication by Mobile Hunters: Chinese Loess Millets

Northern China, particularly the Yellow River basin and hill ranges to its north, was an early center of agriculture founded on millets, which continued to serve the region as the main staple during the Early Bronze Age (Li 1970). The area was the location of the domestication of two millet species, foxtail millet (*Setaria italica*) and broomcorn millet (*Panicum milaceum*). The wild progenitor of foxtail millet is clear, with multiple origins suggested (Meiko et al. 2013), while for *Panicum miliaceum* the progenitor could be extinct, but perhaps is the weedy *Panicum miliaceum* subsp. *ruderale* (De Wet 2000; Hunt et al. 2011) Although foxtail millet is highly drought tolerant, its wild forms tend to favor a range of environments (Douglas et al. 1985). Use of the wild progenitor could have been extensive and nonintensive because the period for flowering, ripening, and shattering in a given stand could last for up to four months, during which time there would always be some spikelets ready to harvest (Lu 2002). Compared with most of the wild grasses of the eastern Eurasian steppe, *Panicum* is relatively large-grained, and thus more grain could be produced per unit of dehusking time than would have been true of many other grasses of the inner Mongolian and Loess plateau steppe (on the grassland composition of northern China, see Wang 1961), which may account for a preference for this grass among early foragers in northern China and other regions. Nevertheless, what were probably dispersed patches of these wild millets would have suited exploitation by mobile hunters, but with cultivation of new artificial patches and storage, these would have become suitable seasonal foods, or foods of need, for both humans and their hunting dogs (Bettinger et al. 2010). With growing sedentism, millets also became suitable feed for kept pigs, which would have reduced reliance on hunted deer for meat (see Figure 6.3).

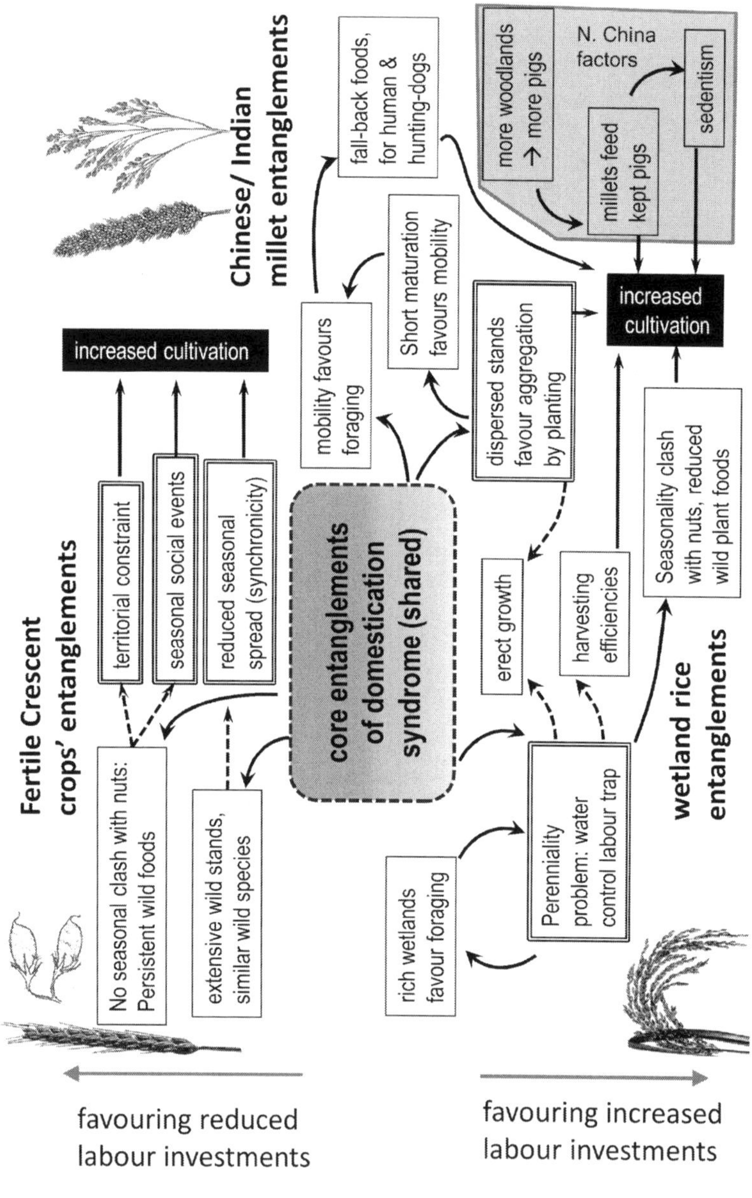

Figure 6.3 Expanded entanglegram with regionally specific factors

The earliest evidence for the possible cultivation of millets is provided from a dispersed set of most likely sedentary cultures, all dating to about 6000 BC and distributed along the southern and eastern margins of the loess plateau. Current research into the origins of millet agriculture focuses on these cultures (e.g., Bettinger et al. 2010; Qin 2012; Yang et al. 2012), while claims for earlier precursors (8000–10,000 BC), based on starch grains and phytoliths, should be treated with caution given the difficulty in determining the identification of their domesticated or cultivated status. Foxtail millet underwent similar changes during domestication to those already discussed for other cereals (Figure 6.2), bringing about major changes in plant architecture. While there is a change from shattering to nonshattering, archaeological evidence that might record this change has been elusive. Changes in shape and increased grain size have much higher potential to be tracked archaeologically, although such studies are still needed. However, identification issues may be compounded by the presence of immature grains (Song et al. 2013).

Present archaeological evidence suggests that harvesting knives, which appear in the Middle Neolithic around 6000 to 5000 calibrated (cal) BC in northern China (Fuller et al. 2008), did not precede cultivation. However, given the eventual emergence of nonshattering forms, it seems probable that harvesting by cutting the plant likely played a similar role to that hypothesized for wheat and barley. Likewise, we can speculate that this change reflected the requirement that foxtail millet be threshed.

For broomtail millet, the pattern is less clear. Ripening of the panicles of *Panicum miliaceum* is often uneven (Matz 1986), and as a consequence, some shattering of the already ripe grain on the panicle occurs if harvested fully ripe. A common solution is to cut the crop while it is still green, then allowing it to ripen/dry prior to threshing (compare with Lyon and Baltensperger 1995). Alternative strategies are harvesting by uprooting or by stripping the seed from the stalk using wooden combs (Bakels 2009:118). Ethnographic work on wild *Panicum* in Australia also records harvesting by stripping the grain, or uprooting the plant somewhat green (Nesbitt 2005).

As with many cereals, domestication resulted in the loss of seed dormancy. Dormancy within wild *Panicum* and *Setaria* species is broken by chilling followed by higher temperatures, for example 25° to 30°C (Baskin and Baskin 2001:378–379), and as with many seeds, there is also a light requirement. Given the colder winter conditions of northern China, such short-term dormancy would promote germination from May to June when temperatures were higher and rainfall at its peak, with plants overwintering during the cold and dry season as seed. Both wild and cultivated foxtail millet can reach maturity from germination in around four months in late summer/early autumn, although seed setting lasts somewhat longer.

Determining the moment when the loss of dormancy occurred during domestication provides interesting food for thought. Wild-type grains that require chilling could be sown (naturally or deliberately) in autumn/winter; however, loss of seed through natural predation meant that cultivators would need to sow larger quantities of grain. Moreover, such practices would not lead to the loss of the dormancy mechanisms seen in domesticated varieties; conversely, seeds lacking dormancy mechanisms are unlikely to have survived to produce viable offspring (compare with Colosi et al. 1988). Thus, the loss of dormancy during domestication could only occur if accompanied by the sowing of the grain from spring to summer. Thus, once dormancy was lost, humans were locked into this sowing regime.

A few scholars have proposed that underground pits, as evidenced at Cishan (8000–5500 BC), for example, were used for millet storage (Bettinger et al. 2010; Lu et al. 2009). Pit storage is often dependent on germination of grain around the edge of a sealed pit so that the remaining oxygen can seal it, preventing both insect pests and the growth of mold (see Reynolds 1974). As such, it is questionable whether people could have developed such grain storage practices until grains had lost their dormancy.

Plant Domestication via Shifting Cultivation: Re-examining the South Deccan, India

Peninsular India, known as the Deccan, has only recently been investigated as a possible center of agricultural origins (Fuller 2011). Recent archaeobotanical analysis reveals that the staple crops of the Neolithic in this region were native domesticates, including horsegram (*Macrotyloma uniflorum*), mungbean (*Vigna radiata*), and browntop millet (*Brachiaria ramosa*). Admittedly, the Neolithic period here is late (from ca. 3000 BC), and introduced pastoral herds, of cattle, sheep, and goats dominated the faunal resources. Thus, an earlier dispersal of mobile pastoral-collectors may precede the development of agricultural economies with plant cultivation and later tendencies towards sedentism. Nevertheless, plant cultivation appears to have been independent in the sense that locally wild species were brought into cultivation and domesticated rather than first developing from introduced crops (Fuller 2011).

These wild progenitors span both the tropical wet to dry deciduous forests on the hills of the Deccan margins and the drier savannah woodland zones of the central peninsula (Fuller 2011:S248). This is like the more Mediterranean habitat of wild pulses in the Neolithic Near East and the drier steppic habitat of wild barley and wheat in its combination of plant cultivars from across adjacent habitats that must have been frequented by earlier mobile collectors. These native species did not form extensive stands as wild wheats, barley, or wild rice did, but rather were likely found in local dense patches in favorable microenvironments. This suited exploitation by transhumant groups, much as was the case for wild Chinese millets. Then again, increased availability would have been possible by aggregating stands, setting in motion the selection of core domestication entanglements (Figures 6.2, 6.3).

The mid-Holocene pastoralists of this region, like the Mesolithic hunter-gatherers that already lived here, must have had a seasonally transhumant pattern tied to the flow and ebb of summer monsoon rains. Dry seasons, primarily from March to May, would have forced herd-following hunters or herders to concentrate on the few perennial water resources; some of these sites became major foci of pastoralist events marked on the landscape by large dung-burning events that left their mark as the ashmounds of south India (Boivin 2004; Fuller et al. 2001; Johansen 2004). The rainy summers encouraged band dispersal, and would have been the season suited to early cultivation, producing post-monsoon harvests focused on social gathering and growing fixed communities that eventually became sedentary. This could fit a "scheduled availability" model (Fuller 2011; Marshall and Hildebrand 2002) of valued foods within a round of annual mobility.

Despite the common sowing period for these native species, there was likely two harvest periods, one for the beans and an earlier one for millets. Millets were likely harvested somewhat green, and perhaps required multiple harvestings. Thus, taken together, the early crops required a protracted harvesting period of as much as two months, reducing the potential to exploit other plant resources and tying cultivators to these resources and sites near the planted stands. In these pulses, size increase was not part of the initial domestication syndrome; seed size increase likely was due to changes in agricultural techniques, such as deeper tillage using ards (Fuller 2007:903, 915–916; Fuller and Harvey 2006:257).

In terms of processing, a common approach to pulse preparation in southern India is to dry roast and then grind into flour, or to prepare flours that are then soaked and fermented. Such flours are mixed with cereal (millet, and in modern times more often rice) flours to prepare batters that become steamed, boiled, or fried for stiff porridge (*uppam*), flatbread (various *roti, papads*), pancakes (*dosa*), or dumplings (*idli, vadai*). Research suggests the high frequency of pulse recovery in southern India compared with that of the Indus region or Mediterranean indicates the likely importance of pulse dry roasting and flours in the prehistoric era (Fuller and Harvey 2006; Fuller and Rowlands 2011). Ceramics for the early Southern Neolithic include a range of bulbous pots that could be used for boiling and large open bowls that suggest communal consumption of served foods rather than individual servings (Boivin et al. 2005). Subsequent innovations included vessels with perforated bottoms, which could indicate that people were steaming food, a common traditional cooking technique for combined batters of pulse and cereal (millet or rice) flour, such as in the production of south Indian *idli* (Kimata and Sakamoto 1992). Thus, over the course of the Neolithic, as sedentism became established and some social differentiation developed, cooking and serving repertoires diversified, as did the range of crops. By contrast, at the start of the Neolithic, ceramic types point toward simple, single-pot meals and the need for a small number of serving dishes, making ceramic use more compatible with a seasonally transhumant lifestyle, or for pastoralist-gatherers turned seasonal cultivators.

Discussion: Fixed and Variable Path Dependencies in Plant Domestication

The transition to agriculture is arguably one of the most decisive periods of human cultural history, one in which the relationship between humans and their food sources undergo changes that echo through to the present, in which new entanglements took form and a series of dependencies between plants and humans began to take shape. Similarities in the basic physical and genetic structure of cereals have undoubtedly led to similarities in the way in which humans interacted with them. The affordances offered by cereal plants to human beings wishing to exploit them for food provide a limited number of interactions; the results of these interactions, such as the development of non-shattering cereal forms and the requirement for threshing, within all four geographical regions suggest that once humans embark upon this pathway, there inevitably comes a point of no return. Thus, the basic cereal domestication syndrome appears to represent a fairly rigid set of path dependencies and inevitable consequences (Figure 6.2), which probably accounts for the recurrence of domestication traits and similarities of evolutionary rates across centres of cereal domestication (Fuller et al. 2014). The requirement for increasing labor to tend soils, harvest, and for threshing locked people into subsistence patterns reliant on a narrow range of crops. This reliance has its own social entanglements, including the storage of surpluses and the consumption of crops, including for feasting.

On the other hand, connections between humans and things also differ in the various regional environments of early cultivation. Each of the geographical areas we explore in this chapter has its own unique climate and flora, which affords certain opportunities for the exploitation of wild plants. In the case of the Yangtze basin and the Neolithic Near East, extensive wild cereal stands and other reliable resources, such as nuts, allow for sedentism; however this cannot suggest a preference for collecting or cultivation without something to tip people toward the labor investment in cultivation. The social importance of cereals, either to support large seasonal gatherings, rituals (compare with Asouti and Fuller 2013), and perhaps competitive feasting (compare with Hayden 2009), or to support emerging craft specialists (Fuller and Qin 2010), could provide such a pull towards cultivation. The Neolithic Near East and China can be contrasted in terms of the potential conflicts between seasonal availability of wild nuts and wild cereals, which are directly in conflict for the harvest period in the Yangtze Valley. As a result, climate-driven declines in woodland acorn sources may have subtly pushed people toward an increased reliance on managing wetland margins and wild rice (Fuller and Qin 2010). Once people started down the path of cultivation, the ensuing unintentional development of the domestication syndrome would have made it harder and harder for people to withdraw from this entanglement. This pull would have been more difficult in the case of rice because of its wild perenniality problem (Figure 6.3).

In the cases of cultivation by mobile hunter-gatherers, the patchy availability of millets would have encouraged the creation of new patches so that they could be available when needed for seasoned social events or as fallback foods for people and their domestic fauna (e.g., dogs). In the case of northern China, environmental factors such as the Early Holocene expansion of woodlands could have pushed people toward increased pig hunting and pig-keeping, which favored sedentism and more reliable sources of millets as pig feed (Figure 6.3). By contrast, in India, the opening of more savannah (see Fuller 2011) with more limited dry-season watering holes might have encouraged the creation of pulse and millet gardens, and the territoriality of these wetter locales. This in turn became entangled with larger groups gathered for harvests, feasts, and investment in creating communities, if only seasonally at first.

In each of these cases, however, there were also unpredictable connections between humans and things, which must be considered in relation to the historical weight of pre-existing cultural traditions rather than determined by environmental context. This is particularly the case in how food plants were processed and transformed into cooked foods. As Fuller and Rowlands (2011) note, there has been a long-term distinction between an East Eurasian focus on boiling and steaming and a West Eurasian focus on production of flours and breads. There is nothing inherent in the cereal species or human digestive needs that predicts this division, and archaeological evidence suggests the origins of this processing division reach back in to the Pleistocene, long (approximately 10,000 years) before crops were chosen for cultivation. However, once cultivation began, these cooking traditions became entwined with and elaborated in relation to early crop plants. Thus, boiled/steamed food in pots provided a context in which a taste for sticky foods, like glutinous rice or millets, could evolve, requiring genetic crop mutation (Fuller and Rowlands 2011). In contrast, bread became a central symbol in metaphors of the Neolithic Near East and derived agricultural traditions. For example, to have a "bun in the oven" as a metaphor for pregnancy was afforded by traditions of grinding and baking. As a growing part of people's lives, both in terms of work and sustenance—the very substance that maintains bodies, families and communities, and food production, both agriculture and cooking—became embedded in ritual and symbolism.

We suggest regional entanglements were determined by pre-existing cultural history and contingent ideologies, and set in place path dependencies in terms of cultural traditions (Figure 6.4). In the case of western Asia, in which cooking traditions focused on heavy grinding stones and ovens, there was strong attachment to the house. Ethnographic accounts indicate that ground stones were rarely moved (Wright 1994), while ovens were fixed. Fuller and Rowlands (2011) argue that these forms of cooking lent themselves to traditions of sacrifice in which distant gods were appeased by rising smoke, and roasted meats and baked breads became foci of sharing within and between houses and across communities, with differential access indicative of social rank. Continuity was embodied in the houses themselves, which were given investment to create permanence and continuity. The continuities of houses at Çatalhöyük have been characterized as representing a "house society" (Hodder 2012:152), and in addition to being locales of crop storage, grinding, and cooking, the dead were also cached here; periodically parts of them, such as skulls, were retrieved for rituals beyond the house. The wider recurrence of skulls in ritual and cached in houses suggests an underlying metaphor of remembered traditions and cultural transmission in the Neolithic Near East (e.g., Kuijt 2008).

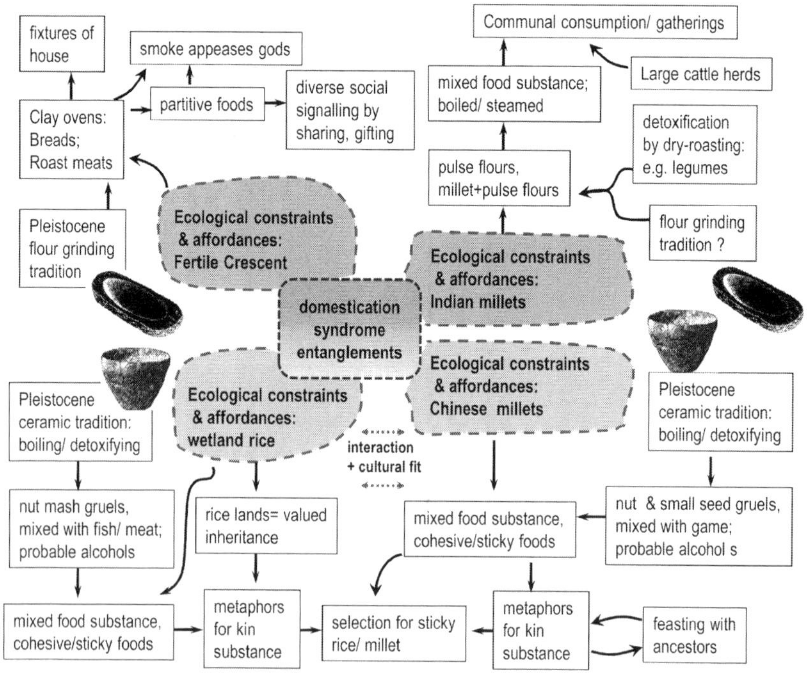

Figure 6.4 Food traditions entanglegram

In Neolithic China, both in rice and millet cultivation areas, the evidence of burial grounds suggests that the ancestors were more fixed. Graves are associated with ceramic vessel sets, which represented food and liquid (i.e., alcohol) offerings that were part of feasting meant to please ancestors and reinforce the continuities of lineages (e.g., Liu 2000; Nelson 2003). The longer-term tradition in China has been the veneration of ancestors, who are kept close to the family through food offerings, while the family shares foods to maintain the substance of kinship. This can be represented metaphorically in cooked foods that are steamed or boiled to be cohesive and sticky, and is therefore fitting that eastern Asia is where literally sticky varieties of rice, millets, and other cereals evolved through selected mutations in the waxy gene (Fuller and Rowlands 2011; Sakamoto 1996).

In southern India, we witness the pull of communal herd gathering and crop processing toward creating appropriate locales for sedentism. Grinding tools were often fixed as bedrock mortars (and querns), tying crop processing to granite outcrops and hills (Fuller et al. 2001). In the wider landscape, seasonal gatherings of cattle herds were memorialized through dung accumulations that were burned in the same spots and developed over a few generations into substantial ashmounds (Boivin 2004; Fuller et al. 2001; Johansen 2004). It is now clear that when more sedentary villages did develop they did so after these events, literally overlying earlier ashmounds (Boivin et al. 2005:70). We consider the memorialized seasonal cattle fairs as consecrating ground for settlement, and where this co-occurred with bedrock crop-processing features, fixed agricultural communities were created. Thus, rather than ancestors or houses linking to past tradition, the physical memorial of past human and cattle gatherings were the focus of communities, grain storage, and feasting events. The centrality of cattle and cattle products in symbolism has persisted since the Neolithic in this region.

These comparisons suggest both parallelism in the coevolution between crops and cultural practices and areas of divergent entanglements. Parallelisms are also found in the rigid path dependencies of the domestication syndrome (Figure 6.2), while regional and species-related ecologies added differing feedbacks and opportunities (Figure 6.3). The evolution of plant exploitation and cultivation was in turn enmeshed in longer-term regional traditions (Figure 6.4) that included cooking, acquired tastes, and the metaphorical connections of these wider-world and belief systems.

Acknowledgments

Our current research on comparative pathways to agriculture is supported by an European Research Council grant (ComPAg, no. 323842). Research on early rice cultivation by D.Q.F. and L.Q. was supported by a grant from UK National Environment Research Council (NE/G005540/1) and a Chinese Education Ministry Grant (to L.Q.).

References

Asouti, Eleni, and Dorian Q. Fuller, 2013. A Contextual Approach to the Emergence of Agriculture in Southwest Asia. *Current Anthropology* 54(3):299–345.

Bakels, Corrie, C., 2009. *The Western European Loess Belt: Agrarian History, 5300 BC–AD 1000.* Springer, Dordrecht, the Netherlands; Heidelberg, Germany; London; New York.

Baskin, Carol C., and Jerry M. Baskin, 2001. *Seeds: Ecology, Biogeography, and Evolution of Dormancy and Germination.* Academic Press, New York.

Barton, Huw, and Tim Denham, 2011. Vegeculture and Social Life in Island Southeast Asia. In *Why Cultivate? Anthropological and Archaeological Approaches to Foraging-Farming Transitions in Southeast Asia*, edited by Graham Barker and Monica Janowski, pp. 17–25. McDonald Institute for Archaeological Research: McDonald Institute Monographs, Cambridge, UK.

Bettinger, Robert L., Loukas Barton, and Christopher Morgan, 2010. The Origins of Food Production in North China: A Different Kind of Agricultural Revolution. *Evolutionary Anthropology* 19(1):9–21.

Bogaard, Amy, Rebecca Fraser, Tim H. E. Heaton, Michael Wallace, Petra Vaiglova, Michael Charles, Glynis Jones, Richard P. Evershed, Amy K. Styring, Niels H. Andersen, Rose-Marie Arbogast, Lászl6 Bartosiewicz, Armelle Gardeisen, Marie Kanstrup, Ursula Maier, Elena Marinova, Lazar Ninov, Marguerita Schäfer, and Elisabeth Stephan, 2013. Crop Manuring and Intensive Land Management by Europe's First Farmers. *Proceedings of the National Academy of Sciences* 110(31):12589–12594.

Boivin, Nicole, 2004. Landscape and Cosmology in the South Indian Neolithic: New Perspectives on the Deccan Ashmounds. *Cambridge Archaeological Journal* 14(2):235–257.

Boivin, Nicole, R. Korisettar, and Dorian Q. Fuller, 2005. Further Research on the Southern Neolithic and the Ashmound Tradition: The Sanganakallu-Kupgal Archaeological Research Project Interim Report. *Journal of Interdisciplinary Studies in History and Archaeology* 2(1):63–89.

Cohen, David Joel, 2011. The Beginnings of Agriculture in China: A Multiregional View. *Current Anthropology* 52(S4):S273–S293.

Colosi, Joseph C., Paul B. Cavers, and Marguerite A. Bough, 1988. Dormancy and Survival in Buried Seeds of Proso Millet (*Panicummiliaceum*). *Canadian Journal of Botany* 66(1):161–168.

Danziger, Edmund J., 1979. *The Chippewa of Lake Superior.* University of Oklahoma Press, Norman.

De Wet, J. M. J., 2000. Millets. In *The Cambridge World History of Food*, edited by Kenneth F. Kiple and Kriemhild Coneè Ornelas, pp. 112–121. Cambridge University Press, Cambridge, UK.

Doolittle, William, E., 2000. *Cultivated Landscapes of Native North America.* Oxford University Press, Oxford, UK.

Douglas, Brian J., Thomas A. Gordon, Ian N. Morrison, and Murray G. Maw, 1985. The Biology of Canadian Weeds. 70. *Setaria viridis* (L.) Beauv. *Canadian Journal of Plant Science* 65(3):669–690.

Doust, Andrew N., 2007. Architectural Evolution and its Implications for Domestication in Grasses. *Annals of Botany* 100(5):941–950.

Elbaum, Rivka, Liron Zaltzman, Ingo Burgert, and Peter Fratzl, 2007. The Role of Wheat Awns in the Seed Dispersal Unit. *Science* 316(5826):884–886.

Fuller, Dorian Q., 2007. Contrasting Patterns in Crop Domestication and Domestication Rates: Recent Archaeobotanical Insights from the Old World. *Annals of Botany* 100(5):903–924.

Fuller, Dorian Q., 2011. Finding Plant Domestication in the Indian Subcontinent. *Current Anthropology* 52(S4):S347–S362.

Fuller, Dorian Q., and Robin G. Allaby, 2009. Seed Dispersal and Crop Domestication: Shattering, Germination and Seasonality in Evolution Under Cultivation. In *Fruit Development and Seed Dispersal, Annual Plant Reviews Volume 38*, edited by Lars Ostergaard, pp. 238–295. Wiley-Blackwell, Oxford, UK.

Fuller, Dorian Q., Robin G. Allaby, and Chris Stevens, 2010. Domestication as Innovation: The Entanglement of Techniques, Technology and Chance in the Domestication of Cereal Crops. *World Archaeology* 42(1):13–28.

Fuller, Dorian Q., Eleni Asouti, and Michael D. Purugganan, 2012. Cultivation as Slow Evolutionary Entanglement: Comparative Data on Rate and Sequence of Domestication. *Vegetation History and Archaeobotany* 21(2):131–145.

Fuller, Dorian Q., Tim Denham, Manuel Arroyo-Kalin, Leilani Lucas, Chris Stevens, Ling Qin, Robin Allaby, and Michael D. Purugganan, 2014. Convergent Evolution and Parallelism in Plant Domestication Revealed by an Expanding Archaeological Record. *Proceedings of the National Academy of Sciences* 111(17):6147–6152.

Fuller, D. Q., and Emma L. Harvey, 2006. The Archaeobotany of Indian Pulses: Identification, Processing and Evidence for Cultivation. *Environmental Archaeology* 11(2):219–246.

Fuller, D., R. Korisettar, and P. C. Venkatasubbaiah, 2001. Southern Neolithic Cultivation Systems: A Reconsideration Based on Archaeobotanical Evidence. *South Asian Studies* 17:149–167.

Fuller, Dorian Q, Qin Ling, and Emma L. Harvey, 2008. Evidence for a Late Onset of Agriculture in the Lower Yangzi Region and Challenges for an Archaeobotany of Rice. In *Past Human Migrations in East Asia: Matching Archaeology, Linguistics and Genetics*, edited by Alicia Sanchez-Mazas, Roger Blench, Malcolm D. Ross, Ilia Peiros, and Marie Lin, pp. 40–83. Routledge, London.

Fuller, Dorian Q., and Ling Qin, 2009. Water Management and Labor in the Origins and Dispersal of Asian Rice. *World Archaeology* 41(1):88–111.

Fuller, Dorian Q., and Ling Qin, 2010. Declining Oaks, Increasing Artistry, and Cultivating Rice: The Environmental and Social Context of the Emergence of Farming in the Lower Yangtze Region. *Environmental Archaeology* 15(2):139–115.

Fuller, Dorian Q., and Michael Rowlands, 2011. Ingestion and Food Technologies: Maintaining Differences over the Long-term in West, South and East Asia. In *Interweaving Worlds Systematic Interactions in Eurasia, 7th to 1st Millennia BC: Essays from a Conference in Memory of Professor Andrew Sherratt*, edited by John Bennet, Susan Sherratt, and Toby C. Wilkinson, pp. 37–60. Oxbow Books Ltd, Oxford, UK.

Gu, Xing-You, Shahryar F. Kianian, Gary A. Hareland, Hoffer, Barry L., and Michael E. Foley, 2005. Genetic Analysis of Adaptive Syndromes Interrelated with Seed Dormancy in Weedy Rice (*Oryza sativa*). *Theoretical and Applied Genetics* 110:1108–1118.

Harlan, Jack R., J. M. J De Wet, and E. Glen Price, 1973. Comparative Evolution of Cereals. *Evolution* 27(2):311–325.

Hayden, Brian, 2009. The Proof Is in the Pudding: Feasting and the Origins of Domestication. *Current Anthropology* 50(5):597–601.

Hodder, Ian, 2012. *Entangled: An Archaeology of the Relationships Between Humans and Things*. Wiley-Blackwell, Malden, MA.

Hunt, Harriet V., Michael G. Campana, Matthews C. Lawes, Yong-Jin Park, Mim A. Bower, Christopher J. Howe, and Martin K. Jones, 2011. Genetic Diversity and Phylogeography of Broomcorn Millet (*Panicum miliaceum* L.) Across Eurasia. *Molecular Ecology* 20(22):4756–4771.

Ishii, Takashige, Koji Numaguchi, Kotaro Miura, Kentaro Yoshida, Pham Thien Thanh, Than Myint Htun, Masanori Yamasaki, Norio Komeda, Takashi Matsumoto, Ryohei Terauchi, Ryo Ishikawa, and Motoyuki Ashikari, 2013. OsLG1 Regulates a Closed Panicle Trait in Domesticated Rice. *Nature Genetics* 45(4):462–465.

Johansen, Peter G., 2004. Landscape, Monumental Architecture and Ritual: A Reconsideration of the South Indian Ashmounds. *Journal of the Anthropological Archaeology* 23(3):309–330.

Kimata, Mikio, and Sadao Sakamoto 1992 Utilization of several species of millet in Eurasia. *Bulletin of Field Studies Institute, Tokyo Gakugei University* 3:1–12.

Kluyver, Thomas, A., Michael Charles, Glynis Jones, Mark Rees, and Colin P. Osborne, 2013. Did Greater Burial Depth Increase the Seed Size of Domesticated Legumes? *Journal of Experimental Botany* 64(3):4101–4108.

Kuijt, Ian, 2008. The Regeneration of Life: Neolithic Structures of Symbolic Remembering and Forgetting. *Current Anthropology* 49(2):171–197.

Li, Hui-Lin, 1970. The Origin of Cultivated Plants in Southeast Asia. *Economic Botany* 24(1):3–19.

Liu, Li, 2000. Ancestor Worship: An Archaeological Investigation of Ritual Activities in Neolithic North China. *Journal of East Asian Archaeology* 2(1):129–164.

Lu, Tracey Lie-Dan, 2002. A Green Foxtail (Setaria viridis) Cultivation Experiment in the Middle Yellow River Valley and Some Related Issues. *Asian Perspectives* 41(1):1–14.

Lu, Houyuan, Jianping Zhang, Kam-biu Liu, Naiqin Wu, Yumei Li, Kunshu Zhou, Maolin Ye, Tianyu Zhang, Haijiang Zhang, Xiaoyan Yang, Licheng Shen, Deke Xu, and Quan Li, 2009. Earliest Domestication of Common Millet (*Panicum miliaceum*) in East Asia Extended to 10,000 Years Ago. *Proceedings of the National Academy of Sciences of the United States of America* 106(18):7367–7372.

Lyon, Drew J., and David D. Baltensperger, 1995. Cropping Systems Control Winter Annual Grass Weeds in Winter Wheat. *Journal of Production Agriculture* 8(4):535–539.

Manning, Katie, Ruth Pelling, Tom Higham, Jean-Luc Schwenninger, and Dorian Q. Fuller, 2011. 4500-year Old Domesticated Pearl Millet (*Pennisetum glaucum*) from the Tilemsi Valley, Mali: New Insights into an Alternative Cereal Domestication Pathway in Africa. *Journal of Archaeological Science* 38(2):312–322.

Marshall, F., and Hildebrand, E., 2002. Cattle before Crops: The Beginnings of Food Production in Africa. *Journal of World Prehistory* 16(2):99–143.

Matz, Samuel A., 1986. *Cereal Science.* AviPress, Westport, CT.

Meiko, Eda, Ayumi Izumitani, Katsuyuki Ichitani, Makoto Kawase, and Kenji Fukunaga, 2013. Geographical Variation of Foxtail Millet, *Setaria italica* (L.) P. Beauv. Based on rDNA PCR–RFLP. *Genetic Resources and Crop Evolution* 60(1):265–274.

Moles, Angela T., David D. Ackerly, John C. Tweddle, John B. Dickie, Roger Smith, Michelle R. Leishman, Margaret M. Mayfield, Andy Pitman, Jeff T. Wood, and Mark Westoby, 2007. Global Patterns in Seed Size. *Global Ecology and Biogeography* 16(1):109–116.

Nelson, Sarah Milledge, 2003. Feasting the Ancestors in Early China. In *The Archaeology and Politics of Food and Feasting in Early States and Empires*, edited by Tamara L. Bray, pp. 65–89. Kluwer/Plenum, New York.

Nesbitt, Mark, 2005. Grains. In *Cultural History of Plants*, edited by Sir Ghillean Prance and Mark Nesbitt, pp. 45–60. Routledge, London.

Qin Ling, 2012. Archaeobotany in the Research of Agriculture Origin in China, Current Status and Future Prospects. In *School of Archaeology and Museology, Peking University, Center for the Study of Chinese Archaeology: A Collection of Studies on Archaeology IX*, edited by Peking University (in Chinese), pp. 260–315. Cultural Relics Press, Beijing.

Reynolds, Peter J., 1974. Experimental Iron Age Storage Pits: An Interim Report. *Proceedings of the Prehistoric Society* 40:118–131.

Sakamoto, Sadao, 1996. Glutinous-endosperm Starch Food Culture Specific to Eastern and Southeastern Asia. In *Redefining Nature: Ecology, Culture and Domestication*, edited by Roy Ellen and Katsuyoshi Fukui, pp. 215–231. Berg, Oxford, UK.

Sherratt, Andrew, 1997. Climatic Cycles and Behavioural Revolutions: The Emergence of Modern Humans and the Beginning of Farming. *Antiquity* 71(272):271–287.

Song, Jixiang, Zhao Zhijun, and Dorian Q. Fuller, 2013. The Archaeobotanical Significance of Immature Millet Grains: An Experimental Case Study of Chinese Millet Crop Processing. *Vegetation History and Archaeobotany* 22(2):141–152.

Tanno, Ken-ichi, and George Willcox, 2012. Distinguishing Wild and Domestic Wheat and Barley Spikelets from Early Holocene Sites in the Near East. *Vegetation History and Archaeobotany* 21(2):107–115.

Vaughan, Duncan Alexander, Bao-Rong Lu, and Norihiko Tomooka, 2008. The Evolving Story of Rice Evolution. *Plant Science* 174(4):394–408.

Vennum, Thomas, 1988. *Wild Rice and the Ojibway People.* Minnesota Historical Society Press, St. Paul, MN.

Wang, Chi-Wu, 1961. *The Forests of China with a Survey of Grassland and Desert Vegetation.* Maria Moors Cabot Foundation, Harvard University, Cambridge, MA.

Willcox, George, 2012. Searching for the Origins of Arable Weeds in the Near East. *Vegetation History and Archaeobotany* 21(2):163–167.

Wright, Karen, 1994. Ground Stone Tools and Hunter-gatherer Subsistence in Southwest Asia: Implications for the Transition to Farming. *American Antiquity* 59(2):238–263.

Yang, Xiaoyan, Zhiwei Wan, Linda Perry, Houyuan Lu, Qiang Wang, Chaohong Zhao, Jun Li, Fei Xie, Jincheng Yu, Tianxing Cui, Tao Wang, Mingqi Li, and Quansheng

Ge, 2012. Early Millet Use in Northern China. *Proceedings of the National Academy of Sciences of the U.S.A.* 109(10):3726–3730.
Zohary, Daniel, 1969. The Progenitors of Wheat and Barley in Relation to Domestication and Agricultural Dispersal in the Old World. In *The Domestication and Exploitation of Plants and Animals*, edited by Peter Ucko and Geoff Dimbleby, pp. 47–66. Duckworth, London.
Zohary, Daniel, Maria Hopf, and Ehud Weiss, 2012. *Domestication of Plants in the Old World*. 4th edition. Oxford University Press, New York, and Oxford, UK.

Chapter 7

Path Dependence and the Long-term Trajectory of Prehistoric Hohokam Irrigation in Arizona

Michelle Hegmon, Jerry B. Howard, Michael O'Hara, and Matthew A. Peeples

This chapter is about how people—and the institutions they create—become entangled (Hodder 2011) in situations from which they cannot easily extricate themselves, a process generally known as *path dependence*. The situations may involve relationships and social institutions as well as material circumstances, and the entanglements develop over time. Thus path dependence is a historical process, a concept ripe for archaeological inquiry.

Here we investigate early farmers in one of the most arid parts of the U.S. Southwest—the Hohokam archaeological region of southern Arizona—who developed enormous, and enormously successful, irrigation systems that watered vast areas and fed tens of thousands of people for centuries. Their success, however, committed them to a path from which it was increasingly difficult to exit, that is, dependence on canal irrigation to take water from large rivers. The irrigation watered fields that could feed many people, but it also required the labor of many people to build, rebuild, and maintain the canals and other infrastructure. Thus the technology, demography, and agricultural productivity became entangled, reducing flexibility and giving people no choice but to continue down the path. Here we investigate the beginnings of this process by investigating the relationships among the construction of larger and larger canal systems, population growth, and agricultural productivity.

Path Dependence (and Technological Momentum): Theory and Archaeological Potential

Path dependence is an intuitively appealing concept that connotes becoming increasingly stuck in a particular way of doing. Archaeologists seem to see potential in the concept and it is increasingly mentioned informally, although it

Archaeology of Entanglement edited by Lindsay Der and Francesca Fernandini, 173–188

is rarely used in archaeological publications (an important exception is Algaze 2008). Path dependence is also a specific theoretical concept developed in economics and political science, and writers in those disciplines argue for a strict definition applicable only to specific kinds of cases (for an excellent review, see Pierson 2000). Because archaeologists should understand the history of the theoretical concepts we use, we begin by reviewing this strict definition. However, we conclude this section with our development of a considerably looser concept for archaeological and historical usage; thus, impatient readers may wish to jump directly to the end of this section.

In economics, path dependence concepts were developed primarily in the study of technology (Arthur 1994), economic geography (Krugman 1991, 1996), and institutional arrangements (North 1990). They entail the radical (for economists) idea that not everything can be explained in terms of ahistorical market forces. Conceptions of path dependence are part of the research that earned North and Krugman Nobel Prizes in 1993 and 2008. For example, Krugman showed how, once established, production facilities attracted other related industries; thus, areas or countries became locked into particular (often disadvantageous) patterns of production and trade.

Key to the economic definition is the idea of *increasing returns* or self-reinforcing processes (which contrasts with the classical economic assumption of negative feedback toward equilibrium). Increasing returns is not necessarily a helpful process (the effects can actually be quite problematic). Rather, it means that the relative benefits of a particular activity—when compared with alternatives—increase over time. Once a manufacturing center has been established, it is cheaper to make a car there than in an isolated factory, and the more the center is established, the more the cost difference increases, even if the actual cost goes up. Brian Arthur (1994) describes four characteristics of path dependent–increasing returns processes:

(1) *Unpredictability*: Early events (such as the initial siting of a major factory) can have a major impact.
(2) *Inflexibility*: The further one goes down a path (the more support industries are built near the major factory), the more difficult it is to change.
(3) *Nonergodicity*: Apparently minor events (such as the travel plans of the CEO who chose the site) can have a major impact.
(4) *Potential path inefficiency*: Once the path becomes locked in, outcomes may have lower payoffs (less profit than a manufacturing center in a more central place), even as they continue to have increasing returns, because of the prohibitive cost of moving the center.

A related concept in science and technology studies is *technological momentum* (Hughes 1994), often used to consider the trajectory of technological systems (such the electric light and power network). Eschewing both technological determinism and pure social constructionism, Hughes sees society and technology as mutually constitutive: once the system is developed—a partly social process—it shapes certain social processes that in turn continue the system. Importantly, Hughes notes that social processes are more important at the origins of a system; that is, before it takes on much momentum.

The research we describe in this chapter began as part of a transdisciplinary project called "Change is Hard: The Challenges of Path Dependence." An initial goal of the project was to use concepts of path dependence to explore the deep and recent history of the Phoenix, Arizona, area. Change is Hard research includes: (1) the work reported here on the archaeological investigation of pre-Hispanic Hohokam canal systems; (2) historical geography of the emergence of a landscape of environmental injustice beginning in the late nineteenth century (Bolin et al. 2005); (3) institutional analysis of the development of land use patterns in the past several decades (York et al. 2011); and (4) the Phoenix Spatial History Project (http://phoenixspatialhistory.asu.edu/home).

Initially, we endeavored to use a strict definition of path dependence, but found that the concept of increasing returns and resulting characteristics were not helpful to our research for at least two reasons. First, in many of our research domains, the concept of "return" had little applicability. Second, not all of Arthur's four characteristics were applicable to cases that seemed—intuitively at least—to be stuck in particular paths. For example, as we describe in this chapter, increasing reliance on large-scale irrigation agriculture locked people into a path from which they could not easily exit. However, the process was fairly predictable (e.g., geologists can pinpoint where irrigation is most feasible) and not obviously influenced by minor events; thus, it violates two of Arthur's four characteristics. Other scholars who have used the concept of path dependence in historical geography or archaeological research also do not explicitly use the concept of increasing returns (e.g., Algaze 2008; Melosi 2000, n.d).

Given these observations and background, Change is Hard researchers established a looser understanding of path dependence. To be useful analytically, it should mean something more than "history matters" (see Pierson 2000), so that it can help us understand why some situations get locked into particular paths. At the same time, for our uses, it must be understandable without a calculus of increasing returns. Therefore, we view *path dependence* as trajectories that are increasingly difficult to exit, because momentum and/or self-reinforcing processes create lock-in. Our research focuses on these processes and especially on identifying *critical junctures,* that is, points at which actions taken or decisions made set the course for path dependence. Contemporary research on anticipatory governance is similarly concerned with anticipating and hopefully avoiding problematic trajectories.

The Research Context

Hohokam is the name, given by archaeologists, to the pre-Hispanic peoples (probably multilingual and multiethnic; see Shaul and Hill 1998) who lived in the deserts of central and southern Arizona until around 1450 CE (Bayman 2001), farming a variety of crops including corn, cotton, and agave. The Hohokam sequence traditionally begins around 1 CE with the Pioneer period, but recent discoveries of earlier irrigation-based villages, especially in the Tucson area (Mabry and Davis 2008), may push this date back substantially. By later times, the densest occupations and largest scale irrigation was in the Phoenix Basin along the Middle Gila and especially the Lower Salt River. At its peak, Hohokam population is estimated to have numbered in the tens of thousands, and they were fed by the largest pre-Hispanic irrigation system in North America (Figure 7.1). Researchers have long noted the enormous amount of labor necessary to build and maintain the canals using only stone tools and human labor. For example, McGuire (1992) concludes that Hohokam social units competed to attract young people (with strong backs). Woodson (2010) argues that labor demands for cleaning and maintaining canals would have been even greater than the labor needed to build them.

Hohokam irrigation in the Phoenix Basin began by the Pioneer period (ca. 1–750 CE); in the subsequent Colonial period (ca. 750–950 CE), Hohokam-style occupations (including distinctive red-on-buff pottery and ballcourts) had spread across most of southern Arizona. During the Sedentary period (ca. 950–1150 CE) there developed an extensive regional system in which ceramics (made by large-scale specialists), produce (probably including corn and cotton), and other staple items (including ground stone and hunted artiodactyls)

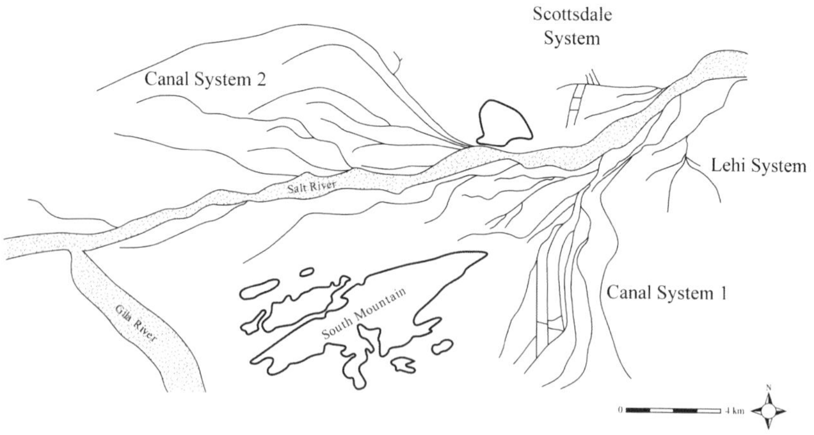

Figure 7.1 Hohokam canal systems in the Phoenix Basin (Courtesy of David Abbott).

were exchanged in markets associated with the ballcourts (Abbott et al. 2007). This system disintegrated abruptly around 1070 CE, some outlying areas were depopulated, and people concentrated in the Phoenix Basin. The Classic period (ca. 1150–1450 CE) is characterized by local rather than regional production and exchange (Abbott 2000), in-migration by peoples from the north, a resident population of 30,000 to 50,000, more evidence of social hierarchy including platform mounds and walled compounds, and continued expansion of the irrigation system. By the time Europeans first saw the area in the sixteenth century, the irrigation systems were no longer in use and the small resident population resided in scattered rancherías.

The end of the Hohokam system is not well understood, and interpretations differ depending on the scale and focus of the analysis. Clearly massive irrigation systems went out of use, and the large population declined. In *Centuries of Decline* (Abbot 2003), which focuses on Pueblo Grande, one of the largest Classic sites, Abbot paints a very bleak picture. Bioarchaeological analyses of Pueblo Grande skeletal material conclude that there were severe health problems, including anemia and nutritional and reproductive stresses; Sheridan (2003) describes the population as "marginal at best [and] doomed to eventual failure" (Sheridan 2003:106). That work was the basis of Hegmon et al.'s conclusion that the Hohokam were caught in a rigidity trap: "As conditions worsened in the Hohokam region, people stayed, in some cases enduring terrible health conditions for generations, until the physical and social infrastructure finally disintegrated" (2008:321). However, a recent re-analysis by McClelland (2015) concludes that the dire descriptions of poor health were not warranted. Finally, important analyses document and compare the decline across the Hohokam pan-region (Clark et al. 2008; Hill et al. 2004), finding evidence for aggregation and social tensions, possibly in reaction to immigrants, but not necessarily violence. They suggest tensions may have been greater at the large headgate sites (such as Pueblo Grande) than in villages with access to more land nearer the ends of canal systems. The larger-scale perspective also makes clear that the population decline (through various processes including lowered reproductive rates and out-migration) was, overall, a gradual process that spanned generations.

Possible explanations for the decline vary as well. Simulation studies show that Classic period systems could have irrigated 112,000 acres, but only once every four years (Howard 2006). Conversely, there were also years with too much water at one time. Stream flow retrodictions (Graybill et al. 2006) show large and probably very destructive flooding in the 1370s CE that could have caused major, and possibly irreparable, damage to some canal systems. Other studies, however, find little evidence for actual damage (Howard and Huckleberry 1991) and see signs of continued occupation after the flooding (Hackbarth 1995).

Despite the lack of consensus regarding the cause of the decline and the human problems it might have entailed, the broad pattern is clear. Over the course of centuries, Hohokam populations grew people, concentrated in the Phoenix Basin, and built larger and larger irrigation systems. Then, in the late pre-Hispanic period, the population declined manifold and the irrigation system fell out of use. The trajectory of growth has the hallmarks of a path-dependent process. The irrigation systems would have fed and also required the labor of a growing population, self-reinforcing processes that might have gained momentum as demand for irrigated crops increased because of the burgeoning exchange (and eventually market) system. The situation would have been difficult to exit because large populations could not gather or grow enough food in that environment without irrigation. In this chapter, we focus on the beginning of this process in the Pioneer and Colonial periods, and investigate how Hohokam society became locked into this trajectory by investigating the mutually reinforcing processes of population growth, crop production, and irrigation labor demands. Specifically, we ask: At what point did the population become so large it could not easily be fed without the canal irrigation? We interpret this as a point of lock-in, when people and the institutions they created became part of a path-dependent trajectory.

Analytical Structure

In our analysis we focus on the large and well-known Canal System 2, which is on the north side of the Salt River and includes the site of Pueblo Grande. The primary data needed for the analysis are the size, gradient, and other characteristics of the canals, as well as their temporal placement. Size data are derived from the excavation and mapping of multiple canal cross-section profiles exposed in numerous projects. These profiles were used to calculate paleohydrologic measures (detailed in Howard 1993) that provide estimates of the amount of water that could be discharged by a canal. The data used here are derived from Howard's earlier work (1993, 2006), supplemented with new calculations based on recently excavated segments of canals (records available through the Pueblo Grande Museum).

Assumptions

In the following procedures, we use data on canal size and discharge to derive estimates of labor requirements, crop production, and population size. To carry out these calculations, we rely on the following assumptions:

1) Hydrological studies show that canals must have specific gradients depending on their size and length and the amount of water they will carry (Howard 1993, 2006). A small canal carrying only a modest amount of water could be built at a slightly different gradient and thus in a slightly different location than a much larger canal. It is unlikely that the canals were built accretionally, or by adding distance and irrigated acreage onto

a short canal. Adding segments onto the end of a canal will eventually require more water (discharge) than the canal carries, so that canals could not be expanded accretionally. Thus, it is likely that a given canal was built over a relatively short period of time; for this study, we assume each canal was built over the course of two years.

2) A large body of ethnographic evidence (summarized in Howard 2006) supports the assumption that the irrigation system was built by the people who used it. In traditional agricultural settings, water allocations and field areas in an irrigation scheme are initially distributed to individuals based not on kinship but on the input of labor into the construction of the system (Chambers 1980; Codrington 1938; Kirkby 1973). By contributing labor to construction, the prospective farmer is securing water rights (Leach 1961; Uphoff 1986, 1992). For water rights to be retained, the farmer must also provide continued annual labor to system maintenance, thus being required to continue to play an active role in the irrigation system.
3) The canals taper in known ways from beginning to end; thus, it is possible to measure their size in cubic meters (Howard 1993). There are numerous estimates in both archaeological and planning literatures for the amount of soil a person can move a day, including recent experiments in Arizona conditions reported by Mabry and colleagues (2008). Following both Howard's earlier work (1993) and Woodson (2010), which summarize the various studies in detail, we estimate that an adult working with digging sticks could excavate 3 cubic meters per day.
4) Labor would have been required to dig the main canals, to build the various water control gates and distribution canals and fields, and to clean and maintain the system. However, not all of these tasks would need to be done simultaneously. Thus, we assume that the labor force needed to dig the main canals (over the course of two years) would have been sufficient to build other parts of the system and maintain it in other years.
5) A person could work 200 days per year excavating canals if others did the agricultural labor. Thus, we assume that a household of five people can provide 200 days of canal-digging labor per year (i.e., one laborer per household).
6) We can develop reasonably accurate calculations for the acreage that could be watered by canal systems and the population that could be supported by this acreage (Howard 1993, 2006). We assume the canals would not have been built unless this amount of irrigation was needed. This assumption is justified based on myriad ethnographic evidence (see assumption 2 for summary). While there was exchange and evidence of hierarchy in Hohokam society, the extensive regional system and the strongly hierarchical society developed in later periods. Thus, at least during the period of interest, we assume most produce was used locally. Using calculations detailed later in this chapter, we estimate the maximum population based on potentially irrigated acreage (see also Woodson 2010). This is

in contrast to other established methods of estimating population based on site size distributions (e.g., Doelle 1995; see also Hill et al. 2004), but those methods are at the most very rough for these early periods because site size information is limited for the early sites, which primarily have pithouse architecture. In the discussion that follows, we tread carefully around issues of potential circularity.

7) Irrigation was used to water fields of maize (probably mixed with beans and squash) as well as cotton. Cotton, a non-food item, was probably an important item for exchange as well as domestic use, though details are not well known. We do not discuss cotton explicitly in our analysis. Rather, our calculations of the acreage that can be watered (which includes loss) assume that some of that "loss" was water used to grow cotton.

Example Calculations

These assumptions can be used to estimate the population needed to provide the labor to build a canal. We illustrate with data from a canal associated with the Dutch Canal Ruins (Greenwald et al. 1988) dating to the Colonial period. Known as Dutch Canal Ruins NM3, it dates to the later (Santa Cruz phase) part of the Colonial period. It is shown as part of the map of the Colonial period system (Figure 7.3). The calculations for this and other canals are summarized in Table 7.1.

The Dutch Canal was 6 km in length (Table 7.1, column C) with a tapering cross-section. Using methods detailed by Howard (1993), we calculate that 15,577 cubic meters had to be excavated to build it (Table 7.1, column D), which would have required 15577/3 = 5,192 person-days of labor (Table 7.1, column E). We assume this labor was distributed over two years, meaning 5192/2 = 2596 person days per year. If an individual worked 200 days per year, it would have required the labor of 2596/200 = 13 people (Table 7.1, column F). Assuming each worker was part of a five-person household, and other members of the household did the work necessary to provide the laborer with food, the total population needed to provide the labor would be 13 × 5 = 65 (Table 7.1, column G).

Using a second series of analyses also detailed in Howard (1993), we calculate the amount of water the canal could supply, known as its discharge (Table 7.1, column H). Because discharge depends on various hydrological factors (including gradient as well as cross-sectional size), it does not correlate directly with soil volume or length. The discharge can then be used to estimate the acreage that can reliably be watered (Table 7.1, column I), a calculation that takes water loss into account and assumes incomplete usage. The Dutch Canal Ruins NM3 canal could reliably water 1,391 acres, which could support 2,319 people (Table 7.1, column J). The figures show that the labor force needed to build and maintain the canal could easily be supported by it.

Table 7.1 Canal characteristics

A	*B*	*C*	*D*	*E*	*F*	*G*	*H*	*I*	*J*
					Labor needed				
Canal	*Phase*	*Canal length, km*	*Soil, m^3*	*Person-days labor*	*Individuals*	w/HHs	*Discharge at head m^3/sec*	*Acres irrigated*	*Population supported*
Dutch Canal Ruins SM1	**Snk**	**14**	**47286**	**15,762**	**39**	**197**	**6.59**	**2119**	**3,531**
AZ:T:12:13 F.1	**Snk-GB**	**10.13**	**77,206**	**25735**	**64**	**322**	**2.333**	**750**	**1,250**
East Papago F.7a	GB	7.0	22,341	7,447	19	93	4.38	1408	2,346
Dutch Canal Ruins NM1	GB	8.0	20,157	6,719	17	84	4.78	1536	2,561
Subtotal	**GB**	**15**	**42,498**	**14,166**	**35**	**177**	**9**	**2944**	**4,907**
East Papago F.57	GB-SC	6.0	18,805	6,268	16	78	4.17	1340	2,234
La Ciudad F.247.01	GB-SC	34.0	222,624	74,208	186	928	8.95	2876	4,794
La Ciudad F.1310	GB-SC	34.0	253,122	84,374	211	1055	12.1	3889	6,482
Subtotal	**GB-SC**	**74**	**494,551**	**164,850**	**412**	**2061**	**8105**	**8105**	**13,509**
Dutch Canal Ruins NM3	SC	6.0	15,577	5,192	13	65	4.33	1391	2,319
East Papago F.7b	SC	7.0	17,973	5,991	15	75	4.12	1324	2,207
Dutch Canal Ruins NM2	SC	7.5	18,805	6,268	16	78	4.62	1485	2,475
Subtotal	**SC**	**21**	**52,355**	**17,451**	**44**	**218**		**4200**	**7,001**

Calculation of columns explained in text. **Bold** indicates total for a given phase; Snk = Snaketown, GB = Gila Butte, SC = Santa Cruz. HH indicates households; F and NM indicate named feature at given site.

The Growth of Canal System 2

Canal System 2 is (along with Canal System 1, which is on the south side of the Salt River; see Figure 7.1) the largest in the Hohokam area. Roughly 50 canals were built as part of Canal System 2 during the overall period of its use (Pioneer through Classic periods). Pueblo Grande (the basis of Abbott's *Centuries of Decline*) is the largest single site along the system and one of the largest platform mounds along the Salt River. Numerous large and smaller villages are situated along and near the ends of the canals.

Drawing on an enormous amount data gathered by hundreds of archaeologists who excavated, mapped, and dated parts of the canals, we can determine the sequence of canal construction. Here we re-present information from Howard (1993) augmented by new information, particularly about the early part of the sequence.

The overall growth of Canal System 2 is illustrated in Figure 7.2. The early Pioneer period system was quite small. The subsequent Colonial period system is much larger, and the size stays roughly the same into the Sedentary period, although it changed in configuration, as canals were built further from the river. In the final, Classic period, the system again expanded significantly.

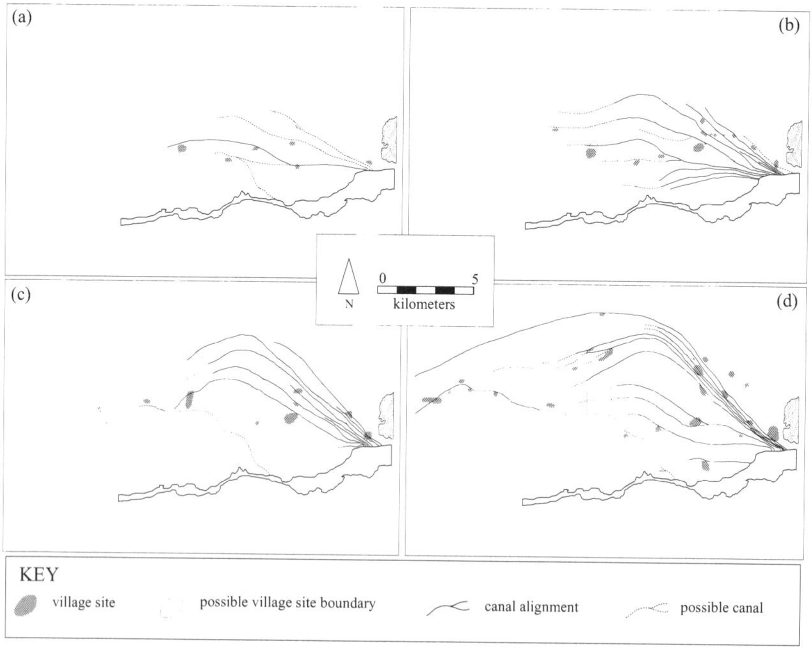

Figure 7.2 Growth of Canal System 2. From (a) to (d): Canals in Pioneer, Colonial, Sedentary, and Classic periods (Prepared by Sophie Kelly).

Our analysis focuses on the early growth that resulted in the full Colonial period system. Not all of these canals were built or used at the same time. Some can only be assigned to the general Colonial period, but others can be dated more precisely. Table 7.1 lists the Colonial (and two earlier) canals and the calculations of labor requirements, water, acreage farmed, and population, as we explain earlier in this chapter. The more precisely dated canals are arranged by phase, and the figures are summed by phase. The Snaketown phase (ca. 700–750 CE) is the latter part of the Pioneer period, and the Gila Butte (ca. 750–850 CE) and Santa Cruz (ca. 850–950 CE) phases are the earlier and later components of the Colonial period. Calculations for each phase are also summed in the subtotal rows.

In Table 7.1, column J shows the population that could be supported by the amount of water the canals carried (a function of discharge [column H] and irrigated acreage [column I]). Because the irrigated acreage is a function of discharge, it does not correlate directly with canal size or labor requirements. As we discuss earlier in this chapter, these population estimates are quite conservative since they take into account water loss and use for purposes other than food crops. We assume that the canals would not have been built if they were not needed to support this many people, so we use these conservative estimates of the population that *could* be fed as estimates of actual population over time. The labor needed to build the canals (column F) and feed the workers (column G) is far less than the total population that could be supported; thus there is no indication (at least in these data) of labor shortages.

The significance of these figures is the change over time, through the late Pioneer and Colonial periods. There is a large increase in labor requirement in the middle of the Colonial period. Together, the two Gila Butte phase canals required "only" 14,166 person-days of labor, whereas just one of the (three total) canals that dates to the middle of the period (transitional between the Gila Butte and Santa Cruz phases) required about six times this much later (more than 84,000 person-days), and all three middle-period canals required a total of 164,850 person-days.

The 10-fold increase in the labor needed to build and maintain the society's vital infrastructure is, in and of itself, a major change. The significance of this change for all aspects of society becomes even more apparent when considered together with the population estimates (Figure 7.3), for the first three phases show a roughly steady state in labor demands and estimates for population that could be fed. Through these times, people probably could have reverted back to an earlier system (Figure 7.3, off the graph to the left), a time of less dependence on irrigation. The changes come with the big jump in the ninth century CE. At that point, the canals could have fed more than 13,000 people and, as we argue previously, they would not have been built if the capacity was not needed. Assuming population grew to at least somewhere close to this level, they could not have reverted to earlier small systems, which would have been barely large enough even to feed the laborers and their families. At this point

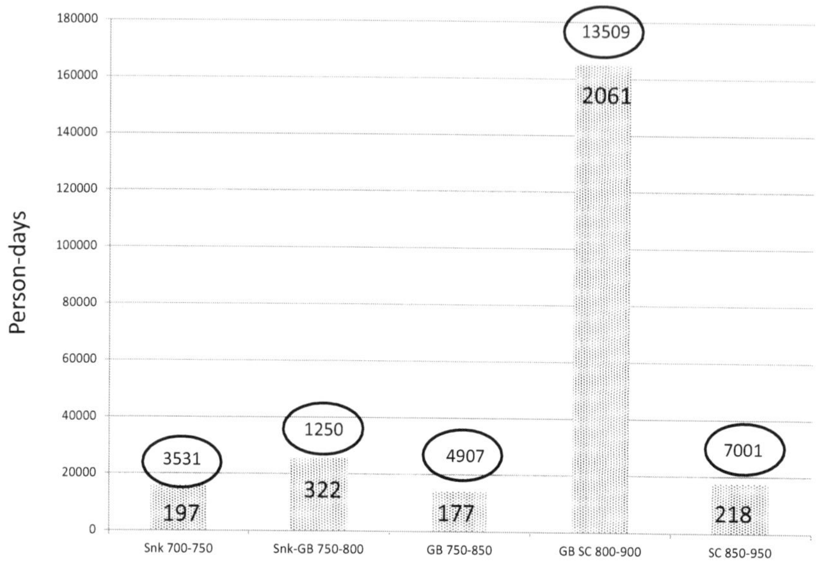

Figure 7.3 Labor requirements and agricultural potential of Canal System 2 through the Snaketown phase and phases of the Colonial period (Gila Butte and Santa Cruz), based on data presented in Table 7.1. Histograms show person-days of labor needed (Table 7.1, column E) to build canal system dated to subphase; numbers in the columns are the population needed to provide the labor (Table 7.1, column G); and numbers in ovals are population that could be fed (Table 7.1, column J).

people would have been locked into depending on these large—and eventually even larger—irrigation systems.

Discussion and Conclusions: Becoming Entangled

Hindsight is a privileged position from which to view Hohokam irrigation, or nearly anything in the past. With hindsight, we can see that from its early beginnings, the size and complexity of the irrigation system grew and grew, and so did the population dependent on it. Before long, the dependent population was so large that there was no alternative way to feed itself except to leave the region. So people stayed and continued to expand the irrigation system until eventually something—or many things—went wrong. Perhaps flooding, perhaps water shortages, perhaps social problems or violence. Some researchers see evidence for a difficult end, with an unhealthy population enduring centuries of decline; others argue for a more benign ending as populations left the region. Either way, the system fell out of use and the society archaeologists know as Hohokam did not continue, although some of their descendants still live in the area in thriving contemporary communities.

From another perspective, nothing lasts forever. However, the Hohokam irrigation system worked for centuries, delivering millions of acre-feet of water that used to grow crops that fed tens—if not hundreds—of thousands of people. It eventually provided food that was distributed in one of the most elaborate market systems known in a pre-state society. It was a marvel of hydroengineering and labor organization.

Concepts of path dependence provide insights into how we can understand and even reconcile these two contrasting but not incompatible perspectives. Instead of simply looking back on the past, we can consider how the past became the future, a perspective advocated by van der Leeuw and colleagues (2011). Such a perspective has obvious humanistic appeal, because it leads us to ask questions about both the actions and motivations of the people who set the trajectory into motion. And even if we cannot (or are not willing to) consider motivations, it at least forces us to consider actions *and their consequences*, a perspective obviously important for imagining our own future. Nelson and colleagues (2011) illuminate this kind of perspective by comparing Hohokam and Zuni (in west-central New Mexico) infrastructure and trajectories. Irrigation was developed early in both areas; however, at Zuni, moderate-scale irrigation became one of a suite of diverse strategies, while in Hohokam an enormous irrigation system became the single dominant strategy. In contrast to Hohokam, the Zuni trajectory is markedly stable; it survived a difficult contact period and is thriving today.

In our research we view path dependence as the development of a trajectory that is increasingly difficult to exit because momentum and/or self-reinforcing processes create lock-in, and we focus on identifying these processes, particularly the *critical junctures*, the points when actions taken or decisions made set the course for path dependence. Here, in this analysis of Hohokam irrigation (focusing on Canal System 2), we see the first large-scale expansion of the system in the Colonial period as a critical juncture that locked people into this trajectory of growth. At that point, the population dependent on the irrigation would have been so large that they could no longer revert back to much smaller-scale irrigation or other forms of subsistence. Later in the sequence there were probably other critical junctures (e.g., when the regional system disintegrated and populations concentrated in the Phoenix Basin) that also contributed to the trajectory.

From the perspective of farmers living near large rivers in the arid deserts of southern and central Arizona, building ditches and eventually canals to bring water from the rivers to their crops must have seemed like an obviously good idea. And the eventual growth indicates that it was successful: irrigation helped them to grow more crops more reliably, at least for a time. Throughout the sequence, the largest sites and eventually platform mounds are associated with the largest irrigation systems, another possible indicator of success. Early benefits—for at least some sectors of society—are part of a path dependent trajectory; the benefits get people on the path and keep them on the path until they are locked in. Then, even if the benefits erode and the path is seen to be problematic, exit is difficult. This is how the entanglement happens.

Acknowledgments

This research was done as part of the "Change is Hard: The Challenges of Path Dependence" project, which was funded through the Late Lessons from Early History program at Arizona State University (ASU). We are grateful to Sander van der Leeuw for creating the Late Lessons program and ASU president Michael Crow for funding it. We also thank Change is Hard lead faculty Bob Bolin, Abby York, and Jamey Wetmore for helping us develop our understanding of path dependence. David Abbott enhanced our understanding of Hohokam archaeology and allowed us to use the map that constitutes our Figure 7.1.

References

Abbott, David R., 2000. *Ceramics and Community Organization among the Hohokam.* University of Arizona Press, Tucson.

Abbott, David R., ed., 2003. *Centuries of Decline during the Hohokam Classic Period at Pueblo Grande.* University of Arizona Press, Tucson.

Abbott, David R., Alexa M. Smith, and Emiliano Gallaga, 2007. Ballcourts and Ceramics: The Case for Hohokam Marketplaces in the Arizona Desert. *American Antiquity* 72:461–484.

Algaze, Guillermo, 2008. *Ancient Mesopotamia at the Dawn of Civilization: The Evolution of an Urban Landscape.* University of Chicago Press, Chicago, IL.

Arthur, W. Brian, 1994. *Increasing Returns and Path Dependence in the Economy.* University of Michigan Press, Ann Arbor.

Bayman, James M., 2001. The Hohokam of Southwest North America. *Journal of World Prehistory* 15(3):257–311.

Bolin, Bob, Sara Grineski, and Timothy Collins, 2005. The Geography of Despair: Environmental Racism and the Making of South Phoenix, Arizona, USA. *Human Ecology Review* 12(2):156–168.

Clark, Jeffery J., Patrick D. Lyons, J. Brett Hill, Anna A. Neuzil, and William H. Doelle, 2008. Immigrants and Population Collapse in the Southern Southwest. *Archaeology Southwest* 22(4):1–15.

Chambers, Robert, 1980. Basic Concepts in the Organization of Irrigation. In *Irrigation and Agricultural Development in Asia: Perspectives from Social Sciences*, edited by E. Walter Coward, pp. 28–50. Cornell University Press, Ithaca, NY.

Codrington, Humphrey William, 1938. *Ancient Land Tenure and Revenue in Ceylon.* Ceylon Government Press, Colombo.

Doelle, William H., 1995. Tonto Basin Demography in a Regional Perspective. In *The Roosevelt Community Development Study: New Perspectives on Tonto Basin Prehistory*, edited by Mark D. Elson, Miriam T. Stark, and David A. Gregory,

pp. 201–226. Anthropological Papers No. 15. Center for Desert Archaeology, Tucson, AZ.
Graybill, Donald K., David A. Gregory, Gary S. Funkhouser, and Fred L. Nials, 2006. Long-Term Streamflow Reconstruction, River Channel Morphology, and Aboriginal Irrigation Systems along the Salt and Gila Rivers. In *Environmental Change and Human Adaptation in the Ancient American Southwest*, edited by David E. Doyel and Jeffrey S. Dean, pp. 69–123. University of Utah Press, Salt Lake City.
Greenwald, David H., Richard Ciolek-Torrello, and James B. Rodgers, 1988. *Archaeological Investigations at the Dutch Canal Ruin, Phoenix, Arizona: Archaeology and History along the Papago Freeway Corridor*. Museum of Northern Arizona, Flagstaff.
Hackbarth, Mark R., 1995. Interpretation of the MTS data with the Late Classic Period Hohokam. In *Archaeology at the Head of the Scottsdale Canal System, Volume 3: Canal and Synthetic Studies*, edited by Mark R. Hackbarth, Douglas B. Craig, T. Kathleen Henderson, and David R. Abbott, pp.173–195. Northland Research, Inc., Flagstaff, AZ.
Hegmon, Michelle, Matthew A. Peeples, Ann P. Kinzig, Stephanie Kulow, Cathryn M. Meegan, and Margaret C. Nelson, 2008. Social Transformation and Its Human Costs in the Prehispanic US Southwest. *American Anthropologist* 110(3):313–324.
Hill, J. Brett, Jeffery J. Clark, William H. Doelle, and Patrick D. Lyons, 2004. Prehistoric Demography in the Southwest: Migration, Coalescence, and Hohokam Population Decline. *American Antiquity* 69:689–716.
Hodder, Ian, 2011. Human-Thing Entanglement: Towards an Integrated Archaeological Perspective. *Journal of the Royal Anthropological Institute* 17(1):154–177.
Howard, Jerry B., 1993. A Paleohydraulic Approach to Examining Agricultural Intensification in Hohokam Irrigation Systems. *Research in Economic Anthropology (Supplement)* 7:263–324.
Howard, Jerry B., 2006. Hohokam Irrigation Communities: A Study of Internal Structure, External Relationships and Sociopolitical Complexity. Unpublished PhD dissertation, Arizona State University, Tempe.
Howard, Jerry B., and Gary Huckleberry, 1991. *The Operation and Evolution of an Irrigation System: The East Papago Canal Study*. Soil Systems, Inc., Phoenix, AZ.
Hughes, Thomas P., 1994. Technological Momentum. In *Does Technology Drive History? The Dilemma of Technological Determinism,* edited by Leo Marx and Merritt Roe Smith, pp. 101–113. MIT Press, Cambridge, MA.
Kirkby, Anne Veronica Tennant, 1973. *The Use of Land and Water Resources in the Past and Present Valley of Oaxaca, Mexico*. Museum of Anthropology, University of Michigan, Ann Arbor.
Krugman, Paul, 1991. History and Industry Location: The Case of the Manufacturing Belt. *The American Economic Review* 81:80–83.
Krugman, Paul, 1997. *Pop Internationalism*. MIT Press, Cambridge, MA.
Leach, Edmund Ronald, 1961. *Pul Eliya: A Village in Ceylon*. Cambridge University Press, Cambridge, UK.
Mabry, J. B., and Owen K. Davis, eds., 2008. *Las Capas: Early Irrigation and Sedentism in a Southwestern Floodplain*. Center for Desert Archaeology, Tucson, AZ.

Mabry, J. B., J. P. Holmlund, F. L. Nials, and M. R. Palacios-Fest, 2008. Modeling Canal Characteristics and Trends. In *Las Capas: Early Irrigation and Sedentism in a Southwestern Floodplain*, edited by J. B. Mabry and Owen K. Davis, pp. 267–282. Center for Desert Archaeology, Tucson, AZ.

McClelland, John A, 2015. Revisiting Hohokam Demography. *American Antiquity* 80(3):492–510.

McGuire, Randall H., 1992. *Death, Society, and Ideology in a Hohokam Community*. Westview Press, Boulder, CO.

Melosi, Martin V., 2000. *The Sanitary City: Urban Infrastructure in America from Colonial Times to the Present*. Johns Hopkins University Press, Baltimore, MD.

Melosi, Martin V., n.d. Path Dependence and Urban History: Is a Marriage Possible? Electronic document, www.geschundkunstgesch.tu-berlin.de/fileadmin/fg95/Melosi_Text.pdf, accessed September 12, 2015.

Nelson, M. C., K. Kintigh, D. R. Abbott, and J. M. Anderies, 2010. The Cross-scale Interplay Between Social and Biophysical Context and the Vulnerability of Irrigation-dependent Societies: Archaeology's Long-term Perspective. *Ecology and Society* 15(3):31. Electronic document, www.ecologyandsociety.org/vol15/iss3/art31/, accessed September 12, 2015.

North, Douglass C., 1990. *Institutions, Institutional Change and Economic Performance*. Cambridge University Press, Cambridge, UK.

Pierson, Paul, 2000. Increasing Returns, Path Dependence, and the Study of Politics. *The American Political Science Review* 94(2):251–267.

Shaul, David Leedom, and Jane H. Hill, 1998. Tepimans, Yumans, and Other Hohokam. *American Antiquity* 63(3):375–396.

Sheridan, Susan Guise, 2003. Childhood Health as an Indicator of Biological Stress. In *Centuries of Decline During the Hohokam Classic Period at Pueblo Grande*, edited by David R. Abbott, pp. 82–106. University of Arizona Press, Tucson.

Uphoff, Norman Thomas, 1986. *Improving International Irrigation Management with Farmer Participation: Getting the Process Right*. Westview Press, Boulder, CO.

Uphoff, Norman Thomas, 1992. *Learning from Gal Oya: Possibilities for Participatory Development and Post-Newtonian Social Science*. Cornell University Press, Ithaca, NY.

Van der Leeuw, S., R. Costanza, S. Aulenbach, S. Brewer, M. Burek, S. Cornell, C. Crumley, J. A. Dearing, C. Downy, L. J. Graumlich, S. Heckbert, M. Hegmon, K. Hibbard, S. T. Jackson, I. Kubiszewski, P. Sinclair, S. Sörlin, and W. Steffen, 2011. Toward an Integrated History to Guide the Future. *Ecology and Society* 16(4):2.

Woodson, Michael Kyle, 2010. The Social Organization of Hohokam Irrigation in the Middle Gila River Valley, Arizona. Unpublished PhD dissertation, Arizona State University, Tempe.

York, Abigail M., Milan Shrestha, Christopher G. Boone, Sainan Zhang, John Harrington, Tom Prebyl, Amaris Swann, Mike Agar, Michael Antolin, Barbara Nolin, John Wright, and Rhonda Skaggs, 2011. Land Fragmentation under Rapid Urbanization: A Cross-site Analysis of Southwestern Cities. *Urban Ecosystems* 14(3):429–455.

Rethinking Dependences and Dependencies: Contemporary Perspectives on Entanglement in Archaeology

Chapter 8

Entangled Histories, Entangled Worlds: Reflections on Time, Space, and Place

Stephen A. Mrozowski

The concept of entanglement commonly refers to the material and social relations that emerge in colonial settings between colonizers and the colonized. In this chapter I explore a different, but not unrelated notion of entanglement: the idea that spaces are often entangled with histories. In particular I explore the notion of historical gravity as a form of cultural perception and representation. Logical examples include places associated with great tragedy or suffering, but there is a large spectrum of events that become attached and identified with particular spaces.

Introduction

In most instances, the notions of entanglement archaeologists employ involve the close relationship between humans and things. This is a welcome addition to the theoretical influences in the field of late since it incorporates a broad-based understanding of things that emphasizes their often vibrant character rather than an inert view (e.g., Bennett 2010; Hodder 2012). One of the values of this broad-based approach is that it helps bridge the gap between social, behavioral sciences and more materials-based, physical science. For archaeologists, the challenge is to be open to both different methods and different epistemologies. Bennett (2010) provides a useful example of this in arguing for the notion of vibrant matter: a material world, literally alive, exhibiting properties that are constantly in flux and in becoming. Thus, metals are not considered inert, but as substances possessing properties humans have taken advantage of in transforming them into things that they rely upon: tools, shelters, transportation devices, items of personal adornment. In its broadest sense, the notion of vibrant matter is a concept that helps bridge the gap between studies of the material and immaterial. This is one of the chief reasons thing theory more generally has become so popular among archaeologists who seek

Archaeology of Entanglement edited by Lindsay Der and Francesca Fernandini, 191–213

to gain a clearer understanding of the relationship between humans and all things material.

Much of the literature on entanglement concentrates on two interwoven themes: the relationship between humans and things, and particular role it plays in colonial contexts (e.g., Gosden 2001; Hodder 2012; Thomas 1991, 1997). Colonial settings are by no means the sole focus of entanglement studies (Hodder 2012); however, the role of material culture and spatial practices in the process of colonialism makes this a particularly fruitful context for conducting such studies. In this chapter I explore the relationship between a rather large class of thing—the landscape, or space writ large—and history. I also outline the notion of historical gravity that can be applied to spaces considered significant largely because of their entanglement with events or a series of events. These events involve moments in history that are long remembered and, in some instances, memorialized. There are, of course, instances when places of deep memory are forgotten, sometimes through the passing of time and in some cases purposely wiped from existence. Places of memory are often considered in relation to issues of heritage; my own interest in the notion of historical gravity can certainly be applied in heritage contexts. What interests me more, however, is the larger meaning attached to places because of their roles in history. For those with whom connections to such places is important, there is an emotional dimension to these attachments that may be difficult, if not impossible, to discern archaeologically. In other words, there may not be a clear archaeological signature of historical gravity, although a long-term attachment to a particular place may result in such a record. A cemetery is a logical example of such a space, with the connection between the living the dead adding to the historical gravity of such a space. Yet we also know that cemeteries are forgotten over time as the historical gravity I have in mind dissipates with time. So the issue of historical gravity and its entanglement with space has several dimensions to consider, including the kinds of events or purposes that might contribute to a place gaining weight and the circumstances that can result in the dissipation of that weight, as well as distinguishing different categories of space and spatial practices that might contribute to the weight of historical gravity attached to a particular place.

Entanglement and Historical Gravity

Perhaps the best way of conceptualizing historical gravity is to begin with a tangible and well-known example. Stonehenge, on the Salisbury Plain of Wiltshire in Britain, provides an obvious example. With its rich heritage and deep history revealed through archaeology, Stonehenge seems like a logical example of a place that exhibits great antiquity. Yet what may seem obvious today was probably not always the case. In this respect, the construction of stone circles and other megalithic structures throughout northern Europe were attempts to interrupt history, to influence its direction. As such, they were places designed by their builders to entangle their followers and their descendants for as long as possible. The effort it took to construct Stonehenge, the cutting and transportation of the megalithic stones, their orientation, and the rich landscapes that accompanied these structures (Bender 1999; Parker Pearson 2012) were purposely designed to ensure their place in the future. The same was true of the large earthen structures constructed in North America that served as temple platforms and burial mounds (see Sassaman 2010, 2012). These too were designed to interrupt history and influence the future. As archaeologists living and working in the early twenty-first century, the intention embedded in such structures and the efforts it took to build them all seem quite obvious to us today. What may seem less obvious is the role entanglement would play in ensuring that the weight of the historical gravity attached to such structures would increase over time. It's unclear whether the builders of such landscapes understood just how far into the future their efforts would be projected. And in the case of Stonehenge, it is easy to imagine that its builders might be impressed to discover how there remain those who even today look to it as a gathering place (Bender 1999; Parker Pearson 2012). It is this power, the power that still attracts neo-Druids today, that typifies what I define as *historical gravity*.

So how should historical gravity be defined? As the combined historical weight of the events and memories that have become entangled with a particular, self-identified space. In many respects, the transformation of space into place involves the conscious entanglement of space with historical gravity. In some instances the accumulation of historical gravity would take time, and result from a single or multiple events, such as the case of a battlefield. In other instances historical gravity can accumulate over time as the direct result of the continuing occupation of a space by its human inhabitants. Longstanding settlements or even urban centers would represent such places. It is important to remember, however, that even in instances where locations have been inhabited for hundreds or thousands of years, events can overtake even the most densely populated settlement, resulting in its abandonment and being forgotten. Archaeologists relish the rediscovery of such places, as well as those where the weight of historical gravity remains part of the conscious entanglement of a particular place and its history. The Neolithic settlement of Çatalhöyük is a good example of a place with tremendous historical gravity that was forgotten until rediscovered by archaeologists (Hodder 1990, 2012). Even a fairly recent settlement such as the fort at Jamestown, Virginia, represents a place that was lost, only to be rediscovered by archaeologists after numerous attempts were made over the better part of a century (Kelso 2006). The literature of archaeology is filled with both such places, and in virtually every instance the weight of historical gravity resulted in these locations maintaining their importance for an extended period of time.

Not all examples of historical gravity involve long, continuous occupations. Longstanding settlements or the sites of memorable events, such as battlefields or disasters, are just two examples of spaces whose entanglements with history have resulted in their weightiness. Earlier I mention the example of Stonehenge and other megalithic structures that were purposefully planned with the intent to ensnare humans to a particular location. There are other, less obvious examples of such places that are equally commonplace in the field research archaeologists carry out across the globe. On a small scale, a single burial can represent a location of historical gravity, especially when compared with a less deliberate form of archaeological site such as a butchering location or a stone tool quarry. The latter represents a class of archaeological site found continuously, yet which does not intrinsically exhibit much historical gravity because their spatial form was not consciously planned with a purpose in mind. Ironically this only happens when archaeologists rediscover the sites. There are, however, other classes of archaeological site that contain evidence suggesting their inhabitants had some notion of the future when building their settlements. Such sites are important for a variety of reasons, but in particular they demonstrate the conscious effort to entangle history to a specific location. The evidence of such efforts is not always obvious, as in the case of Stonehenge, for example, or other notable, large-scale structures that often involved the organization of labor on a massive scale such as the earthen mounds of North America, the monumental cities of ancient Mesoamerica or the Near East, or the pyramids of Egypt. Again, these are obvious examples. There are also less obvious, but no less significant, examples of conscious efforts made to tether a deeper past to a specific location. In Africa, for example, there are instances of what Paul Lane (2013) calls a "presencing of the past" in which material culture from earlier periods appear to be purposely gathered and buried as a way of carrying forward the past into the future. Kenneth Sassaman (2010, 2012) also argues that certain classes of material culture went from being valued for their functional qualities to being valued for their connections to a deeper past in North American Archaic contexts. In my own work I find evidence to suggest people in the past took steps to link deeper practices, as represented by particular classes of material culture, to locations in such a way as to influence a particular future. Each of these examples involves conscious efforts to entangle history and space. By examining them more closely we can develop a better understanding of the role entanglement plays in adding to the historical gravity of a particular place for those who lived there and for those expected to live there in the future. In some instances there are other forms of entanglement that influence the experiences of individuals and groups connected with specific places. An example of the latter is the way notions such as *primitive*, *prehistoric*, *indigenous*, or *authentic* become entangled with particular groups of people in such a way that it can have a profound influence on the relationships that develop between these groups and governments or other communities.

When archaeologists rediscover sites that were constructed, lived in, and abandoned in the past, it is normal for us to think of everything in the past tense. But this not actually the case; many of the sites we excavate include manifestations of actions that were purposefully designed to affect a specific future. In this regard, archaeologists rediscover futures as often as we find pasts (see Mrozowski 2013, 2014; Sassaman 2010, 2012). The difference between archaeological deposits created to influence the future and those linked to daily practice is obviously one of intent and agency in a larger sense. One way of conceptualizing the difference revolves around residual intent: actions taken to purposely affect an outcome or aspiration. So, when an individual was sitting producing stone tools some 10,000 years ago in what is today Finnish Lapland, it seems safe to infer that the spatial patterning of activities at the site (Kankaanpää and Rankama 2011:43–63) was not the result of activities purposely designed to implicate a particular future. I am not saying such deposits hold no information about past activities; indeed they do, and their spatial patterning may reveal social behavior. But this is very different from evidence that appears to be linked with purposeful forethought. Although ideas concerning the precise character of the beliefs behind such actions may be difficult to discern with great confidence, it is nevertheless possible to infer the purpose behind those actions. In some instances even the subtlest of material evidence can suggest attempts to sow the seeds of historical gravity by entangling things with places and the people who do—and potentially will—inhabit those places. To illustrate these points I provide three vignettes that demonstrate different examples of the manner in which space and history become entangled, leading ultimately to a further entanglement with archaeology. The first two are drawn from my own research over the past decade that has focused on the Christian Indian communities of Magunkaquog and Hassanamesit in Massachusetts and Connecticut.

Planning the Futures of Magunkaquog and Hassanamesit

The Nipmuc communities of Magunkaquag and Hassanamesit were two of seven "Christian Indian" settlements established as part of the English missionary John Eliot's attempts to convert the native peoples of southern New England to Christianity during the seventeenth century (Figure 8.1).

The first such community, Natick, was established in 1650, followed by Hassanamesit a few years later. Magunkaquag, the seventh such community, was established by 1669. Each of these communities was different, yet all shared a connection to Eliot's larger enterprise of converting native peoples to Christianity. Eliot's particular vision of religious conversion was part of an eschatology that held that the conversion of all non-Christian believers would

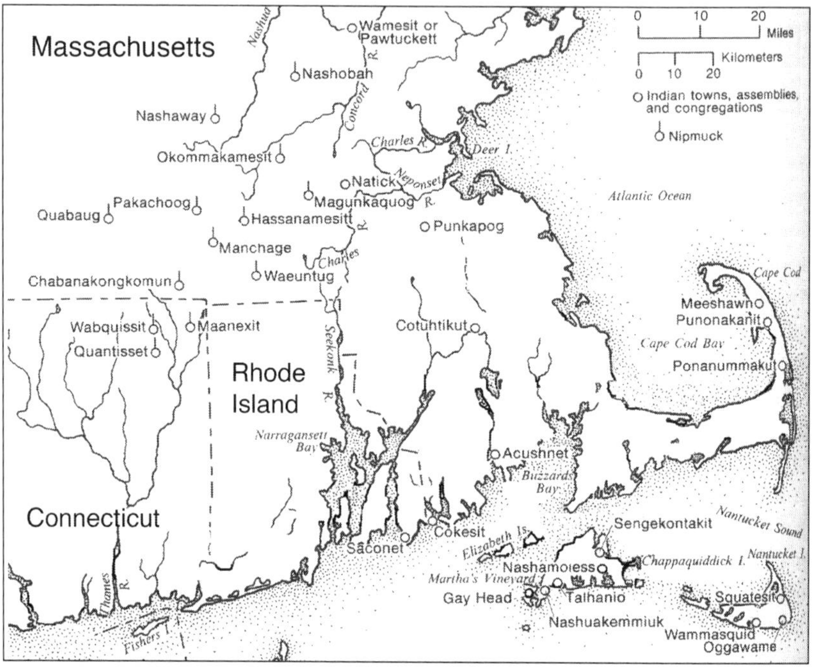

Figure 8.1 Seventeenth-century Christian Indian Communities in New England (Adapted from Conkey, Boissevain and Goddard 1978).

happen during the latter stages of the seventeenth century (Cogley 1999:9–22). This process was to follow a particular path, with Jews and Muslims converting first. Like many religious figures of this period, Eliot was not sure where the native peoples of North America fit into this larger scheme. Therefore, he chose a particular path for their conversion beginning with their adopting English cultural practices. This was the primary purpose of what would come to be called the "Praying Indian" communities of Massachusetts and Connecticut. The outbreak of war in 1675 between the native peoples of southern New England and the English, commonly known as King Philip's War, temporarily put a halt to Eliot's work. Once the war ended in 1676, he returned to establishing such communities. Eventually, he helped found a total of 14 settlements; however, most of the original seven communities had their daily lives severely disrupted by the war.

Historians (e.g., Calloway 1997; Cogley 1999; Kellaway 1961; O'Brien 1997, 2010; Wyss 2000) and archaeologists (Brenner 1980, 1986; Carlson 1986; Handsman 2003) have written much about this period, focusing on issues such as the disposition of indigenous lands as a result of colonization, indigenous use of writing, and the inability of archaeologists to discover any remains of the Christian Indian settlements until quite recently. Although each of these topics provides an important vantage point from which to examine the history of colonization and entanglement, for the purposes of this chapter I focus more narrowly on the particular histories surrounding the communities of Magunkaquog and Hassanemesit.

Magunkaguog

Magunkaguog, which never had been much larger than 50 to 60 people, never regained its prewar vitality, although it seems to have remained viable until the middle of the eighteenth century (Mrozowski et al. 2005, 2009). Evidence for the later history of Magunkaquog is less clear than the events surrounding its establishment. There is real drama in this history, which reveals the deep fissures within a community that was making efforts to cope with a changing world. The impacts of European exploration and fishing during the sixteenth century and the eventual colonization of New England by the Dutch and English during the seventeenth century involved disease, warfare, and general cultural dislocation. By the middle of the seventeenth century, when Eliot's efforts began, the indigenous peoples of New England understood the seriousness of the threat Europeans represented well enough to begin entertaining the possibility of converting to Christianity.

At the conclusion of King Philip's War, the English governments of both the Massachusetts and Connecticut colonies moved to limit the control the remaining Native American communities had over their own destinies. Most important, they passed laws establishing boards of overseers for each Native American community with responsibilities to handle the legal and commercial affairs of the various groups and then dole out the proceeds of land sales and other economic activities to the native inhabitants. Both Magunkaquog and Hassanamesit worked with overseers, but there is little in the documentary record concerning Magunkaquog before the eventual takeover of the community's lands by Harvard College (today Harvard University). The documentary evidence that does exist reveals a complex set of entanglements characterized by struggle, duplicity, and general inequality. More detailed discussions of these histories, their production, and implications can be read elsewhere (Herbster 2005; Law 2008; Law et al. 2008; Law-Pezzarossi 2014; Mrozowski et al. 2005, 2009); however for the purposes of this discussion, I focus on a single event in 1715 concerning the disposition of Magunkaquog lands after King Philip's War: Harvard College's acquisition of the Magunco Lands, as they were called. Harvard leased some of this land to English settlers to provide the college with income. The archaeological discovery of what I believe was the meeting house/fair house at Magunkaquog—the community did not have a church, as was the case at both Natick and Hassanamesit—suggests that some of the community's residents remained on the land after this purchase (Mrozowski et al. 2005, 2009). Before addressing this history, however,

I focus first on the archaeological evidence from Magunkaquag before returning to the documented later history of the settlement.

The excavations conducted at Magunco Hill revealed the remains of a dry-laid foundation purposely built into the hillside so that one floor of the building could be entered from the ground while a second lower room/cellar could be accessed through an opening on the southwest, downhill side of the yard (Figures 8.2, 8.3). Excavations of the foundation and surrounding yard unearthed a rich assemblage of material culture that extended into a small yard area north of the foundation. Much of the assemblage was composed of items manufactured in Europe, primarily Britain. There is also a small but highly significant collection of artifacts that exhibit evidence of native technology. Based on the manufacturing dates of the ceramics discovered on the site and other diagnostic artifacts, it appears to have been established sometime during the second half of the seventeenth century—documents suggest circa 1669—with occupation ending by the middle of the eighteenth century (Mrozowski et al. 2005, 2009).

No evidence of an interior hearth was unearthed during our excavations of the foundation. The remains of a fairly substantial hearth were discovered immediately southwest of the foundation that contained charred faunal remains and a substantial assemblage of lithic debitage. Much of the debitage appears to be the remains of quartz cobbles that were heated and worked. The assemblage of European items recovered from inside the foundation,

Figure 8.2 Foundation believed to be Magunkaquog meeting house (Magunco Hill Site), Ashland, Massachusetts

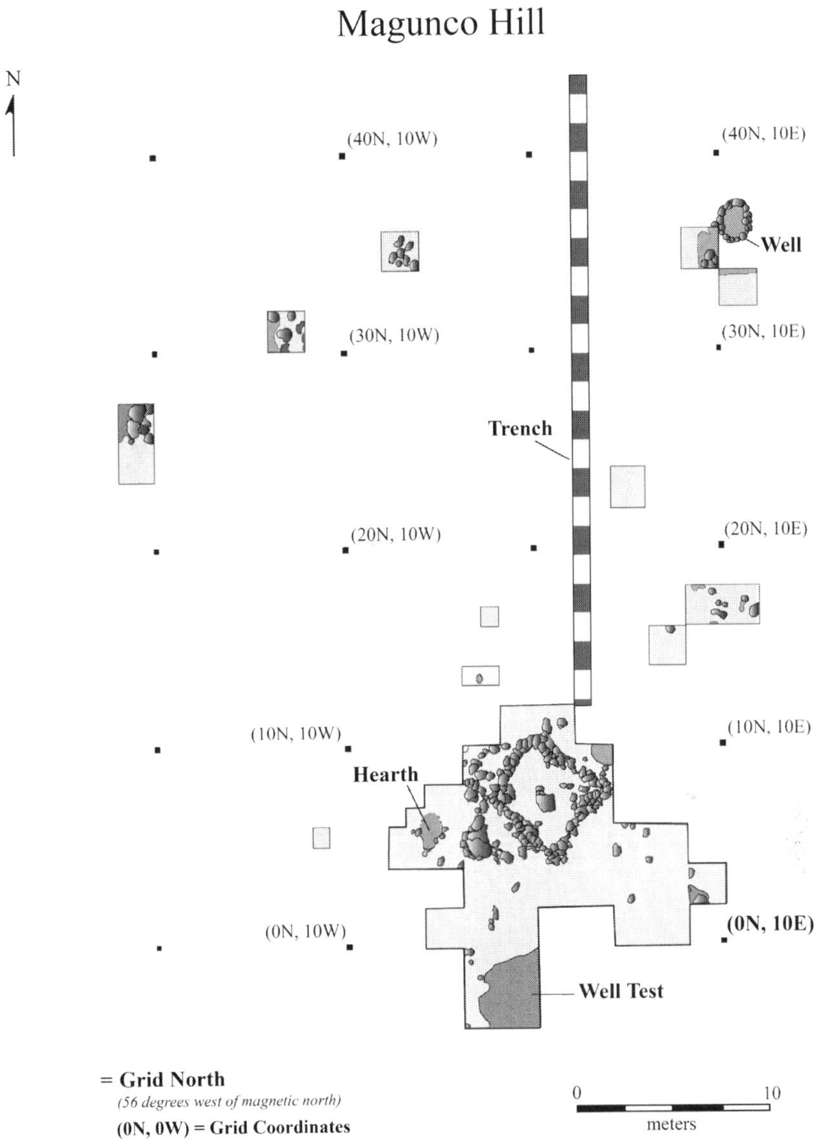

Figure 8.3 Magunco Hill site plan, Ashland, Massachusetts

and the yard area to the south of the structure, suggest that the structure served as the community's meetinghouse. In his description of Natick, Eliot referenced a "fair house" as a place where valuables would have been stored (Whitfield 1834 [1652]:138–143; a fair house referred to a well-built, substantial structure in seventeenth-century England [Steane 2004:50–51]). It seems safe to assume that Eliot would have considered the English material culture stored in such a building valuable. The material culture recovered from the site includes items associated with furniture such as bed curtain rings, ornamental chair tacks, and matching drawer pulls for a chest with possibly a single drawer. Harness hardware from both a saddle and bridle were also recovered as well as a discrete assemblage of eight identical thimbles. Much of the remaining assemblage included ceramics, glassware, faunal material, and lithic artifacts including several gunflints, quartz debitage, and quartz crystals (Mrozowski et al. 2005, 2009).

It is possible that the foundation discovered on Magunco Hill also could have served as a dwelling for either Ponhamen or Job, the religious leader and teacher for the community, respectively. Or could it have been used as a gathering place where young native women were taught how to sew, as evidenced by the thimbles (Loren and Beaudry 2006:258)? As a central place in the settlement, the meetinghouse would have served many purposes, but chief among them appears to be an outward expression of English ways. In some respects, one might expect that of all the locations in the settlement, this had the closest appearance to an English building. This assertion is based on the dearth of evidence for Native American structures in southern New England that used stone foundations. Instead, most Native structures used wooden support posts without foundations of any kind, calling into question whether the stone foundation could be that of a Native structure. However, the recovery of quartz crystals purposely placed in three corners of the foundation strongly counters this assumption. These crystals were extracted from larger quartz cobbles heated in a hearth immediately outside the foundation. If the building on Magunco Hill served as a teaching place for the most pious of their community, the presence of the crystals suggests that the lessons here were steeped in a native spirituality of great antiquity, possibly as deep as 4,000 years ago (Mrozowski 2013).

We can easily interpret the bulk of material culture recovered from the foundation as an English household. Yet the presence of quartz crystals, as well as an assemblage of quartz gunflints that Luedtke (1999, 2000) and Murphy (2002) both ascribe to native lithic traditions, reveal a more complex picture. Murphy's analysis clearly links the quartz crystals at Magunkaguog to spiritual and religious practices in southern New England at least 4,000 years ago. The adoption of specific technologies such as metal cooking vessels and English ceramic pots by Native groups throughout southern New England (see Bradgon 1996; Crosby 1988) represents actions designed to incorporate new elements into a cultural lexicon with deep, but not static, historical roots. In the minds of those adopting the technology, the goal was to maintain identity, not relinquish it. Part of that identity seems to have included embracing beliefs that actions taken in the present paid homage to a deeper past while simultaneously sowing the seeds of a continuing future. In this regard, the crystals placed in the foundation represent an informative example of the multidimensional character of things and places, histories and spaces. It also suggests the residents of Magunkaquog had a view of time as a continuous part of life in which past, present, and future were intertwined.

There is, however, tragic irony in the placement of crystals, entangling past and present in this one space, and the future that would unfold after their deposition. The documentary record concerning Harvard's negotiations to purchase the Magunkaquog lands points to fissures in the greater Massachusetts indigenous community concerning the sale. The purchase of the property is fairly well documented because Harvard had been granted a bequest that provided them with funds as long as they were used to promote English colonization of the area. In ingenious fashion Harvard used the funds to purchase lands that it then leased to English colonists, thereby providing them with an income while adhering to the requirements of the gift they had received (Mrozowski et al. 2009:435–438). Fifteen residents of Natick signed the final deed for the transaction, noted to have taken place on October 15, 1715; however, in the same month a group of Natives from Magunkaquog sent a letter to Samuel Sewell, who was in charge of the negotiations for Harvard, expressing their misgivings about the sale of the land: "Mr. most hai and ounorabol Samuel Sewell and all the gentlemon that is With you we had the touwn meting Monday last we desire you [consl] us that We are poor indias we are not will to sal our landes or debate with it in any ways" (Sewall 1973:801–802). The day after the agreement was signed, Sewell was informed that one of the signatories, Issac Nehemiah, had hanged himself with his own belt. The struggles evident in such an event were felt by many of the Christian community's residents including Ponampam, one of the religious leaders of Magunkaquog. He expressed his own ambivalence when questioned by Eliot as part of a program to record the convert's proclamations of faith. Ponampam stated: "When you (Eliot) always came to us ... I found that al my doings were sins against God ... I saw that in every thing I did, I sinned: & when I saw these sins against God ... I was weary of my self, & angry with my self in my heart" (cited in Wyss 2000:26).

The ambivalence and struggle expressed by Magunkaquog's religious leader seems consistent with the presence of crystals in seeking to continue entanglements with a deeper past and older religious practices. The "stickiness" (see Hodder 2012:94) of the crystals and their association with a living space remained powerful enough to have them incorporated into a novel set of religious and cultural practices that converged at Magunkaquog. Combined with European material culture that was itself used in ways more consistent with indigenous foodways, the archaeological remains at Magunkaquog provide an example of the multidimensional character of such entanglements that linked people, place, and history in such a manner that it contributed to its initial, yet subsequently truncated, historical gravity.

Hassanamesit

The sale of much of Hassanamesit to white settlers in 1727 resulted in the allotment of land parcels to prominent members of the remaining Hassanamesit community in what is today Grafton, Massachusetts. One such plot was allotted in 1727 to the daughter of a Nipmuc leader, a woman named Sarah Robins and her Narragansett husband Peter Muckamugg. The history of these 106 acres is a testament to the persistence of Sarah's family and the larger native community at Hassanamesit (Figure 8.4).

The size and orientation of the Muckamugg lot, like that of other Nipmuc lots visible on the map illustrating the 1727 reallotment, is markedly different from the numbered lots allotted to English colonists. I believe these different orientations reflect earlier settlement patterns that may be linked to a deeper landscape, one whose historical gravity resulted in its continued entanglement with Nipmuc life in the eighteenth and nineteenth centuries. By tracing the ownership of the land from 1727 to 1837, when the death of Robins's great-granddaughter Sarah Boston appears to have marked the end of daily occupation of the property, it is clear that several generations of Nipmuc women observed a strong tradition of matrilineal naming and inheritance of land. The land passed from Robins to her daughter Sarah Muckamugg, from Muckamugg to her daughter Sarah Burnee, and finally to Burnee's daughter

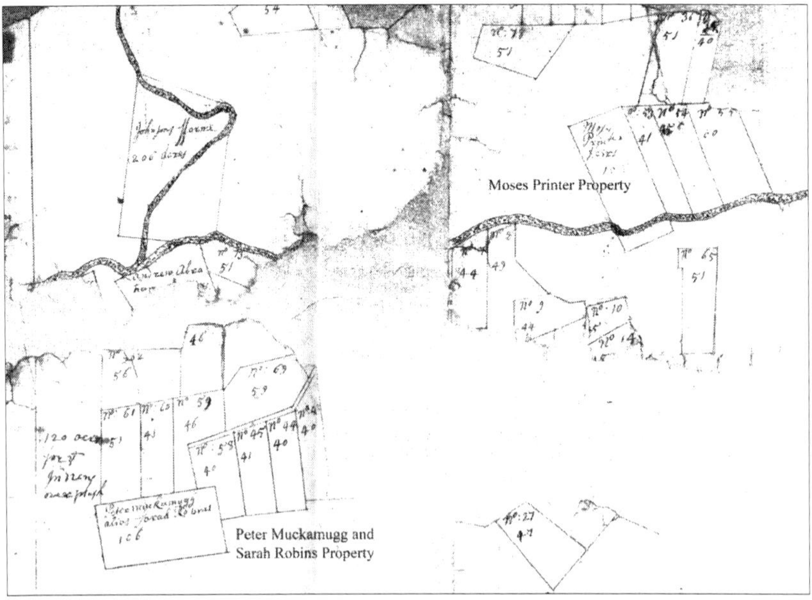

Figure 8.4 1727 land redistribution map, including Peter Muckamugg and Sarah Robins's lot as well as the Moses Printer property

Sarah "Boston" Phillips. These women all faced aggressive colonial land encroachment in the form of patriarchal challenges to their matrilineal rights. Racial and class distinctions of the time further challenged their gender roles, yet they persisted on the land for more than 125 years after the colonial campaign targeted them in earnest.

As was the case at Magunkaquog, the bulk of the material culture recovered from the site is of English or European manufacture, and much of it was recovered either from within or in the yard of a single stone foundation (Figure 8.5).

Figure 8.5 Foundation of the Sarah Burnee/Sarah Boston Farmstead, Grafton, Massachusetts

These similarities do not extend to the size of the material assemblage recovered from the two sites: more than 120,000 artifacts have been recovered from the Sarah Burnee/Sarah Boston farmstead. The overwhelming majority of the site materials dates to roughly 1750 to 1850, but is much more tightly associated with a period of between 1770 and 1830. There are a few items dating to the late seventeenth century, including a single silver-plated spoon and a small, but consistent assemblage that dates to the mid-eighteenth century. Therefore, the bulk of the site assemblage dates to the periods of the Sarah Burnee and Sarah Boston households. The large number of eating utensils, serving dishes, and drinking vessels—many more than are normally found on Anglo sites—combined with the faunal assemblage suggest that the household served as a community gathering place for the local Hassanamisco (Allard 2010; Law 2008; Law et al. 2008; Pezzarossi 2014; Pezzarrosi et al. 2012). This interpretation is also supported by Rae Gould's investigation of the Printer property, which became the focus of Nipmuc gatherings starting in the mid-nineteenth century and continues to serve as the tribal reservation today (Gould 2010; Mrozowski et al. 2015). The Printer lot also was illustrated on the 1727 allotment map (Figure 8.3) and, like the Muckamugg lot, was much larger than the numbered lots for English use.

Although the majority of the material culture recovered from the Sarah Burnee/Sarah Boston farmstead was of English and European manufacture, like at Magunkaquog, there was a notable assemblage of lithic artifacts that suggests a deeper entanglement with earlier practices. Of the more than 120,000 artifacts recovered from the site, 216 appear to be of Native manufacture and use (Bagley 2013). These include 169 lithic items, the majority of which are quartz; 17 gunflints made from European flints; and 30 sherds of Native American ceramics. One of the more noteworthy discoveries from the site is the remains of a soapstone crucible or small bowl. The bowl fragments were recovered from a midden that contained European ceramics and other material culture including metals that date to the late late eighteenth/early nineteenth centuries. Precisely how the bowl may have functioned is unclear; however, x-ray fluorescence (XRF) analysis did reveal evidence of both copper and zinc, suggesting the bowl may have been used to heat metal items such as buttons, which were recovered in abundance from the site. Soapstone was used extensively through out eastern North American between approximately 3,900 and 2,600 years before present (BP; Sassaman 1999, 2010). Although there remain questions concerning its use in the processing of mast products (e.g., Hart et al. 2008; Truncer 2004) and its continued use after the development of ceramic technologies (see Sassaman 2010:202–203), its importance is perhaps best exemplified by its intensified inclusion in burial contexts during both the Coburn (ca. 3,550–3,150 years BP) and Orient (ca. 3,150–2,600 years BP) cultural manifestations (Sassaman 2010:203).

Although the precise purpose of the soapstone bowl remains unclear, the presence of metal traces suggests Sarah Burnee and her daughter Sarah Boston used the bowl in the same period of occupation. The broader question is whether this item represents a repurposing of an older vessel found by the site's inhabitants, or whether it represents an example of "presencing," the purposeful transportation of materials known to be associated with ancestors and deposited purposely as a way of entangling past and present. In his discussion of presencing in African contexts, Paul Lane (2013) draws on the work of Keith Ray (1987), who suggests that metal artifacts recovered from archaeological sites represent proxies of ancestors. Could the soapstone bowl represent a similar example of presencing by the Nipmuc, who sought to add to the historical gravity of their homestead by incorporating earlier materials into the daily lives?

Recently completed analysis suggests that the answer to this question is yes. Joseph Bagley, who conducts research as part of the larger Hassanmesit Woods Project, has examined this very question. In his analysis of lithic and ceramic artifacts from the Sarah Burnee/Sarah Boston farmstead, Bagley (2013) concludes that longstanding lithic technologies continued to be used to shape materials such as quartz, which has a long history of use in New England, as well as European flints that appear both as gunflints and as ballast flint. More important, Bagley (2013) argues that many of the Nipmuc homesteads in the area surrounding Hassanemesit were located on parcels that had deep histories of indigenous use. Much of this entanglement revolved around lithic quarries—one of which is a mere 2,000 yards from the Sarah Burnee/Sarah Boston farmstead—that had been used for millennia and appear to have been parts of landscapes that served to ensnare Nipmuc descendants in ways that transcended functionality—the need for lithic materials such as quartz—to incorporate examples of presencing the past as I note earlier in this chapter. In particular, Bagley argues that quartz, including quartz crystals, may have represented a category of material culture that area inhabitants purposefully spread over sites during the eighteenth or nineteenth century as a way of further entangling themselves with their ancestors. Such steps do not represent attempts to maintain cultural continuity in the sense of maintaining ancient technologies in the face of changes brought about by colonialism. Instead, the repurposing of the soapstone bowl, the continuing us of lithic technologies, or the purposeful presencing of homesteads established during the colonial period need to be examined within the broader context of New World studies that demonstrate the innovative character of indigenous populations in adopting new technologies rather than seeing such steps as representing a loss of indigenous identity (e.g., Cornell and Galle 2003; Hayes 2013; Lowawaima 1989; Mills 2008; Mrozowski 2013; Mrozowski et al. 2015; Mrozowski et al. 2009, 2015; Silliman 2009, 2010).

The results from both Magunkaquog and Hassanmesit provide numerous and varied examples of different forms of entanglement and historical gravity. Both communities appear to have been established on properties that had long, but not continuous, occupations that represented long entanglements of history and space. In the case of Hassanemesit, the lithic quarries may have been the key element of the landscape that served to continuously ensnare Nipmuc populations. There was also evidence of earlier occupations at Magunkaquog, but here again, the evidence is not continuous, creating questions concerning the nature of the entanglements and the discontinuous (forgetting) that may or may not affect the power of historical gravity to continue to entangle populations to a particular location. Bagley (2013) openly questions whether links to earlier histories were rediscovered by site inhabitants, or whether the presence of nearby quarries represented a resource that served as the chief reason indigenous populations returned to the area time and time again over the course of some 7,000 to 8,000 years. The use of quartz, in particular quartz crystals, represents yet another example of materials that may represent the catalyst for continuing entanglements. Because their use in indigenous religious practices has a history and geographical scope covering the New World more generally (see Mrozowski 2013), it is more than plausible such materials served as conduits of religious expression that when purposely buried, such as at Magunkaquog, or spread across a site, such as at the Sarah Burnee/Sarah Boston farmstead, may well have represented actions taken to reconnect pasts with presents.

What makes communities such as Magunkaquog and Hassanmesit so intriguing is both their small scale and colonial contexts. Both appear to have served as gathering places for small groups of Nipmuc, but they were not of the scale of much larger, more visible spaces that served as centers of entanglement for long periods of time. This does not make them less important or less informative with regards to what they can tell us about larger processes, but comparing them with larger-scale, better-known examples may be useful in revealing in greater depth the power of entanglement between histories and spaces. To provide such a comparison I briefly return to the well-known site of Stonehenge in Britain as an example of how history and space were purposely entangled to produce the conditions necessary for the accumulation of historical gravity.

Stonehenge

Stonehenge, a Neolithic megalith, is a World Heritage property and has been the focus of human curiosity for millennia. In his recent summary of his and his colleagues' work, Mike Parker Pearson (2012) provides a comprehensive overview of the archaeological investigations conducted at Stonehenge as well as an interesting summary of how the site has been the focus on human activity almost continuously since its initial phase of construction approximately 5,000 years ago. Obviously there is much to this story; however, I want to focus on one comment Parker Pearson makes and its implications concerning entanglement and historical gravity. He states the following: "The designers of that first Stonehenge had big plans ... it wasn't just a unification of people and places, drawing bluestones from an ancestral place of power in Wales, but also a unification of the entire cosmos—the earth, the sun, and the moon" (Parker Pearson 2012:331). This unification of "people and places" and its extension to the cosmos provide a powerful example of historical gravity and the intention on the part of Stonehenge's builders to ensnare and entangle people for centuries to come. Whether its builders were thinking about this kind of time frame is difficult to say, but given their efforts and the edifice they constructed, it seems their aspirations had a long shadow.

Parker Pearson's summary is rich and has tremendous implications for our understanding of the British and European Neolithic and the role of such structures in drawing people together, sometimes in celebration of celestial events, as appears to have been the case at Stonehenge, but also for other social purposes. In his discussion of the sequencing of Stonehenge's construction he leaves little doubt concerning the link between the megalith's early history and the commemoration of the dead (Parker Pearson 2012:309–313). The numerous cremations spread across the site confirm its function as a repository for the dead. There is also ample evidence of the role that Stonehenge and the other earthen structures that comprise the World Heritage Site as gathering places for groups that Parker Pearson believes could have come from southern England, Wales, and possibly further in Britain (2012:328). The work he and his colleagues carried out at Durrington Walls, further along the Avon River from Stonehenge, confirms a village-sized settlement near the earthen structure that likely was a gathering place for large groups of visitors. Their analysis of faunal remains and pottery residues suggests that these gatherings did coincide with celestial events, whose timing was incorporated into Stonehenge's alignment (Parker Pearson 2012:343). What is equally fascinating is the manner in which Parker Pearson documents earlier archaeological excavations at the site, many of which were carried out in the twentieth century (2012:181–198), as well as other evidence of use after the end of formative activity at the site during the Middle Bronze Age that he dates to between 1680 and 1520 BC (2012:311–313). This included evidence of reuse, off and on, from the Middle Bronze Age to the present.

Conclusion

I seriously doubt whether the builders of Stonehenge had in mind that neo-Druids would still see the site as a gathering place some 5,000 years after the beginnings of its construction. Yet, that aspiration has been realized (Bender

1999; Parker Pearson 2012). Even today, Stonehenge remains a gathering place that has captured the world's attention; as such, it represents a historical gravity not unlike that of a black hole in that it draws in whoever comes near it. The cumulative weight of its history serves to enhance its "stickiness," to use Hodder's term (2012:94). Although Hodder is primarily interested in exploring the dependences between people and things, the same sorts of dependences exist between people and specific places, especially those weighted down by history: by the events that have shaped them or unfolded in a specific space. In the examples I discuss here there is ample evidence of people taking actions to purposely entangle themselves and others to specific locations. As was the case at Hassanmesit, the attraction of lithic resources may have been enough to continuously draw the area's inhabitants to the same quarries, apparently even after nonlithic alternatives became available. People continued to use quartz from these quarries to make tools for more than 7,000 years. The extraction of high-quality quartz crystals continues even today at one of the quarries within a mile of the Sarah Burnee/Sarah Boston farmstead (Joseph Bagley, personal communication, 2013). The importance of these lithic materials, such as quartz, for the indigenous peoples of New England is something difficult to appreciate for archaeologists living in the twenty-first century. Yet their white color, workability, and crystalline structure all represent vibrant qualities (see Bennett 2010) that contribute to their stickiness, their attraction, and their continuous entanglement with human societies throughout the New World (Mrozowski 2013) and beyond.

The entanglement of people, things, and spaces throughout history has resulted in the world's archaeological legacy. Archaeologists likely owe a debt of gratitude to the people of the past for so assiduously entangling themselves with things. There are, however, other questions that arise from this notion of entanglement that extend beyond our aspirations to theorize these relationships. In closing, I offer two such points of departure. First, although things have always played an important role in the development of human society, they have also become an immense drain on the resources of the earth. The effort required to transport massive stones from Wales to the Salisbury Plain was done in large measure because its builders sought to "control something akin to the *omphalos*, the navel of the world, or the birthplace of the Gods—the place where the movement of the sun was marked in the land" (Parker Pearson 2012:331; emphasis in original). And as Parker Pearson notes, this was no small enterprise, involving "an entire society, possibly a growing political domain or kingdom" (Parker Pearson 2012:331). Much less physical effort and enterprise was needed to bury the quartz crystals in the cellar at Magunkaquog, but it would be a mistake to believe that the depth of the intent or the aspiration to control the future was any less meaningful or concrete. Whether the same can be said of the 120,000 artifacts recovered from the Sarah Burnee/Sarah Boston farmstead raises other questions concerning the immense productive power of industry to leave the earth awash in material culture. The presence of such a large assemblage, as noted earlier, suggests that the Sarah Burnee/Sarah Boston farmstead served as a gathering place for the local Nipmuc. Yet it also speaks to the entanglement of indigenous peoples with mass-produced goods and the market that facilitated their spread across the earth (see Pezarrossi 2008; Pezarrossi et al. 2012). We should not lose this facet of entanglement and its implications for a world awash in commodities in our search for more refined theories concerning entanglement and historical gravity.

The final point concerns the need to better understand the forces behind such entanglements and their implications for the world's dwindling resources. The historical gravity that contributes to pulling in people to a particular place has helped to support an ever-growing number of urban centers. The dependences that rest at the heart of such communities extend to a global network of energy- and food-producing facilities that cannot be sustained. The cities of modern era offer important vantage points from which to examine issues including global environmental decay, global warming, and the neverending thirst for commodities and energy that fuel these problems (Mrozowski 2012). The conditions that have contributed to historical gravity, its sustainability in some places, and its loss (forgetting) in others, suggest that archaeology's greatest contribution may come in its ability to examine the many futures embedded in the pasts we examine on a regular basis (Mrozowski 2013). The entanglements between pasts, presents, and futures, exemplified by places such as Stonehenge and Magukaquog, represent opportunities for archaeologists to extract from them a notion of where we have been as a species and where we are going: it is this entanglement, between us and our future, that remains our most pressing challenge.

References

Allard, Amalie, 2010. Foodways, Commensality, and Nipmuc Identity: An Analysis of Faunal Remains from Sarah Boston's Farmstead, Grafton, Massachusetts 1790–1840. Unpublished M.A. thesis, Department of Anthropology, University of Massachusetts, Boston.

Bagley, Joseph, 2013. Cultural Continuity in a Nipmuc Landscape. Unpublished M.A. thesis, Department of Anthropology, University of Massachusetts, Boston.

Bender, Barbara, 1999. *Stonehenge: Making Space*. Berg, New York.

Bennett, Jane, 2010. *Vibrant Matter: The Political Ecology of Things*. Duke University Press, Durham, NC.

Bragdon, Kathleen J., 1996. *Native People of Southern New England 1500–1650*. University of Oklahoma Press, Norman.

Brenner, Elise, 1980. To Pray or to Prey: That is the Question, Strategies for Cultural Autonomy of Massachusetts Praying Town Indians. *Ethnohistory* 27(2):135–152.

Brenner, Elise, 1986. Archaeological Investigations at a Massachusetts Praying Indian Town. *Bulletin of the Massachusetts Archaeological Society* 47(2):69–78.

Calloway, Colin, 1997. *After King Philip's War: Presence and Persistence in Indian New England.* University Press of New England, Hanover, NH.

Carlson, Catherine, 1986. Archival and Archaeological Research Report on the Configuration of the Seven Original Seventeenth Century Praying Indian Towns of the Massachusetts Bay Colony. University of Massachusetts Archaeological Services, Amherst.

Cogley, Richard W., 1999. *John Eliot's Mission to the Indians before King Philip's War.* Harvard University Press, Cambridge, MA.

Conkey, Laura E., Ethel Boissevain, and Ives Goddard, 1978. Indians of Southern New England and Long Island: Late Period. In *Handbook of North American Indians: Volume 15, Northeast,* edited by Bruce Trigger, pp. 177–189. Smithsonian Institution, Washington, DC.

Cornell, Per, and Hermann Galle, 2003. El fenómeno Inka y su articulación local: Reflexiones desde el sitio de El Pichao, Valle de Santa María (Tucumán). In *Local, Regional, Global: Prehistoria, protohistoria e historia en los valles calchaquies,* edited by Per Cornell and Per Stenborg, pp. 211–217. Instituto Iberoamericano Universidad de Göteborg, Sweden.

Crosby, Constance A., 1988. From Myth to History, or Why King Philip's Ghost Walks Abroad. In *The Recovery of Meaning: Historical Archaeology in the Eastern United States,* edited by M. P. Leone and P. B. Potter, pp. 193–209. Smithsonian Institution Press, Washington, DC.

Gosden, Christopher, 2001. Postcolonial Archaeological: Issues of Culture, Identity and Knowledge. In *Archaeological Theory Today,* edited by Ian Hodder, pp. 241–226. Polity Press, Cambridge, UK.

Gould, Donna R., 2010. Contested Places: The History and Meaning of Hassanamisco. Unpublished Ph.D. dissertation, Department of Anthropology, University of Connecticut, Mansfield.

Handsman, Russell G., 2003. Towards Archaeological Histories of the Nipmuc Indian Community in the "Lost Century" (1820–1920). In *Indigenous People and Archaeology: Honouring the Past, Discussing the Present, Building for the Future: Proceedings of the 32nd Annual Chacmool Conference,* edited by T. Peck, E. Siegfried, and G. Oetelaar, pp. 28–42. The Archaeological Association of the University of Calgary, Saskatchewan, Canada.

Hart, John P., Eleanora A. Reber, Robert G. Thompson, and Robert Lusteck, 2008. Taking Variation Seriously: Testing the Steatite Mast-Processing Hypothesis with Macrobotanical Data from the Hunter's Home Site, New York. *American Antiquity* 73(4):729–741.

Hayes, Katherine H., 2013. *Slavery Before Race: Europeans, Africans, and Indians on Long Island's Sylvester Manor Plantation, 1651–1821.* New York University Press, New York.

Herbster, Holly, *2005. A Documentary Archaeology of Magunkaquog.* Unpublished M.A. thesis, University of Massachusetts, Boston.

Hodder, Ian, 1990. *The Domestication of Europe.* Blackwell, Oxford, UK.

Hodder, Ian, 2012. *Entangled: An Archaeology of the Relationships Between Humans and Things.* Wiley-Blackwell, Malden, MA.

Kankaanpää, Jarmo, and Tuija Rankama, 2011. Spatial Patterns of the Early Mesolithic Sujala Site, Utsjoki, Finnish Lapland. In *Mesolithic Interfaces: Variability in Lithic*

Technologies in Eastern Fennoscandia, edited by Tuija Rankama, pp. 43–63. Monographs of the Archaeological Society of Finland, Oulu.

Kellaway, William, 1961. *The New England Company 1649–1776: Missionary Society to the American Indians*. Barnes and Noble, New York.

Kelso, William, 2006. *Jamestown: The Buried Truth*. University of Virginia Press, Charlottesville.

Lane, Paul, 2013. Presencing the Past: Implications for Bridging the History-Prehistory Divide. In *The Death of Prehistory*, edited by Peter R. Schmidt and Stephen A. Mrozowski, pp. 47–68. Oxford University Press, Oxford, UK.

Law, Heather, 2008. Daily Negotiations and the Creation of an Alternative Discourse: The Legacy of a Colonial Nipmuc Farmstead. Unpublished M.A. thesis, Department of Anthropology, University of Massachusetts, Boston.

Law, Heather, Guido Pezzarossi, and Stephen A. Mrozowski, 2008. *Archaeological Intensive Excavations: Hassanamesit Woods Property, The Sarah Boston farmstead, Grafton, Massachusetts*. Cultural Resource Management Study No. 26, Andrew Fiske Memorial Center for Archaeological Research, University of Massachusetts, Boston.

Law-Pezzarossi, Heather, 2014. Traces of Residence: Indigenous Mobility and Materiality in 19th c. New England. Unpublished PhD dissertation, Department of Anthropology, University of California, Berkeley.

Lomawaima, Hartman H., 1989. Hopification, a Strategy for Cultural Preservation. In *Columbian Consequences Volume 1: Archaeological and Historical Perspectives on the Spanish Borderlands West*, edited by David H. Thomas, pp. 93–99. Smithsonian Institution Press, Washington, DC.

Loren, Diana D., and Mary C. Beaudry, 2006. Becoming American: Small Things Remembered. In *Historical Archaeology*, edited by M. Hall and S. W. Silliman, pp. 251–271. Blackwell, Malden, MA.

Luedtke, Barbara E., 1999, Gunflints in the Northeast. *Northeast Anthropology* 57:27–43.

Luedtke, Barbara E. 2000. Gunflints from Magunco. Paper presented at the Annual Meeting of the Society for Historical Archaeology, January 4–9, Quebec, Ontario, Canada.

Mills, Barbara, 2008. Colonialism and Cuisine: Cultural Transmission, Agency, and History at Zuni Pueblo. In *Cultural Transmission and Material Culture: Breaking Down Boundaries*, edited by Miriam Stark, Brenda Bowser, and Lee Horne, pp. 245–262. University of Arizona Press, Tucson.

Mrozowski, Stephen A., 2012. Ethnobiology for a Diverse World: Spaces and Natures: Archaeology and the Political Ecology of Modern Cities. *Journal of Ethnobiology* 32(2):129–133.

Mrozowski, Stephen A., 2013. The Tyranny of Prehistory and the Search for a Deeper History. In *The Death of Prehistory*, edited by Peter R. Schmidt and Stephen A. Mrozowski, pp. 220–240. Oxford University Press, Oxford, UK.

Mrozowski, Stephen A., 2014. Imagining an Archaeology of the Future: Capitalism and Colonialism Past and Present. *International Journal of Historical Archaeology* 18(2):340–360.

Mrozowski, Stephen A., D. Rae Gould, and Heather Law Pezzarossi, 2015. Rethinking Colonialism: Indigenous Innovation and Colonial Inevitability. In *Rethinking Colonialism: Comparative Archaeological Approaches*, edited by Katherine

Howlett-Hayes and Craig N. Cipolla, pp. 121–142. Gainsville, FL: University Press of Florida.

Mrozowski, Stephen A., Holly Herbster, David Brown, and Katherine L. Priddy, 2005. Magunkaquog: Native American Conversion and Cultural Persistence. In *Eighteenth-Century Native Communities of Southern New England in the Colonial Context*, edited by J. Campsi, pp. 57–71. The Mashantucket Museum and Research Center, Mashantucket, CT.

Mrozowski, Stephen A., Holly Herbster, David Brown, and Katherine L. Priddy, 2009. Magunkaquog Materiality, Federal Recognition, and the Search for a Deeper History. *International Journal of Historical Archaeology* 13(4):430–463.

Murphy, John. P., 2002. Crystal Quartz from Magunco. Unpublished M.A. thesis, Department of Anthropology, University of Massachusetts, Boston.

O'Brien, Jean M., 1997. *Dispossession by Degrees: Indian Land and Identity in Natick, Massachusetts, 1650–1790*. Cambridge University Press, Cambridge, UK.

O'Brien, Jean M., 2010. *Firsting and Lasting: Writing Indians Out of Existence in New England*. University of Minnesota Press, Minneapolis.

Parker Pearson, Michael, 2012, *Stonehenge: Exploring the Greatest Stone Age Mystery*. Simon and Schuster, London.

Pezzarossi, Guido, 2014. Camouflaging Consumption and Colonial Mimicry: The Materiality of a Colonial Nipmuc Household. *International Journal of Historical Archaeology* 18(1):146–174.

Pezzarossi, Guido, Ryan Kennedy, and Heather Law, 2012. "Hoe Cakes and Pickerel": Cooking Traditions and Community at a Nineteenth Century Nipmuc Farmstead. In *The Menial Art of Cooking: Archaeological Studies of Cooking and Food Preparation*, edited by S. Graff and E. Rodriguez-Alegria, pp. 201–230. University of Colorado Press, Boulder.

Ray, Keith W., 1987. Material Metaphor, Social Interaction and Historical Reconstructions: Exploring Patterns of Association and Symbolism in the Igbo-Ukwu Corpus. In *The Archaeology of Contextual Meanings*, edited by Ian Hodder, pp. 66–78. Cambridge University Press, Cambridge, UK.

Sassaman, Kenneth E., 1999. A Southeastern Perspective on Soapstone Vessel Technology in the Northeast. In *The Archaeological Northeast*, edited by M. A. Levine, K. E. Sassaman, and M. S. Nassaney, pp. 75–95. Bergin and Garvey, Westport, CT.

Sassaman, Kenneth E., 2010. *The Eastern Archaic, Historicized*. AltaMira Press, Lanham, MD.

Sassaman, Kenneth E., 2012. Futurologists Look Back. *Archaeologies* 8(3):250–268.

Sewall, Samuel, 1973. *The Diary of Samuel Sewall, 1674–1729*. Reprinted. Farrar, Strauss, and Giroux, New York. Originally published 1878–1882, Massachusetts Historical Society, Boston.

Silliman, Stephen W., 2009. Change and Continuity, Practice and Memory: Native American Persistence in Colonial New England. *American Antiquity* 74(2):211–230.

Silliman, Stephen W., 2010. The Value and Diversity of Indigenous Archaeology: A Response to McGhee. *American Antiquity* 75(2):217–220.

Steane, Mary A., 2004. Building in the Climate of the New World: A Cultural or Environmental Response. *Traditional Dwellings and Settlements Review* 15(2):49–60.

Thomas, Nicholas, 1991. *Entangled Objects: Exchange, Material Culture, and Colonialism in the Pacific.* Harvard University Press, Cambridge, MA.

Thomas, Nicholas, 1997. *In Oceania: Visions, Artifacts, Histories.* Duke University Press, Durham, NC.

Truncer, James, 2004. Steatite Vessel Age and Occurrence in Temperate Eastern North America. *American Antiquity* 69(3):587–514.

Whitfield, Henry, 1834 (1652). Strength Out of Weakness; or a Glorious Manifestation of the Further Progress of the Gospel among the Indians in New England. Simmons for J. Blague and S. Howes, London. 1834 facsimile edition. *Massachusetts Historical Society Collections* 35(4):149–196.

Wyss, Hilary E., 2000. *Writing Indians: Literacy, Christianity and Native Community in Early America.* University of Massachusetts Press, Amherst.

Chapter 9

Looting: Archaeology's Dirty Little Secret

Lindsay Der

As you may have already surmised from the title of this chapter, what I am about to suggest over the course of my argument is somewhat scandalizing. It will almost surely offend the sensibilities of at least some, if not a good many, archaeologists and outrage others. I only ask that you look beyond what on the surface seems like a completely ludicrous idea—that archaeology is intrinsically and irrevocably entangled with the illicit antiquities market—and consider its merits. Is it counterintuitive that archaeologists, the investigators and caretakers of the ancient past, are culpable in the very system of practices that they decry? Yes, but my point is not to accuse anyone of knowing complicity. Instead, I assert that it is the invisible connective tissues, lurking beneath the surface, between antiquities trafficking and archaeology that are at the root of the problem. More simply stated, these connections are the values that produce and are reproduced by archaeology. If we expand the circle outward, we can see that contemporary social values (largely driven by Western systems) as well as political and economic elements are also entangled in this web.

A Valuable Past

The practice of selling or exporting cultural properties has materially aided the promotion of many important values: the preservation of priceless artifacts, the enrichment of aesthetic sensibilities, the advancement of education and scholarships, the breakdown of parochialism, the encouragement of cultural pluralism, and the role of art as a goodwill ambassador (Warren 1989).

The single most crucial link between archaeology and the black market for antiquities is forged from the belief that the past is valuable. This notion is fundamental to the justification of the existence of archaeology. Without value, the past has no worth (either tangibly or intangibly), so there is no reason to research it or to attempt to understand ancient societies. Archaeology

Archaeology of Entanglement edited by Lindsay Der and Francesca Fernandini, 215–234

as a discipline grew out of a fascination with old things. Enthusiastic collectors, such as Augustus Pitt-Rivers, accumulated artifacts and were curious about the histories behind these objects. Although interest and worth attributed to the past led to the creation of archaeology as a science, archaeology in turn produced and reinforced the idea that the past was something worth knowing. As Chip Colwell-Chanthaphonh (2004:575) notes, "When people begin to see objects not merely as things, but as things past, objects become imbued with new and special meanings." This circular feedback system is further complicated by a bidirectional connection between archaeology and antiquities (Figure 9.1). Archaeology is only possible so long as there are artifacts to study: it is a thing-based science. Artifacts as we know them (as opposed to considering these objects garbage, natural parts of the landscape, etc.) only exist with the classification and special status that archaeology ascribes them. Furthermore, archaeologists excavate and identify artifacts on a practical level.

The past intersects with values in many different ways: the collecting of artifacts may be a way to engage in identity building, to connect to one's ancestors, or as a way to gain knowledge and satisfy curiosity. Through artifacts, we may satisfy these intangible values in a tangible way. They are a conduit through which to interact with the inalienable (Hollowell 2006). Inalienable possessions are embedded with memory and endure through time; as such, they may be linked to the valuation of stability in a fast-paced, changing world. According to Weiner (1992:33), they are "symbolic repositories of genealogies and historical events ... their unique, subjective identity gives them absolute value." It is this authority derived from the past that makes antiquities inalienable and highly sought. And, if we follow the strands of Weiner further,

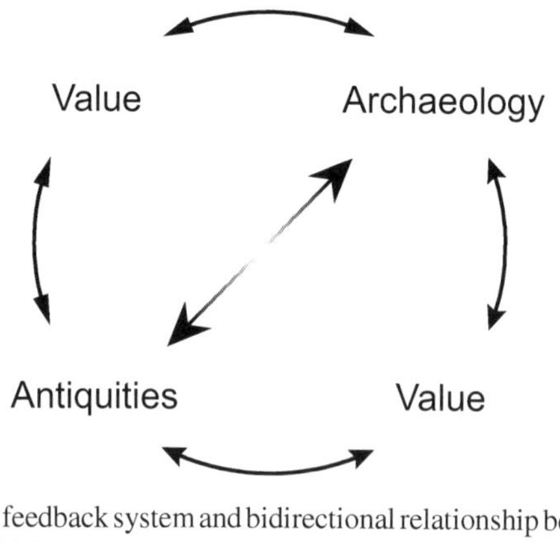

Figure 9.1 Circular feedback system and bidirectional relationship between archaeology and antiquities. This bidirectionality is representative of the interdependencies between the two elements.

we may conclude that antiquities, once possessed and transformed into private property, are often returned only under extenuating circumstance. For instance, many museums are reluctant to relinquish looted goods within their collections unless forced by public pressure, legislation, or legal battles. In the case of subsistence looters who often belong to source communities, the lack of alternative economic means creates a situation in which antiquities must be sold for income (Hollowell 2006).

Furthermore, there are cultural values of adventurism, mystery, fame, and the thrill of discovery associated with commonly held ideas of archaeology as treasure hunting. In this sense, looting is sensationalized. The quest for that "special find" and the resulting prestige may even overtake hard profits as a driving factor for unauthorized digging (Early 1989). Western ideals maintain that cultural property is universally owned and thus should be accessible by all peoples. These ideals may often be invoked to justify the exhibition, study, or removal of antiquities from their home countries through illegal channels. Even the perception that looting is a negative act is a value judgment. To someone outside our own sphere of morality, there may well be no obvious difference between archaeological excavations and looting (Stuart 1989). Pyburn (2003:214) tells us that "all archaeological sites are endangered," but are they really? That is a subjective, value-loaded statement that positions archaeological sites as needing to be saved from something else. It is only our own values, formed in relation to our own society and culture, that tell us to care about looting! This in turn is connected to the assumed universal significance of antiquities, which in and of itself is a projection of our own ethics onto others. This privileging of the past and its subsequent need to be protected is a product of our present time. For instance, the development of excavation as a systematic and recorded investigation with the goal of retaining the maximum amount of information, regardless of personal research questions, is relatively recent. In comparison, the tunneling and massive trenching carried out by earlier archaeologists, such as Heinrich Schliemann, showed little regard for the preservation of sites and context. Likewise, after World War II there was a significant increase in interest in cultural and ancient property that is often linked to the emergence of the antiquities black market (Bator 1988). In addition, the capitalist economies of Western countries facilitate the free market system within which antiquities are legally sold (Herscher 1989). This market then helps to create the socially acceptable ideology that old things have monetary value, which in turn creates impetus for looting and trafficking of illicit goods. One striking example of this contemporary ideology is presented in the Public Broadcasting Service (PBS) program *Antiques Roadshow*, on which everyday citizens have their family heirlooms and collections appraised by consultants from auction houses. Episodes routinely feature historical artifacts both foreign and domestic, including Native American crafts, Egyptian bronzes, and Civil War documents; frequently these objects are of unknown provenance. The exoticization of archaeology into a treasure-hunting and commercial endeavor has proven popular appeal, breeding even more controversial television programs such as Spike TV's *American Digger* and the National Geographic Channel's *Diggers*. These latter two television series have met with widespread condemnation from the archaeological community for their promotion of the commodification of artifacts and what many see as the glorification of digging and high potential for looting (see Limp 2012a, 2012b). It is clear that many kinds of values anchor the chains of entanglements that proliferate in the trade of illicit antiquities, but who are the agents embedded in these chains? I now turn to a consideration of the people caught up in the web of the black market.

Major Players

Collectors

Although the role that archaeologists play in enabling looting is somewhat below the radar, there are many players in the trafficking of artifacts who are more overtly involved. The first of these is the private collector who creates demand for antiquities and thus the belief that they hold value. He or she may be an amateur archaeologist. For sure, both the discipline and its related institutions have their forefathers in the form of collectors (see Impey and MacGregor 1985). Museums in particular have been established by and continue to rely upon the donation and loan of artifacts. Bator (1988) notes that collectors sometimes pursue the kinds of things that museums have not yet recognized as having value so they can diversify the antiquities being traded and also provide a potential source to supplement future museum collections. If private collectors and museums are so closely intertwined, isn't the difference between collectors creating exhibits or acquiring antiquities and museums engaging in the same activities just an abstraction? Somehow, it seems more legitimate and laudable when museums do it, but this is a false impression that points to the elite and privileged position of academia and public institutions. Moreover, consider that the Western mode of science practiced by archaeology is but one type of knowledge system. That it is the dominant (in terms of both the legal and social) way of knowing (as opposed to other systems such as traditional ecological knowledge) is a function of differential power relations telling us that archaeologists are "the experts"; that is, archaeologists are ultimately privileged based on a system that revolves around scientific ontology. As Griffin points out, "The archaeologist and the collectors are embarked, essentially, on the same journey. Both assemble materials and attempt to deduce from them certain ideas about ancient American civilizations" (1989:103). Both claim that they are fulfilling their roles as guardians of ancient artifacts; it is that overlap in roles that leads to the blurred lines between expert and hobbyist.

Institutions

Conservation is a justification that institutions such as museums frequently point to for the acquisition and/or exhibition of looted artifacts. Even when looting results in the mutilation of antiquities during the process of removal, some may argue this is still better than in situ preservation. The clout and resources that institutions command and have at their disposal can at times far outweigh the resources available on the ground in conflict- or poverty-stricken countries rich in archaeological materials. It is this great discrepancy between the West and the rest of the world that gives museums the power and the money that feed the illicit antiquities trade and eventually the destruction of sites. The very existence of these monolithic institutions, devoted to the display and admiration of old things, again points to the value that we as a society ascribe to the past. These objects have so much potency that we have produced dedicated structures (both physically and socially) within which to house them. The field of archaeology has certainly spurred the erection and growth of an increasing number of museums. It has furnished them with materials, information, and staff. Museums serve the archaeological mantra that cultural heritage is universally owned, that the past has an educational value, and that artifacts need to be kept safe.

The relationship between museums and looting is interdependent, like that between archaeology and antiquities (Figure 9.2). Museums pump cash into the illicit market and the looted artifacts, in return, generate income and

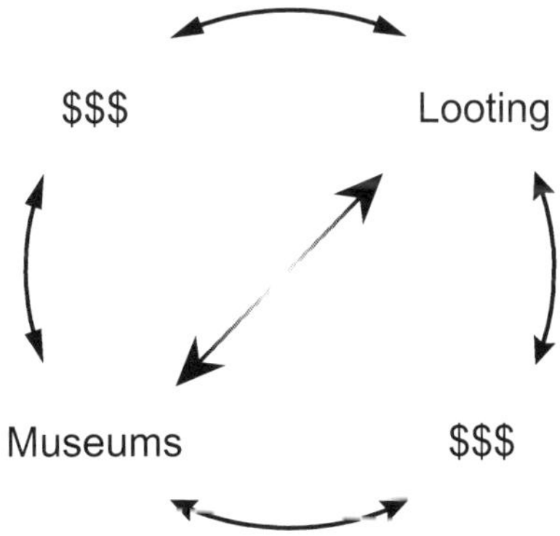

Figure 9.2 Relationship between museums and looting. Each generates income for the other. Compare with the interdependent relationship between archaeology and antiquities (Figure 9.1).

net worth for museums. To illustrate how pervasive this liaison is, we have only to consider the assertion of John D. Cooney, curator at the Cleveland Art Museum in 1972, that "95% of all antiquities in the United States had been smuggled" (Brodie et al. 2000:8). In addition, the exhibition of stolen goods by museums is akin to "academic laundering": it is a way to legitimize the illegitimate via unspoken endorsement and complicity (Renfrew 2000). The museums in the United States alone that have dealt with illicit antiquities reads like a laundry list of high-profile stakeholders: the Cleveland Art Museum, the Houston Museum of Fine Arts, the Minneapolis Institution of Art, the Brooklyn Museum, Nelson Rockefeller's Museum of Primitive Art, Boston's Museum of Fine arts, the J. Paul Getty Museum, and the Metropolitan Museum of Art in New York (Bator 1988).

Despite ethical guidelines of associations such as the International Council of Museums (ICOM), many museums continue to engage in licentious acquisition schemes, often in violation of their own official policies. One such example that made headlines concerns the Getty Museum and the scandal surrounding the notorious dealer Giacomo Medici. Italian authorities alleged that Marion True, a curator at the Getty Museum, had engaged in a conspiracy with Medici and his partner to traffic and purchase looted antiquities (Povoledo 2009). During her time at the Getty, True had implemented a strict acquisition policy and had actively repatriated several stolen pieces. Yet, it seems that the allure of certain artifacts may have been too tempting for True to resist. Similarly, the Boston Museum of Fine Arts has had an ethical acquisition code in place since 1983, but has since then faced accusations of adding antiquities of questionable provenance to its collections, including a donation of looted Maya pottery in 1996 (Brodie et al. 2000). It is clear that museums value public perception in their adoption of collections policies. However, this same public perception spawns the reality that museums are in constant competition for patrons. The livelihoods of curators and directors are directly related to the prestige, money, and reputation of an institution, which makes for a high-pressure atmosphere in which the refusal of looted goods may amount to "professional suicide" (Mackenzie 2011).

This contradiction is then defended by the values that compete with the principle of looting as a negative act. These values include the "rescuing" of artifacts from the hands of private collectors or poor source communities, the accessibility of cultural heritage to all peoples, and the physical preservation of archaeological materials. It is made easier by ignorance, willful or otherwise, of the provenance or documentation of acquisitions. Museums affiliated with universities, such as Dumbarton Oaks, a Harvard University institution in Washington, D.C., also have a storied history of enriching their collections with illegal artifacts (Matsuda 1998). Institutions host archaeologists, scholars, and conservators whose consultation may augment the monetary and historic value of objects through their authentication. In return for their silence and complicity, these people may receive funding or access to research materials, as in the case of one University of Oxford laboratory paid to date illicit Malian ceramics (Brodie et al. 2000).

Auction Houses

Auction houses also authenticate provenance while simultaneously laundering dirty antiquities into the legal market with relative ease (Hollowell 2006; Prott 1983). A quantitative study of Sotheby's and Christie's revealed that between 1958 and 1998, almost 90% of antiquities sold had not been known before auction, and that 95% had no archaeological information (Chippindale et al. 2001). Auction houses, as private for-profit businesses, are essentially left to police themselves. Monitoring the backgrounds of the innumerous things that pass through their doors is not good business, especially given the statistics suggesting a high proportion of auctioned objects may have links to the black market. This likelihood is supported by British journalist Peter Watson's 1997 book in which a former cataloguer for Sotheby's, James Hodges, reveals that Sotheby's dealt with numerous dirty dealers on an international scale. Notably, the auction house, along with the same Giacomo Medici implicated in the Getty scandal, are alleged to have knowingly trafficked unprovenanced antiquities from Italy to Switzerland and then finally to Sotheby's in London in a multimillion dollar plot (Watson 1997). Finally, in March 2015, Sotheby's acknowledged it must shoulder some of the responsibility in preventing the future circulation of illicit cultural objects, bowing to soft pressure and joining a United Nations Educational, Scientific and Cultural Organization (UNESCO) coalition for the prevention of archaeological trafficking (UNESCO 2015).

The Criminal Element

High profit margins with relatively little risk compared with other black markets (for example, the drug trade) lure shifty characters such as Medici to traffic antiquities. A 2013 UNESCO report estimates the overall value of the antiquities market at US$60 billion, with the most recent figures for the illicit sector at more than US$6 billion in 2000 (UNESCO 2013). Such a valuation gives the illicit trafficking of antiquities the dubious honor of being one of the top five transnational crimes, falling only behind the movement of arms, drugs, and counterfeiting (World Customs Organization 2015). Nonetheless, this figure is likely under-represented because data are difficult to obtain for underground activities and are based only on known criminal activities. The structure of the antiquities trade is unique in that goods are laundered in the gray market, where illegal and legal acquisitions comingle (Campbell 2013; Dietzler 2013; Mackenzie 2011; Proulx 2011). It is here that the appearance and documentation of looted items can be

Figure 9.3 Chain through which antiquities, which must be illicitly obtained (due to legal restrictions such as export laws), flow. Is this any different than the flows of drugs or human trafficking?

manipulated to give the appearance of legitimacy. Further, the large quantity of unprovenanced items moving through venues such as auction houses is conducive to another crime, forgery (Bator 1988; Bauer 2007; Brodie et al. 2000; Prott 1983). The chains of players and conditions (such as the lack of a legal market for looted material) involved in the trafficking of artifacts create a structural organization susceptible to organized crime (Bonn-Muller 2010; Mackenzie 2011; see Figure 9.3). In this flow of goods, the law may be continually violated or circumvented through means such as bribery of corrupt government officials.

What's more, the illicit antiquities market is caught up in other types of organized crime. Drug bosses may use artifacts to launder cash or to buy product (Mackenzie 2011). One such smuggling ring was busted in Spain in 1999 after criminals attempted to trade artifacts for cocaine (Brodie et al. 2000). Seizures of weapons, narcotics, and cultural property often occur together. Matsuda (1998) contends that Belizean marijuana growers use looting as a supplemental source of income, one that can be quickly mobilized into a full-fledged operation in the event that their cannabis supply is interrupted. On a smaller scale, individual methamphetamine addicts have turned to digging up Native American artifacts. Coined "twiggers" (a combination of "tweakers" and "diggers") by law enforcement, the American authorities note this is an increasingly pervasive problem aided by the ease with which these types of objects can be fenced (Patel 2009).

Conflict and Inequality

Unsavory connections to the illicit trade of cultural property abound even more when we consider not just the human players, but also the sociopolitical factors. As Patron observes, "economic strife and political unrest exacerbate the profit-driven looting market" (2008:467). Political dissension and mistrust of the government may trigger communities to deliberately participate in looting. For instance, Migliore (1991) asserts that Sicilian looters believe that the Italian government is conspiring to sell antiquities to rich foreigners, and that this is the real reason for excavation regulations, so they take no issue in unearthing artifacts themselves.

Another way that power comes into play is apparent in how the actual diggers of looted materials receive nominal compensation even though they

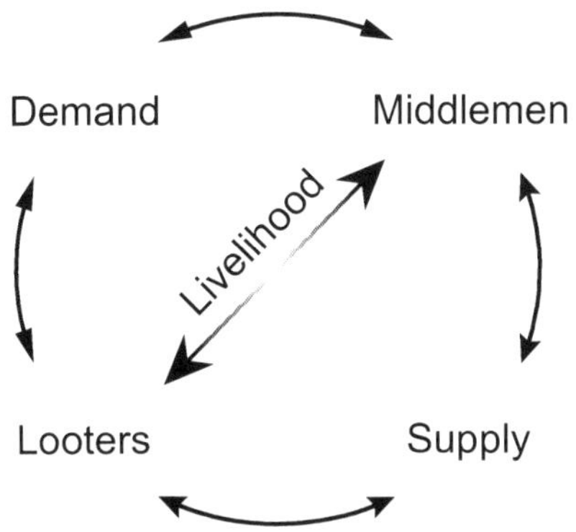

Figure 9.4 Interdependent relationship between looters and middlemen

absorb the highest degree of risk (since prosecution and penalties for the actual act of removal from the ground are generally much greater than those for violating export/import laws). According to Brodie, approximately 98% of the final sale price goes into the pockets of middlemen (1998). This results in a vicious circle in which the on-the-ground looters, who are typically poor and without alternative sources of income, are exploited by middlemen; they are never able to make enough money to remove themselves from the chain but are instead dependent on the middlemen who pay their salaries. The middlemen, in return, become dependent on laborers to supply them with product. The livelihoods of both players are interdependently connected (Figure 9.4).

The illicit trade of cultural property involves unequal power relations not just at the level of middlemen and looters, but also at the international level. Artifacts most predominantly move from poor, developing, or conflict-stricken nations to developed, wealthy, and stable ones. This discrepancy in power and wealth creates chains of supply and demand as consumers in privileged positions have the luxury of acquiring possessions of want, rather than merely of need. One ongoing case in point is the looting of Iraq. After the Gulf War, there was a sudden flood of Iraqi artifacts onto the antiquities market that correlated with the disappearance of more than 3,000 items from that country's regional museums (Brodie et al. 2000). Likewise, since the 2003 U.S.-led invasion of Iraq, approximately US$10 million to $20 million worth of Iraqi antiquities has entered the international market each year (Patron 2008). The common thread here is that war has left Iraq without the infrastructure and authoritative government to enact the strict anti-looting policies that previous regimes had executed. These circumstances are coupled with economic strife directly related to conflict and unrest, so many civilians have no alternative but to engage in subsistence digging (Adams 2005). Iraq's instability has also led to the increasing forays of terrorist networks into the illicit cultural property market. In 2005, 9/11 terrorist Mohammed Atta attempted to sell artifacts to facilitate his purchase of an airplane, and Marine Reserve Colonel Matthew Bogdanos maintains that al-Qaeda, Shiite militias, and Hezbollah all fund their operations with dirty antiquities, along with ransom kidnappings and extortion fees (Becatoros 2008; Bogdanos 2008).

Ten years later, it seems little has changed; the repatriation of items continues as American agencies work to dismantle organized trafficking networks with connections to prominent cultural institutions (Northam 2015). The theft and desecration of cultural property continues to occur in Iraq and the Middle East although it is now the Islamic State (IS or DAESH) who is brazenly making headlines (*Al Jazeera* 2015; Lawler 2015). The ravaging of the archaeological sites of Hatra, Nimrud, Nineveh, and Khorsabad along with the pillaging of the Mosul Museum have served simultaneously as war crimes in the erasure of the culture, identity, and history of the Iraqi people; as weapons of propaganda for the doctrine of Islamic State extremism; and as a means to generate revenue for terrorist activities. (A British Broadcasting Corporation [BBC] investigation traced the movement of artifacts looted and sold by IS, uncovering a middleman who described antiquities stolen from Aleppo and fetching prices as high as $US1 million [Cox 2015].) In this show of force, the Islamic State has asserted its power and dominance in the region.

Subsistence Looting

As I briefly mention in the previous section, subsistence looting is linked to oppression, unequal power relations, civil unrest, and poverty. It may also be connected to land speculation, limited business opportunities, displacement from traditional lands, colonialism, and class (Matsuda 1998). Archaeologists may themselves unintentionally trigger this practice, as in the case of the St. Lawrence Islands. There, indigenous beliefs about the dead initially prevented digging. However, after the archaeologists Otto Geist and Henry Collins paid locals per artifact found, community values shifted to view excavation as profitable (Staley 1993). The undervaluing of local labor by archaeologists is reflected in the poor working conditions of excavations or low salaries that may prompt communities to run their own illegitimate digs instead. The proliferation of subsistence looters should not be underscored. Rough estimates count more than 500,000 individuals practicing subsistence digging in Mexico, the same number in the El Salvador and Guatemala region, and 50,000 in Belize (Matsuda 1998). Many of these people are not connected to organized crime, but participate in the illicit market by default since unauthorized excavation is against the law (and there is no legal market for ancient artifacts). Others, such as the St. Lawrence Islands populations, do have legal avenues within which to sell unearthed objects. In either case, subsistence looting may intersect with intangible as well as tangible

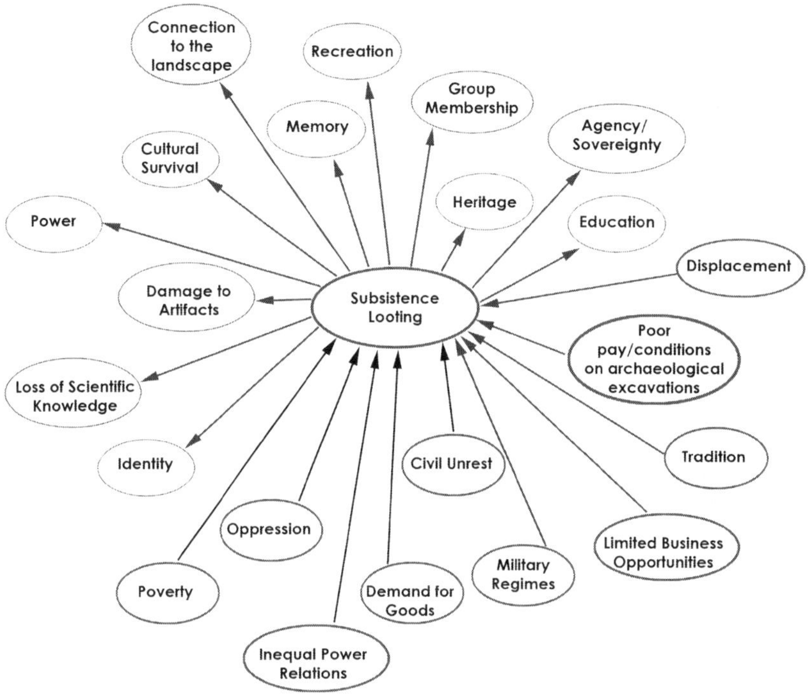

Figure 9.5 Tangibles and intangibles connected to subsistence looting

values (Figure 9.5). People may feel a sense of community and closeness to their ancestors, of agency, and of self-determination (Colwell-Chanthaphonh 2004). They may use this practice as a way to build identity, educate their children, reinforce ideologies, sustain traditions (or traditional subsistence strategies), or simply for recreation (Hollowell 2006).

The innumerable chains linked to subsistence looting make it hard for us, as outsiders, to judge. Even if communities are not digging for purely economic reasons, who are we to tell them that they must instead do hard labor or demeaning jobs for less money? Archaeology itself is equally guilty of destroying the material record since older excavation methodologies do not differentiate much from those of modern-day looters (Matsuda 1998). For sure, we face a dilemma of competing values. On the one hand, we want to protect archaeological data and keep artifacts in context. On the other hand, to deprive other human beings of their livelihood is also immoral. And if we are to make allowance and exceptions, who gets to decide where the ethical boundaries lie? For example, surface scatters contain limited information because they are no longer in situ, so is the procurement of these types of artifacts more justifiable?

Looting as an Unsolvable Problem

The first reason that looting is an unsolvable problem is that it is interconnected with a supply and demand system. At base level, "the art buyer makes the market. If art plunderers knew there would be no buyers for their spoils, there would be no spoils" (Koczka 1989:191). To completely eradicate looting, we would have to eliminate, at the very least, the demand for antiquities. This is no short order considering the profusion of things in our highly commoditized contemporary society and the fetishization of inalienable objects that connect us to the past (Baudrillard 1996, 1998). The desire to collect is strong, and all the interconnected values inherent in collecting help to justify one's ignorance or dismissal of the actual means by which pieces are acquired. Ever-increasing populations produce a culture where individuality is actively sought. The exclusivity of illicit artifacts increases their appeal so that "the black market, in sum, is a product of scarcity" (Bator 1988; see also Bator 1982). Differentiation is a means of empowerment, a way to climb social ladders and generate identity (Bauer 2007).

If anything, history has shown that the trafficking of illicit antiquities is on the upswing and now involves such a complicated consortium of players that it would be nearly impossible to cut the head off of the hydra at this point. Antiquities are big business for auction houses, museums and research institutions, criminals, local laborers, *and* for archaeologists. All these stakeholders attribute different kinds of value to the past and therefore create demand for it in its physical form. If it were possible to operate "business as usual" purely within the legal cultural property market, why would any of these players risk their reputations and livelihoods by supporting the illicit one? Although complete deregulation may help to reduce the level of illicit dealings, it is unlikely to eliminate it altogether. Hollowell's work on subsistence looting suggests that legal markets only diversify and expand the consumer base to include average Joes in addition to connoisseur collectors, and it does nothing to reduce the monetary value (Hollowell 2006). Besides, to do so would require a drastic shake-up of conservation values so that any and every artifact, regardless of provenance or scientific significance, would come into fair play.

On the potential of the law to curb the cultural property black market, the crux of the problem here is that there is a lack of consistency among various nation-states, making it difficult to tackle the antiquities market as a united front (Patron 2008). Until all countries unequivocally come together to hammer out a consistent, interlocked, all-encompassing plan for legally dealing with illicit trafficking, widely divergent import and export regulations will only continue to undermine one another. This event is unlikely to happen given attitudes about sovereignty and the poor track record of the international community on reaching consensus in other matters such as global warming and war crimes. Even laws within individual countries are contradictory. Take for example Israel, where the state is said to own all artifacts yet has a loophole in their Antiquities Law that allows for the licensed sale of works (Bonn-Muller 2010). Or consider the vast differences in laws concerning ancient finds on land versus underwater. Even when legal mechanisms exist to deter and penalize violators, these are wholly ineffective without enforcement. Legislation may even backfire by creating a false sense of security (Pendergast and Graham 1989). Since the 1970 UNESCO Convention on the Means of Prohibiting and Preventing the Illicit Import, Export and Transfer of Ownership and Cultural Property, looting has increased, not decreased (Renfrew 2001). Moreover, it is difficult to legally deal with retroactive looting. Current laws allow for exemptions of items that fall outside the statute of limitations, but this loophole is a vulnerability easily exploited with fraudulent provenances or forged documentation.

Legislation is only as good as enforcement, but this assumes there is the will and commitment to enforce, which Patron (2008) contends rarely happens in source nations. Also, enforcement is simply a Band-Aid solution that fails to address the actual root of the problem (which I argue is the valuation of the past). The consumer, who is responsible for the demand for black market goods, is rarely prosecuted and given any meaningful punishment. Most often it is the middlemen or looting laborers who take the fall, not the museum director, curator, or private collector. The resources available to stop the trafficking of illicit antiquities pale in comparison to the purchasing power of high-profile consumers (Bator 1988). Looters often have bigger and better crews and funding than do legitimate excavations. They also have the advantages of unlimited time and higher profits without the responsibility to record and detail archaeological sites, or even to meticulously excavate them (Pendergast and Graham 1989). The exponential growth of technology opens up the illicit market even further as Internet stores and sites such as Amazon, Craigslist, and eBay provide new, unmonitored ways of selling antiquities (Hollowell-Zimmer 2003).

To get to the real source of the problem from which looting stems, we have to look at ourselves. No impetus can exist for the trafficking of cultural property so long as old things lying in the ground do not have value. As archaeologists, our entire profession and existence depends on this assignment of worth to the material remnants of past societies. But if we remove this value, we remove the motivation to loot. Stuart notes that "both archaeologists and collectors must share in the blame for such practices—archaeologists for providing the knowledge that gives a piece more 'meaning' and hence more value as a collectible; collectors for competing in the sales galleries or auction houses" (1989:249). The nature of research funding requires archaeologists to market not only themselves, but their excavation sites and artifacts of study. The ascription of significance to these things justifies our position in the world. Our relationship with antiquities is such that we profit (Bauer 2007).

This profit may take the shape of a career, reputation, livelihood, or the personal satisfaction obtained from investigating the unknown.

The role that archaeologists play in enabling looting is further compounded when we agree to study or consult on questionable collections in return for money or access. Our research and publications especially augment the value of black market antiquities when we engage in these sorts of behaviors, despite the best of intentions. Even the "purists" who argue that archaeology is solely about the quest for knowledge must be cognizant of the contradictions inherent in associations with institutions borne from collections of looted pieces or that accept disputed donations (Matsuda 1998). For example, Chris Donnan, a University of California, Los Angeles (UCLA) professor, came under fire when he exchanged his silence for photographic access to Moche artifacts he wanted to add to the UCLA Cultural History Museum archive (Alexander 1990). Though Donnan maintained that his disclosure (rather than his silence) would have done nothing to reverse the looting of these pieces, such complicity and apathy can only help the illegal market to endure. Brodie (2011) argues that the discipline of archaeology is essential to the antiquities market, and thereby the illicit gray market, in four ways: publication, which legitimizes and increases demand; identification, which helps to ascribe monetary value; authentication, which builds consumer confidence and desire; and the concealment of or silence on provenance, inhibiting legal enforcement. The documentation and study of objects is a double-edged sword, at once an endeavor of salvage and preservation while at the same time proliferating the very system of harm from which archaeologists wish to protect these things.

In its niche production of experts, archaeology reinforces the idea that access to the past is exclusive. It problematizes looting through its construction of "proper" procedures and conservation values. Moral codes are not objectively, but rather, subjectively created. Looting is wrong only because we (archaeologists and Western society-at-large) have deemed it so: it is an ethical issue at heart, and thus easy solutions do not exist. When we try to fix something, we imply that something *needs* to be fixed in the first place. Likewise, when we try to stop looting (through mechanisms such as discourse, regulations, etc.), we imply that there is something broken in our world that *needs* to be mended. *We* have shaped things to fit our values, produced endless chains between different facets of our lives, and jumbled them together into one giant, knotted heap of intersections. We are essentially entangled in a web of our own creation, one that is only growing with time. In a Heideggerian fashion, archaeology gathers, as does the antiquities market, as do artifacts (Heidegger 1971). Hodder notes, "The defining aspect of human entanglement with made things is that humans get caught in a double-bind, depending on things that depend on humans" (2011:154). Archaeologists and artifacts, as I show in this chapter, have a relationship of interdependency that facilitates illicit antiquities trafficking. And this relationship extends outward into the larger sphere of the black market, which subsumes and is continually produced by interdependencies among human players (for example, looters and criminal middlemen or dealers) and nonhuman elements (such as looting and museums).

Concluding Remarks

The illicit antiquities trade is not cut and dried, but messy and intricately complicated by various interdependencies; the practice of archaeology is but one cog in the wheel. At first glance, the notion that archaeology fundamentally enables the illicit antiquities market may seem absurd, but is it really all that crazy? Archaeologists live, work, and research in an increasingly complex world of connected interfaces. There are no vacuums within which we can operate. My point here is not to accuse archaeologists of consciously facilitating looting, but that this is a hidden, unintended, and even unavoidable consequence of the discipline. The web and chains of things and people entangled in the black market are so proliferate that it is impossible at this point to segregate each variable (Figure 9.6). As it grows with the propagation of more and more emergent chains and interdependencies, we give up more and more control.

My intention is not to cast a cloud of gloom over the discipline. The interweaving of archaeology and the antiquities market does not preclude the premise that the pursuit of knowledge about the past and academia are worthwhile undertakings. Nor does it necessarily suggest that we should give up on our ethical codes or cease to fight to remove cultural objects from illicit trafficking rings. I simply strive to recognize that as archaeologists, our actions have far-reaching consequences, and that we should endeavor to be mindful of how something as innocuous as artifact identification can be appropriated for more nefarious ambitions. Moreover, this uneasy entanglement at times brings forth positive unintended consequences. For instance, the highly publicized sacking of Iraqi sites and museums, while unmistakably a travesty, has helped to mobilize the international community to take more concrete and united action to combat illicit artifact trafficking and the destruction of archaeological sites in conflict zones, brought recognition of the gravity and extent of the problem to the public arena, and elicited discourse on the value of cultural heritage. The acquisition of looted objects by museums, galleries, and private collectors may very well save some antiquities from deterioration and far worse fates, although whether this justifies their initial theft is arguable. Along these lines, the presence of artifacts in museums in particular makes these objects publicly accessible and available for scientific study, furthering educational goals of archaeology. Last, we cannot ignore that some people rely on their participation in the illicit antiquities market to subsist, especially in regions with widespread poverty, unemployment, and unstable economies.

In the end, however, there is no absolute manner in which archaeology can continue without in some way participating in the ascription of value to

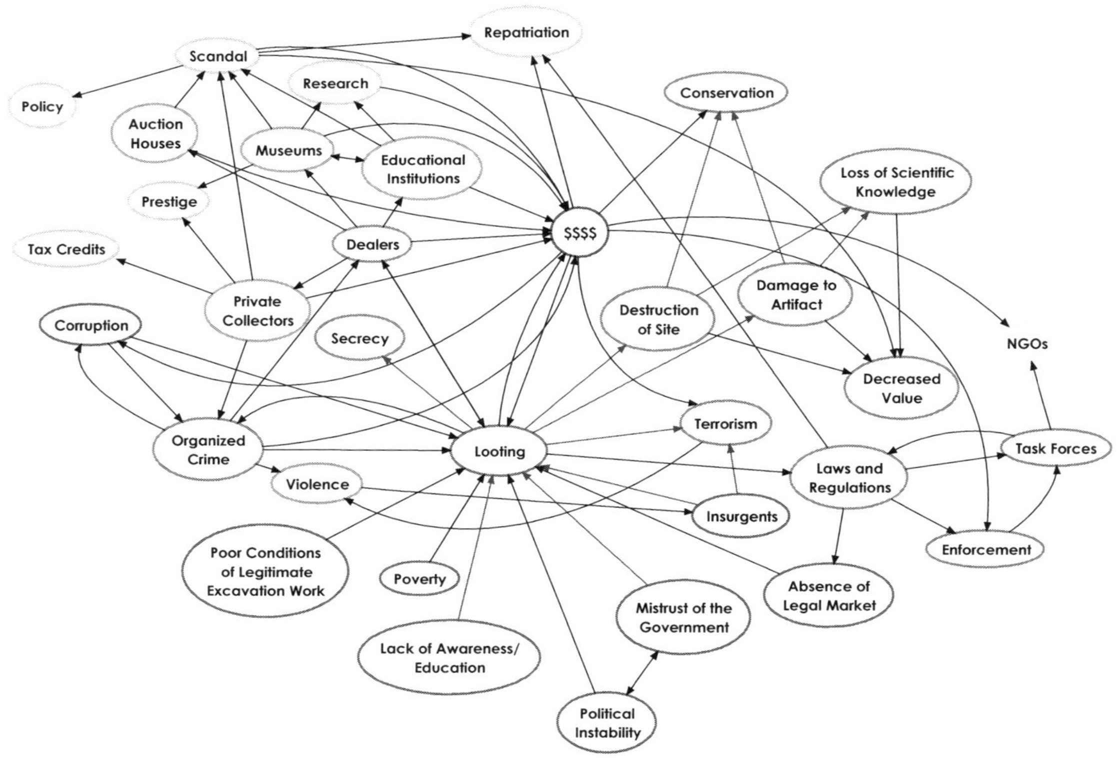

Figure 9.6 Messiness of some of the elements entangled and interdependent with looting. Since archaeology enables looting, these elements are all linked by various degrees of separation from archaeology.

things. This is the double-bind within which we find ourselves: archaeology gives the past value, which in turn affords the looting and trafficking of antiquities, but this value and the existence of antiquities afford archaeology's very being. Entanglements are contradictory and full of incestuous relationships. Archaeology is at the epicenter of the collision of competing values held by the past and the present. It is easier not to think of the hand we play in looting; perhaps it would be best, for our own peace of mind, to just keep it our own dirty little secret.

References

Adams, Robert M., 2005. Contexts of Iraqi Looting. *Proceedings of the American Philosophical Society* 149(1):56–62.

Al Jazeera, 2015. Iraq Officials Say ISIL Ransacked Ancient Assyrian Site: Looting and Razing in Khorsabad Follows Attacks on Heritage Sites of Nineveh, Nimrud and Hatra. *Al Jazeera,* March 12. Electronic document, www.aljazeera.com/news/2015/03/iraq-officials-isil-ransacked-ancient-assyrian-site-150312024652948.html, accessed March 20, 2015.

Alexander, Brian, 1990. Archeology and Looting Make a Volatile Mix. *Science* 250(4984):1074–1075.

Bator, Paul M., 1982. An Essay on the International Trade in Art. *Stanford Law Review* 34(2):275–384.

Bator, Paul M., 1988. *The International Trade in Art.* University of Chicago Press, Chicago, IL.

Baudrillard, Jean, 1996. *The System of Objects.* Verso, London; New York.

Baudrillard, Jean, 1998. *The Consumer Society: Myths and Structures.* Sage, London; Thousand Oaks, CA.

Bauer, A. A., 2007. New Ways of Thinking About Cultural Property: A Critical Appraisal of the Antiques Trade Debates. *Fordham International Law Journal* 31:690–741.

Becatoros, Elena, 2008. Smuggled Antiquities Funding Iraq Extremists, U.S. says. *National Geographic News,* March 19. Electronic document, http://news.nationalgeographic.com/news/2008/03/080319-AP-iraq-insurg.html, accessed June 6, 2011.

Bogdanos, Matthew, 2008. Thieves of Baghdad. In *The Destruction of Cultural Heritage in Iraq,* edited by Peter G. Stone, Joanne Farchakh Bajjaly, and Robert Fisk, pp. 109–134. Boydell Press, Woodbridge, UK.

Bonn-Muller, Eti, 2010. Inside the Israel Antiquities Authority—Amir Ganor, Director, Robbery Prevention Division. *Archaeology.* Electronic document, www.archaeology.org/israel_antiquities_authority/ganor.html, accessed March 28, 2015.

Brodie, Neil, 1998. Pity the Poor Middlemen. *Culture Without Context* (3):7–9.

Brodie, Neil, 2011. Congenial Bedfellows? The Academy and the Antiquities Trade. *Journal of Contemporary Criminal Justice* 27(4):408–437.

Brodie, Neil, Jennifer Doole, Peter Watson, Museums Association, and International Council of Museums United Kingdom, 2000. *Stealing History: The Illicit Trade in*

Cultural Material. McDonald Institute for Archaeological Research, Cambridge, UK.

Campbell, Peter B., 2013. The Illicit Antiquities Trade as a Transnational Criminal Network: Characterizing and Anticipating Trafficking of Cultural Heritage. *International Journal of Cultural Property* 20(2):113–153.

Chippindale, C., D. Gill, E. Salter, and C. Hamilton, 2001. Collecting the Classical World: First Steps in a Quantitative History. *International Journal of Cultural Property* 10(1):1–31.

Colwell-Chanthaphonh, Chip, 2004. Those Obscure Objects of Desire. *Journal of Contemporary Ethnography* 33(5):571–601.

Cox, Simon, 2015. The Men who Smuggle the Loot that Funds IS. *BBC News,* February 17. Electronic document, www.bbc.com/news/magazine-31485439, accessed February 20, 2015.

Dietzler, Jessica, 2013. On "Organized Crime" in the Illicit Antiquities Trade: Moving Beyond the Definitional Debate. *Trends in Organized Crime* 16(3):329–342.

Early, Ann M., 1989. Profiteers and Public Archaeology: Antiquities Trafficking in Arkansas. In *The Ethics of Collecting Cultural Property: Whose Culture? Whose Property?*, edited by Phyllis M. Messenger, pp. 39–50. University of New Mexico Press, Albuquerque.

Griffin, Gillett, 1989. Collecting Pre-Columbian Art. In *The Ethics of Collecting Cultural Property: Whose Culture? Whose Property?*, edited by Phyllis M. Messenger, pp. 103–115. University of New Mexico Press, Albuquerque.

Heidegger, Martin, 1971. *Poetry, Language, Thought.* Harper & Row, New York.

Herscher, Ellen, 1989. International Control Efforts: Are There Any Good Solutions? In *The Ethics of Collecting Cultural Property: Whose Culture? Whose Property?*, edited by Phyllis M. Messenger, pp. 117–128. University of New Mexico Press, Albuquerque.

Hodder, Ian, 2011. Human-thing Entanglement: Towards an Integrated Archaeological Perspective. *Journal of the Royal Anthropological Institute* 17(1):154–177.

Hollowell, Julia J., 2006. St. Lawrence Island's Legal Market in Archaeological Goods. In *Archaeology, Cultural Heritage and the Antiquities Trade,* edited by Neil Brodie, M. Kersel, C. Luke and K. W. Tubb, pp. 98–132. University Press of Florida, Gainesville.

Hollowell-Zimmer, Julie, 2003. Digging in the Dirt: Ethics and "Low-end Looting". In *Ethical Issues in Archaeology,* edited by Larry J. Zimmerman, Karen D. Vitelli, and Julia J. Hollowell, pp. 45–56. AltaMira Press in cooperation with the Society for American Archaeology, Walnut Creek, CA.

Impey, Oliver R., and Arthur MacGregor, 1985. *The Origins of Museums: the Cabinet of Curiosities in Sixteenth and Seventeenth-Century Europe.* Clarendon Press, Oxford, UK.

Koczka, Charles S., 1989. The Need for Enforcing Regulations on the International Art Trade. In *The Ethics of Collecting Cultural Property: Whose Culture? Whose Property?*, edited by Phyllis M. Messenger, pp. 185–198. University of New Mexico Press, Albuquerque.

Lawler, Andrew, 2015. Updated: Islamic State Group Seeks to Erase History in Iraq. *Science,* March 10. Electronic document, http://news.sciencemag.org/archaeology/2015/03/updated-islamic-state-group-seeks-erase-history-iraqLimp,

William F. 2012a. Letters to Spike TV, MTV, Viacom, and Gerny Productions opposing the "American Digger" show. Society for American Archaeology, February 12. Electronic document, www.saa.org/Portals/0/SAA/new/American%20Digger%20 Letter%20-%20Spike%20TV.pdf, accessed March 29, 2015.

Limp, William F., 2012b. Letter to the National Geographic Society opposing the "Diggers" show. Society for American Archaeology, February 27. Electronic document, www.saa.org/Portals/0/SAA/Press/Diggers.pdf, accessed March 29, 2015.

Mackenzie, Simon, 2011. *The Market as Criminal and Criminals in the Market: Reducing Opportunities for Organised Crime in the International Antiquities Market.* Springer, New York.

Matsuda, D., 1998. The Ethics of Archaeology, Subsistence Digging, and Artifact Looting in Latin America: Point Muted Counterpoint. *International Journal of Cultural Property* 7(01):87–97.

Migliore, Sam, 1991. Treasure Hunting and Pillaging in Sicily: Acquiring a Deviant Identity. *Anthropologica* 33(1/2):161–175.

Northam, Jackie, 2015. U.S. Returns Dozens of Looted Artifacts To Iraq. *NPR*, March 17. Electronic document, www.npr.org/blogs/thetwo-way/2015/03/17/393403937/u-s-returns-dozens-of-looted-artifacts-to-iraq, accessed March 17, 2015.

Patel, Samir, 2009. Drugs, Guns and Dirt. *Archaeology* 62(2). Electronic document, www.archaeology.org/0903/etc/drugs.html, accessed December 5, 2011.

Patron, Raisa E., 2008. The Looting of Iraqi Archaeological Sites: Global Implications and Support for an International Approach to Regulating the Antiquities Market. *George Washington International Law Review* 40:465–496.

Pendergast, David M., and Elizabeth Graham, 1989. The Battle for the Maya Past: The Effects of International Looting and Collecting in Belize. In *The Ethics of Collecting Cultural Property: Whose Culture? Whose Property?*, edited by Phyllis M. Messenger, pp. 51–60. University of New Mexico Press, Albuquerque.

Povoledo, Elisabetta, 2009. Getty Ex-Curator Testifies in Rome Antiquities Trial. *The New York Times,* March 21, p. C3.

Prott, Lyndel V., 1983. International Control of Illicit Movement of the Cultural Heritage: The 1970 UNESCO Convention and Some Possible Alternatives. *Syracuse Journal of International Law and Commerce* 102:333–351.

Proulx, Blythe B., 2011. Organized Criminal Involvement in the Illicit Antiquities Trade. *Trends in Organized Crime* 14(1):1–29.

Pyburn, K. A., 2003. What Are We Really Teaching in Archaeological Field Schools? In *Ethical Issues in Archaeology,* edited by Larry J. Zimmerman, Karen D. Vitelli, and Julia J. Hollowell, pp. 213–223. AltaMira Press in cooperation with the Society for American Archaeology, Walnut Creek, CA.

Renfrew, Colin, 2000. *Loot, Legitimacy, and Ownership: The Ethical Crisis in Archaeology.* Duckworth, London.

Renfrew, Colin, 2001. Foreword. In *Trade in Illicit Antiquities: The Destruction of the World's Archaeological Heritage*, edited by Neil Brodie, Jennifer Doole, and Colin, pp. xi. McDonald Institute for Archaeological Research; David Brown [distributor], Cambridge, UK; Oakville, ON, Canada.

Staley, David P., 1993. St. Lawrence Island's Subsistence Diggers: A New Perspective on Human Effects on Archaeological Sites. *Journal of Field Archaeology* 20(3):347–355.

Stuart, George E., 1989. Conclusion: Working Together to Preserve Our Past. In *The Ethics of Collecting Cultural Property: Whose Culture? Whose Property?*, edited by Phyllis M. Messenger, pp. 243–252. University of New Mexico Press, Albuquerque.

United Nations Educational, Scientific and Cultural Organization (UNESCO), 2013 *The Fight Against the Illicit Trafficking of Cultural Objects. The 1970 Convention: Past and Future. Information Kit.* UNESCO. Electronic document, www.unesco.org/new/fileadmin/MULTIMEDIA/HQ/CLT/pdf/2013_INFOKIT_1970_EN.pdf, accessed March 30, 2015.

United Nations Educational, Scientific and Cultural Organization (UNESCO), 2015. The Director-General Meets with Sotheby's Director of Compliance over Illicit Trafficking of Cultural Heritage. UNESCO, March 9. Electronic document, www.unesco.org/new/en/media-services/single-view/news/the_director_general_meets_with_sothebys_director_of_compliance_over_illicit_trafficking_of_cultural_heritage/#.VRjv—HxGJ1, accessed March 9, 2015.

Warren, Karen J., 1989. A Philosophical Perspective on the Ethics and Resolution of Cultural Issues. In *The Ethics of Collecting Cultural Property: Whose Culture? Whose Property?*, edited by Phyllis M. Messenger, pp. 1–26. University of New Mexico Press, Albuquerque.

Watson, Peter, 1997. *Sotheby's: The Inside Story.* Random House, New York.

Weiner, Annette B., 1992. *Inalienable Possessions the Paradox of Keeping-while-Giving.* University of California Press, Berkeley.

World Customs Organization, 2015. *Trafficking of Cultural Property.* Electronic document, www.wcoomd.org/en/topics/enforcement-and-compliance/activities-and-programmes/other-activities/protection-of-cultural-heritage.aspx, accessed March 17, 2015.

Chapter 10

Degrees of Dependence: The Example of the Introduction of Pottery in the Middle East and at Çatalhöyük

Ian Hodder

One definition of *entanglement* (Hodder 2012) is that it is the dialectic of dependence and dependency between humans and things. Dependence (and for the plural I shall use *dependences*) recognizes that the human use of things is enabling and productive, cognitively, psychologically, socially, and economically. I use *dependence* here in the sense of "reliance on." But dependence also often involves a second focus that I call *dependency* (and its plural *dependencies*). Dependency involves some form of constraint. Humans become involved in various dependencies that limit their abilities to develop, as societies or as individuals. These notions of dependence and dependency draw attention to the tensions between humans and things that lead to entrapment and the human sense of being caught up in the world. Some notions of entanglement deal with the historical dimensions of power inequalities in colonial and postcolonial settings (Thomas 1991). I generalize from these colonial aspects of entanglements to refer to the overall condition of humans in their dependence and dependency in relation to things.

If the notion of dependence is central to entanglement theory, then it merits closer scrutiny. Broader discussions of dependence include ontological considerations about substance, existence, and how we carve up reality into entities of various sorts (Correia 2008). For my purposes in this chapter I take from these broader discussions the notion that entities are not self-sufficient and that there are types and degrees of sufficiency. Regarding forms of insufficiency, there are functional insufficiencies in which an entity cannot function in relation to some purpose without another entity; thus a wheel cannot function to transport goods without an axle, and a pot cannot function to transfer liquids without an opening. Another form of insufficiency is structural and derives from part-whole relations. Thus in cuisine, a pot may be part of a set

Archaeology of Entanglement edited by Lindsay Der and Francesca Fernandini, 235–250

that includes plates, or cups may go with saucers. In poststructuralist terms, there is always the "lack," the need for other entities to complete meaning (Derrida 1998).

There are also degrees of lack or insufficiency. In discussing a tanglegram of dependences and dependencies for the Neolithic site of Çatalhöyük, some things seem more central in that they had more dependence and dependency relations with other entities (Hodder 2012: Figure 9.2). For example, the house was involved in many aspects of social, symbolic, and material life. Burials occurred there, as did daily production of food, as did the main art and ritual activities. Through time, whether wider change could take place depended on whether change occurred in the house. Everything seemed very dependent on the house. But dogs or ash or wooden objects seemed more sufficient to themselves, and change could occur in these realms without major change in other realms. So what does it mean to say that some things are more entangled than others? How might one define degrees of dependency? To explore this question I use the example of the introduction of pottery in the Middle East.

The Introduction of Pottery

"Pottery," or fired ceramic containers, first appear in the Middle East at a relatively late date compared with its emergence in China (Liu and Chen 2012). Undecorated ceramics are found at a number of sites in many parts of the Middle East by 7000 BCE, although not in the southern Levant until about 6400 BCE. The first examples occur at Ganj Dareh in highland Iran at around 8000 BCE (Bar-Yosef and Meadow 1995, 79; Smith 1976; Zeder 2009). The first pottery throughout the region is undecorated, although decoration and painting quickly emerge. The earliest pottery often occurs in small numbers and shows low levels of skill in production.

In many ways, the adoption of pottery was part of a gradual continuum. We know that communities had the ability to heat clays and minerals to high temperatures from well before the Pottery Neolithic in the Middle East. Fired-lime production was widespread in the Levant and Anatolia in the early Neolithic from 10,000 BCE (Garfinkel 1987; Goren et al. 2001; Kingery et al. 1988), reaching temperatures of 750°C to 900°C. So, for 2,000 to 3,000 years, communities had the ability to reach very high temperatures with mineral materials, but they did not make pottery. They did make other ceramic objects such as figurines, and when their unfired mud-brick buildings accidentally burned, they saw that hard, fired mud bricks had been produced.

And they also made containers well before they made pottery containers. Stone vessels, often decorated, were made in the northern Levant and southeast Turkey from 10,000 BCE. For example, decorated stone bowls occurred at Hallan Çemi in the mid-tenth millennium BCE (Rosenberg 2011), and stone vessels with elaborate figurative designs occurred at Körtik Tepe in the Early

Pre-Pottery Neolithic A (EPPNA) (Özkaya and Coşkun 2011). "White ware" vessels of chalk or gypsum were found in central and eastern parts of the Fertile Crescent region by 8000 BCE (Bar-Yosef and Meadow 1995:79; Zeder 2009). There is extensive evidence throughout the region of the use of baskets (Wendrich 2005) and wooden vessels (Asouti 2013; Mellaart 1967).

The first pottery appears in northern Mesopotamia at around 7000 BCE in different and diverse cultural contexts and with different specific forms (Bernbeck and Nieuwenhuyse 2013). For example, early examples of pottery in the middle Euphrates occur at 7000 BCE at Akarçay (Özbaşaran and Duru 2011). At Mezraa-Teleilat on the Euphrates (Özdoğan 2011), there is a gradual adoption of pottery with at first a small number of sherds, mainly made of coarse, chaff-tempered wares, and then a shift to plain, grit-tempered wares, followed by the appearance of decorated impressed and painted wares. There is an overall process of increasing pottery quality and complexity at this and other sites through the seventh millennium BCE.

Pottery was adopted slowly and gradually and may initially have had little impact on overall economies and social systems. Containers already existed, as did fired clay. Early pottery was used in small numbers and may often have had specific uses (Bernbeck and Nieuwenhuyse 2013).

The Introduction and Adoption of Pottery at Çatalhöyük

Certainly this is the pattern of adoption and use we see at Çatalhöyük. Last et al. (2005) showed that the introduction of pottery at Çatalhöyük in South I or H was part of a wider first use of vegetable-tempered pottery in the Middle East around 7000 BCE (Aurenche et al. 2001; Moore 1995; Vandiver 1987). This initial use of organic tempered pottery at Çatalhöyük was then followed by a series of changes around South M that involved more use of pottery, more controlled firing and better pastes, mineral temper, and thinner walls. Last and colleagues related the major South M shift to the increased use of pottery in cooking.

The earliest pottery at Çatalhöyük shows little evidence of fire clouding on the outer surfaces and, given the vegetable temper and thick walls, it is unlikely that the pottery was used extensively in cooking. We presume that the earliest pots were used as containers and for consuming food. In the lower levels at the site up to South M, fired clay balls dominate the deposits. The existence of the balls again shows that firing of clay occurred before pottery. Research by Atalay (2005) convincingly demonstrates that prior to the use of cooking pottery at Çatalhöyük, people cooked by heating clay balls in ovens and then placing them in baskets or wooden or skin containers to cook liquids and solids; they may also have placed meat and other foods directly onto the heated balls.

So in asking why this method of cooking with clay balls, or at other sites with stone boilers, was abandoned in favor of fired-clay pots, it is important to

Table 10.1 Chronological system of levels at Çatalhöyük

Levels		
Mellart	*South-4040*	
0,I,II	TP6	6400–6000
	South T - 4040.J	
	South S - 4040.J	
	South R - 4040.I	
	South Q - 4040.H	
(V)	South P - 4040.H	
VIA	South O - 4040.G	6500–6400
VIB	South N - 4040.G	
VII	South M - 4040.F	6700–6500
VIII	South L - 4040.F	
IX	South K	7100–6800
X	South J	
XI	South I	
XII	South H	
Pre XII	South G1,G2,G3,G4	

understand the various performance characteristics or affordances of the two methods (Knappett 2005; Skibo et al. 1989). As Atalay demonstrated, cooking with clay balls is very efficient, but requires a lot of attention from the cook as balls are added and changed during the cooking. Cooking with pottery demands less attention, thus allowing the cook to undertake other tasks. To some degree, the pot can be left on the fire, where it acts as a delegate for humans (Latour 2005). We know that throughout the sequence at Çatalhöyük, houses got larger and more activities took place in and around them. They became increasingly the focus of multiple productive tasks. Cooking with pots on hearths may have saved time in the cooking process, even if it increased the amount of labor needed to make and obtain pots. (I discuss other entangled factors involved in these changes later in this chapter.) Mineral temper allows more efficient cooking and heat transfer than vegetable temper (Skibo et al. 1989), and so the shift to thin-walled vessels with mineral temper and with external surface clouding suggests a gradual shift from clay balls to cooking pots. The main changeover occurs in South M.

What was being cooked in these new mineral-tempered pots? We have some phytolith evidence of plant residues, but our main residue evidence suggests the presence of lipids from ruminant fats (Pitter et al. 2013). We know from the faunal evidence that domestic sheep bones were very intensively processed in domestic contexts. They were broken up and processed for marrows and fats. Given the small size of the pottery, it seems reasonable to conclude that the pots were used in the processing of sheep meat and bones (since large cattle bones were often processed differently, in larger-scale, feasting-type contexts).

Around South M–P we also have the first evidence of use of pots for milk, though not to the degree found in northwestern Anatolia (Evershed et al. 2008; Pitter et al. 2013). For milk residues to survive in pot matrices, it had to have been heated in the pots. Given the presumed lactose intolerance of human populations in Anatolia in the Neolithic, heat-related processing of milk into yoghurt, sour milk, and cheese seems likely (see Schoop 1998). Milk residues in northwestern Anatolia are related to a predominance of cattle remains, and it is notable that milk residues and domestic cattle appear at about the same time in South M–P at Çatalhöyük.

South P also sees a major increase in the density of sheep bones on site. It is possible that the increased herding of sheep at Çatalhöyük as well as the adoption of domestic cattle were linked to the increased milk- and meat-processing power provided by the use of mineral-tempered pottery. The increased dependence on domestic sheep and domestic cattle would have been associated with a greater workload in the domestic context to process meat, fats, and milk products. The pots as delegate cooks would have facilitated this increased workload.

This use of mineral-tempered pottery continued from South M to at least South T. During this period, pottery played a key role in the domestic economy. In an analysis of cut marks on animal bones, Demirergi et al. (2013) show that the frequency of filleting cuts at Çatalhöyük increases on both sheep-size and cattle-size animals during the middle and later phases of the site. One possible explanation is that these later inhabitants were processing more of their meat prior to cooking it, perhaps for drying (i.e., meat storage). But another possibility is that they were removing meat from the bone for stewing, and boiling in pots. The increased range of pot types in the upper levels at the site would certainly allow for this second interpretation.

It is notable that the pottery after South M remained undecorated, like many aspects of domestic production. Hearths and ovens too were undecorated; they occurred in the south side of main rooms in buildings where the walls too were usually unpainted and without reliefs. Most of the elaborate symbolism in the main rooms in houses at Çatalhöyük occurred on the northern, western, and eastern walls. As I argue elsewhere (Hodder 2006), the main symbolic focus up to South O was on burial, feasting, and prowess in relation to wild animals, especially wild bulls. Domestic cooking was a largely "unmarked" area (Keane 2011).

But gradually through time after South O, there was an increasing diversity of pottery forms and fabrics. While mineral-tempered pottery was initially undecorated and largely involved in food preparation in the house, through time it became diversified. From South P and Q onwards, a wider range of pottery shapes and an increasing amount of decoration are found. There is a greater variety of forms, bases, lugs, etc. in the upper levels (Yalman et al. 2013). Doherty and Tarkan Özbudak (2013) also note a general increase in the quality of firing. In these upper levels, a greater diversity of pottery likely was needed to differentiate functions, occasions, users, and so on.

As the inhabitants of Çatalhöyük increasingly came to depend on pottery for a wide range of tasks and needs, they were drawn into additional costs and increased labor. For example, the earliest pottery at Çatalhöyük makes use of local clays, but from South M there was a switch to predominantly nonlocal clays, probably obtained from volcanic regions to the west (Doherty and Tarkan Özbudak 2013). A second transition at about South R sees another increase in the diversity of raw materials, perhaps reflecting a period of experimentation as suggested by Last et al. (2005). Chaff-tempered fabrics make a brief return in the upper levels, as do a series of higher-fired silty wares. From this point into the Early Chalcolithic, there is an increasing return to the use of more local clay sources, although the nonlocal volcanic fabrics are still important.

The return to the use of local clays in the Early Chalcolithic of the West Mound is associated with another form of increased labor input: larger-scale production and the emergence of pottery workshops. The early phases of occupation on the West Mound in the early sixth millennium BCE show a gradual transition between the relatively undecorated wares of the East Mound and the elaborately painted ceramics of the later occupation of the West Mound. We know less about the early levels on the West Mound, but by the time of the upper levels, we find a wide range of wares. Franz (2011) describes the strong evidence for large-scale workshop production of pottery in these upper levels. For example, a cache of unfired clay balls was found in Space 449 in 2010. These were almost certainly the ready raw material for making pots, as is indicated by the associations with unfired pottery as well as vitrified sherds from a number of contexts. Also found were bone tools and burnishing stones used in pottery production and pieces of pigment used in painting pottery.

We have little evidence of pottery residues from these later time periods, but it seems likely that some types of pottery were used in processing sheep and cattle fat and milk as in the upper levels of the East Mound. Clearly identifiable cooking pots can be identified. There are also pot stands on which cooking pots could have been placed. But there are also other new functions for pottery in the Chalcolithic. For example, very large storage jars appear for the first time. The undecorated bowls and holemouth jars of South M to T on the East Mound remained relatively small. But on the West Mound there are storage jars that are substantially larger in size, allowing both greater independence of individual households and greater exchange between households.

In addition to the cooking and storage pots in the Chalcolithic levels, there is also a great diversity of fine wares painted with an ebullient decoration. These pots are associated with rooms with well-made and sometimes painted floors in which there is a central hearth; by this time, the oven has often been marginalized to side rooms. There seems to be a new focus on commensalism and exchange in the house-based social process. Stone vessels too were dragooned into the new emphasis on exchange around the hearth and social display. Andesite trays become more common in TP (the uppermost levels on the East Mound in the Team Poznan area) and on the West Mound, where also they become footed. The symbols that had earlier occurred on house walls now occur on pottery. There are images of dancing women as well as headless figures and bulls and animal horns. It is no longer the fabric and continuity of the house itself that is the social focus; now, there is an emphasis on symbolism linked to domestic production and display (Hodder 2006), even if the symbolic themes hark back to earlier times. By the Chalcolithic levels in the upper West Mound, pottery has become a central social focus, depended on for cooking, storage, and social display. It had increased in quantity and quality, requiring more labor, and was integrally linked into the social process.

The Changing Entanglements of Pottery at Çatalhöyük

I summarize the above process in terms of a series of entanglements in Figure 10.1, from (a) the earliest levels at Çatalhöyük when pottery was largely absent and cooking was achieved with clay balls, to (b) when cooking with clay balls continued and organic-tempered pottery was used as a container, to (c) when mineral tempered pottery was used in cooking, to (d) in the Chalcolithic when pottery was produced on a large scale for a wide range of functions and was elaborately painted. For images of the clay balls and pottery at each of these phases, see Figure 10.2. Through the sequence we see a gradually increased dependence between pottery and other things and humans. Pottery becomes increasingly central and involved in ever-greater dependences and dependencies. It becomes increasingly insufficient.

In the earliest levels on the East Mound, prior to the introduction of pottery, inhabitants cooked with the help of clay balls made from local clays and grits. The forming and production processes were relatively simple (in contrast to forming pots), although finding the right mix of clay and temper so that the balls did not explode when heated or placed in pots would have involved considerable skill. The balls were used in conjunction with and had to stay close to the hearths and ovens in which they were heated. They were also used with baskets and other containers made of wood and skin in which the balls were placed to heat food. Overall, the links in Figure 10.1a are relatively constrained; there are not large numbers of dependences.

Much the same can be said of the early use of pottery as diagrammed in Figure 10.1b. Since the first pottery was not much used for cooking, it was relatively self-sufficient and had few dependences. There must have been other links of which we know little; for example, the pots may have been used as containers and for consuming food, and so the pots were linked in to various food pathways. But it is not clear that at this stage pots had great advantages

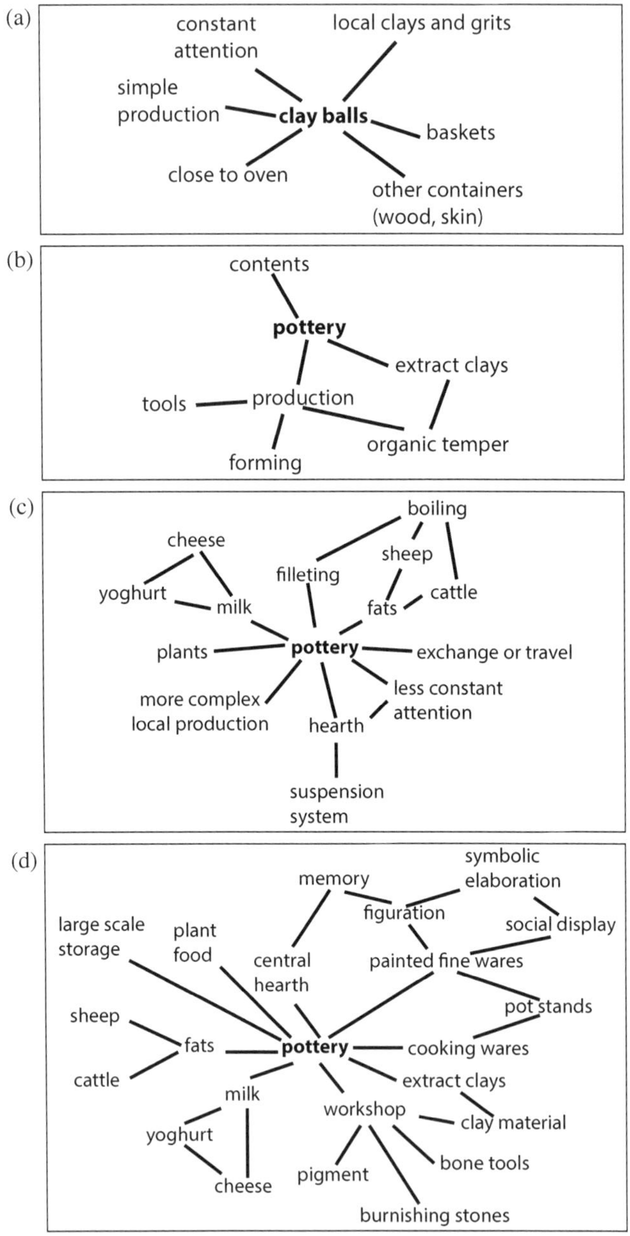

Figure 10.1 Dependent relationships of clay ball and pottery containers at different phases during the occupation of Çatalhöyük. (a) Clay ball use in South G–M. (b) Early pottery use in South H–M. (c) Later Neolithic pottery use in South M–T. (d) Chalcolithic pottery use in the upper levels of the West Mound at Çatalhöyük.

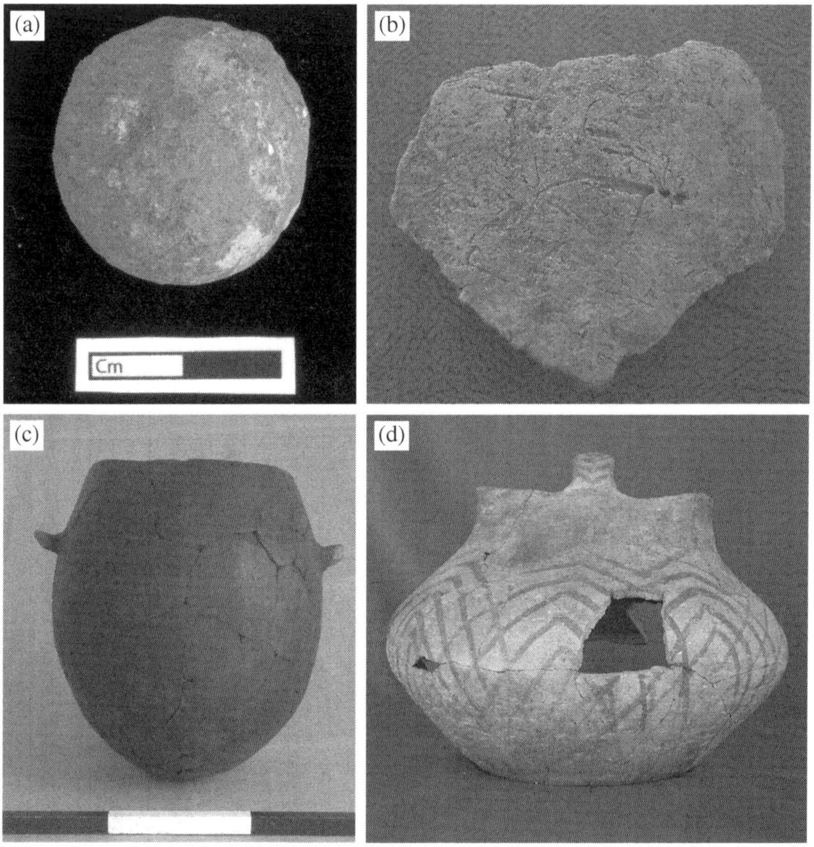

Figure 10.2 Examples of clay balls and pottery at different phases during the occupation of Çatalhöyük. (a) Clay ball. (b) Early organic tempered pottery. (c) Mineral tempered holemouth cooking vessel. (d) Painted Chalcolithic pottery (All images courtesy of the Çatalhöyük Research Project and Jason Quinlan).

over baskets and wood and skin containers. We do not know why pottery containers were introduced. Perhaps they were just experiments, in the same way that communities elsewhere tried out stone and chalk containers (see above). Perhaps people needed a greater diversity of containers as more activities were brought inside the house and the levels of activity in houses increased. But, overall, the introduction of pottery seems to have had little impact at Çatalhöyük. Few other changes occur in South H and I: pottery slipped in with little initial impact.

It is a different story for the introduction of cooking pottery in South M. As shown in Figure 10.1c, there are many more dependences associated with the thin-walled, mineral-tempered, undecorated cooking wares from South M–T.

And there are concomitant changes throughout many aspects of life. Compared with clay balls, the cooking pots demanded less supervision because they were placed on hearths or hung above hearths using their lug handles. They allowed more activities to take place and be managed inside the house. They were used for cooking plants, but also for the processing of meat, fat, and milk products, probably including the boiling of filleted meat. This greater ability to process animal products was associated with an economic shift at Çatalhöyük to greater dependence on sheep and domestic cattle. But the use of pots involved more complex pottery production and the securing of pottery from elsewhere by travel, trade, and exchange. The earliest pottery at Çatalhöyük made use of local clays, but from South M there was a switch to predominantly nonlocal clays, probably obtained from volcanic regions to the west. Thus, the use of pottery solved some problems but added new demands.

As pottery became increasingly drawn into the social process in South M–T, so new forms and fabrics gradually emerged, leading towards the next major phase diagrammed in Figure 10.1d. By the later levels in the Çatalhöyük West Mound, a wide range of forms, several of them elaborately decorated with painted geometric designs, had emerged. Some pot types were used for cooking, others for large-scale storage, and yet others for consumption and social display. There was a whole paraphernalia of pots, including pot stands. As part of the emphasis on consumption and social display, hearths moved into the centers of large rooms. While there is some evidence that walls continued to be painted, there is no evidence that the wall paintings were as complex as those in the East Mound. Rather, pottery seems to have taken on the symbolic role previously given to walls. Given the greater emphasis on pottery production and use, there is more evidence for large-scale production of pottery, using local clays. There is workshop production in which inhabitants used a wide range of tools. Pottery had now become much less self-sufficient; it had come to be nodal in many aspects of life at Çatalhöyük.

Degrees of Entanglement

What can we learn from this example of degrees of entanglement? What is "increased entanglement"? We have seen that it can be defined as the extent to which parts of an entanglement can function independently of other parts. Early pottery at Çatalhöyük and in the Middle East did not have a major impact, and it was not caught up (entangled) in many spheres of life. But later in the sequence, this initially insignificant new cultural trait took on a major and central role. It became involved in multiple dependences, such as with plant cooking and symbolic representation. But it also became involved in dependencies such as that among pottery and meat and milk and sheep and domestic cattle. For example, increased household production throughout the Middle East depended on more intensive sheepherding and on the use of domestic cattle, including for milk. Because many humans were lactose intolerant, they and domestic cattle depended on pots to process milk into consumable yoghurts and cheeses. But the increased dependence on pots in this way meant that humans had to invest more energy to produce pots locally on a larger scale, leading to workshop production of pottery with all the associated equipment. Humans were thus drawn into dependency relationships with cattle and milk and pottery.

The notion that there are degrees of entanglement underpins wider discussion about differences between biological and cultural evolution. Ecological interactions in the biological "natural" world differ fundamentally from the dependencies within entanglements. As much as species are linked and dependent, they do nevertheless reproduce themselves; they have life that generates new life. Many, if not all, organic and inorganic things also have the opposite tendency—to decay, disintegrate, die out—so if humans are dependent on them they are drawn into their care. Domestic animals and crops differ from wild animals and plants in that they can no longer reproduce themselves: they become less self-sufficient (and more entangled) in relation to human goals. Of course, all the wild species in Darwin's entangled bank are highly connected and depend on each other, yet they have a life force that is more sufficient than many of the artifacts made by humans. John Maynard Smith puts the difference very well in his book *The Theory of Evolution* (1993:317–318): "Whereas random change in one part of a machine would almost certainly mean that the machine as a whole would not fit together, a random change in one part of an organism (or strictly, in one of the developmental processes of that organism) may well be compensated for by adaptive changes in other parts."

The degree of insufficiency can be measured in terms of numbers of links going into nodes, and the numbers of connections along chains. Figure 10.1 shows these differences very well as the numbers of links and nodes proliferate. But degrees of dependence are not simply measurable in these terms; there is also entrapment created by the dialectic of dependence and dependency. Where there are many dependency relationships, humans get caught in particular historical binds from which it is difficult to become extricated. Thus, once humans became dependent on cattle milk and sheep meat to support larger houses and a greater emphasis on household production, it would have been difficult to give up cooking pottery and go back to cooking with clay balls. The latter path would have involved such massive production of clay balls, so much time and effort in using them to cook, and so much space to lay them out, that there would not have been sufficient time for other tasks, such as tending sheep and cattle. Once humans started down a particular path, it became difficult to turn back.

One aspect of entanglement that the pottery example obscures is the social tensions and changes that must have been involved. We know little of the gender, age, and status dimensions of using clay balls and cooking pots. We cannot see what social relations were transformed as pots came into greater use. But it is important to recognize that relations of dependence and dependency also exist between humans. Degrees of entanglement equate strongly to social inequality: dominant groups are often less entangled than subordinate groups, and their dominance is often based on the degree to which others are entangled. It is possible that as pots were increasingly entangled in the processing of milk, meat, and fat, and as humans were increasingly entrapped in the production of more pottery, it was actually just one segment of society caught up and constrained. For example, it may have been young women's labor that was drawn in and exploited in the interests of dominant groups (perhaps elders and household heads). For the moment, we have no evidence of the social realm implicated in the pottery entanglements I describe. But in general terms we can say that degrees of entanglement as experienced by different community members are closely related to power and resources; entanglement is both produced by and is productive of power.

Degrees of entanglement are also related to the ways in which human-thing dependences are tied to cultural abstractions and bodily resonances (Hodder 2012). Through much of the sequence at Çatalhöyük there were strong constraints on social differentiation. There were strong leveling mechanisms, and certainly the largely undecorated cooking wares of the East Mound allow little expression of social difference in terms of their size or treatment. In addition, on the East Mound the undecorated ceramics were part of a set of symbolic differences in which the domestic arena was unmarked in contrast to the elaborate ritual energy expended in those areas of social life surrounding death and feasting and wild animals. The differences between the north and south parts of main rooms in houses remained throughout the sequence at Çatalhöyük and suggest deeply embedded concepts and practices in which undecorated pottery, undecorated ovens and hearths, and undecorated storage bins and storage areas all played their parts. Individual houses seem to have had their own local versions of these rules; for example, in the 65-56-44-10 sequence of houses in the South Area, undecorated pots were repeatedly buried into floors at the bottom of ladders in the south parts of main rooms (Regan and Taylor 2013). These general and specific constraints seem to have been loosened—or at least transformed—by the time of the upper levels on the Chalcolithic West Mound. Although there remains much evidence of leveling mechanisms, one significantly larger building (B.25) has been excavated (Last and Gibson, personal communication, January 2001). The elaborately decorated pottery allows more opportunity for display of difference, and mace-heads appear, perhaps as markers of distinction.

Conclusion

We have seen that the early entanglements of pottery at Çatalhöyük lead later on to quite different entanglements. And this same trend seems relevant for the introduction of pottery in the Middle East more widely. Things invented for one purpose become useful for another. A similar process has been noted in evolutionary theory. As Pigliucci and Kaplan (2006) argue, all adaptations are originally exaptations (i.e., had some other purpose). Natural selection does not influence what variations are produced, and evolution is not forward-looking. As a result, traits can be selected for over time whatever their initial role. Of course, human societies usually are forward-looking in the sense that they envisage and work toward imagined futures. But the ensuing actions often lead to unpredicted and unexpected consequences. As new situations unfold, traits developed for one purpose often are used for others. Certainly pottery containers may initially have been used like stone or basket containers: to keep things separate, and to carry them around. But over time, the cooking purpose came to dominate, and as a result, undecorated mineral-tempered pottery was drawn into a wide range of needs and activities, as shown in Figure 10.1c. Still later, pottery was used for yet other purposes, particularly large-scale storage and social display in the Chalcolithic West Mound, as shown in Figure 10.1d.

Through time, then, pottery became increasingly entangled. In this chapter I explore what might be meant by the notion that there are degrees of entanglement. The question returns us to the notion of dependence and the various types and degrees of dependence. It might be possible to argue that the earliest pottery played a mainly functional role, whereas through time it became additionally involved in a different form of dependence: the part-whole relationships that had symbolic, social, and productive dimensions. But also through time the degree of dependence on pottery increased. I have tried to show that degrees of dependence might be defined as the extents to which parts of an entanglement can function independently of other parts. Through time we seem to see more aspects of the overall entanglements dependent on pottery; indeed, pottery seems to become essential to many primary processes, such as the processing of meat and plant nutrients and later the display of social generosity around the hearth.

But it is not enough simply to argue that increases in entanglement can be measured in terms of the number and lengths of links into specific nodes. Certainly Figure 10.1d looks much more entangled than Figure 10.1b, but entanglement also refers to the degree of entrapment; that is, the degree of constraint or dependency within a larger system of dependence or reliance between humans and things. Figures 10.1c and 10.1d show a lot of reliance, but the hidden dependencies create the main entanglement. The diagrams include a number of double-binds in which humans and things not only rely on each other, but also develop dependency relationships in which humans are trapped into the maintenance and control of things. For example, the greater human dependence on sheep and domestic cattle itself depends on the use of cooking pottery, but the production of cooking pottery requires more labor; this then conflicts with the investment of labor in looking after sheep and domestic cattle. While assessment of entanglement is in part quantitative, it also involves interpretation of constraints and double-binds that occur within human-thing relationships.

References

Asouti, E., 2013. Woodland Vegetation, Firewood Management and Woodcrafts at Neolithic Çatalhöyük. In *Humans and Landscapes of Çatalhöyük: Reports from the 2000–2008 Seasons*, edited by Ian Hodder, pp. 129–161. Cotsen Institute of Archaeology, Los Angeles, CA.

Atalay, S., 2005. Domesticating Clay: The Role of Clay Balls, Mini Balls and Geometric Objects in Daily Life at Çatalhöyük. In *Changing Materialities at Çatalhöyük: Reports from the 1995–1999 Seasons*, edited by Ian Hodder, pp. 139–168. McDonald Institute for Archaeological Research, London; British Institute for Archaeology at Ankara, Cambridge, UK.

Aurenche, O., P. Galet, E. Régagnon-Carolie, and J. Evin, 2001. Proto-Neolithic and Neolithic Cultures in the Middle East—The Birth of Agriculture, Livestock Raising and Ceramics: A Calibrated 14C Chronology, 12,500–5,500 cal BC. *Radiocarbon* 43(3):1191–1202.

Bar-Yosef, O., and R. H. Meadow, 1995. The Origins of Agriculture in the Near East. In *Last Hunters, First Farmers: New Perspectives on the Transition to Agriculture*, edited by T. D. Price and A. B. Gebauer, pp. 39–94. School of American Research Press, Santa Fe, NM.

Bernbeck, R., and O. Nieuwenhuyse, 2013. Established Paradigms, Current Disputes and Emerging Themes: The State of Research on the Late Neolithic in Upper Mesopotamia. In *Interpreting the Late Neolithic in Upper Mesopotamia*, edited by R. Bernbeck, O. Nieuwennhuyse, P. Akkermans, P., and J. Rogasch, pp. 17–37. Brepols, Turnhout, Belgium.

Correia, F., 2008. Ontological Dependence. *Philosophy Compass* 3(5):1013–1032.

Demirergi, G. A., K. T. Twiss, A. Bogaard, L. Green, P. Ryan, and S. Farid, 2013. Of Bins, Basins and Banquets: Storing, Handling and Sharing at Neolithic Çatalhöyük. In *Integrating Çatalhöyük: Themes from the 2000–2008 Seasons*, edited by Ian Hodder, pp. 89–106. Cotsen Institute of Archaeology, Los Angeles, CA.

Derrida, J., 1998. *Of Grammatology.* John Hopkins University Press, Baltimore, MD.

Doherty, C., and Tarkan Özbudak, D., 2013. Pottery Production at Çatalhöyük: A Petrographic Perspective. In *Substantive Technologies at Çatalhöyük: Reports from the 2000–2008 Seasons*, edited by Ian Hodder, pp. 181–192. Cotsen Institute of Archaeology, Los Angeles, CA.

Evershed, R. P., S. Payne, A. G. Sherratt, M. S. Copley, J. Coolidge, D. Urem-Kotsu, K. Kotsakis, M. Özdogan, A. Özdogan, O. Nieuwenhuyse, P. M. M. G. Akkermans, D. Bailey, R. R. Andeescu, S. Campbell, S. Farid, I. Hodder, N. Yalman, M. Özbarasan,

E. Bicakci, Y. Garfinkel, T. Levy, and M. M. Burton, 2008. Earliest Date for Milk Use in the Near East and Southeastern Europe Linked to Cattle Herding. *Nature* 455:528–531.

Franz, I., 2011. Ceramics Report West Mound Trench 5-7. Çatalhöyük Archive Report: 79–80. Electronic document, www.catalhoyuk.com/downloads/Archive_Report_2011.pdf, accessed September 15, 2015.

Garfinkel, Y., 1987. Burnt Lime Products and Social Implications in the Pre-pottery Neolithic B Villages of the Near East. *Paléorient* 13:69–76.

Goren, Y., N. Goring-Morris, and I. Segal, 2001. The Technology of Skull Modelling in the Pre-Pottery Neolithic B (PPNB): Regional Variability, the Relation of Technology and Iconography and Their Archaeological Implications. *Journal of Archaeological Science* 28(7):671–679.

Hodder, Ian, 2006. *The Leopard's Tale: Revealing the Mysteries of Çatalhöyük*. Thames and Hudson, New York.

Hodder, Ian, 2012. *Entangled: An Archaeology of the Relationships Between Humans and Things*. Wiley-Blackwell, Malden, MA.

Keane, W., 2011. Marked, Absent, Habitual: Approaches to Neolithic Religion at Çatalhöyük. In *Religion in the Emergence of Civilization: Çatalhöyük as a Case* Study, edited by Ian Hodder pp. 187–219. Cambridge University Press, Cambridge, UK.

Kingery, D., P. Vandiver, and M. Prickett, 1988. The Beginning of Pyrotechnology, Part II: Production and Use of Lime and Gypsum Plaster in the Prepottery Neolithic Near East. *Journal of Field Archaeology* 15(2):219–244.

Knappett, C., 2005. *Thinking Through Material Culture*. University of Pennsylvania Press, Philadelphia.

Last, J., S. Özdöl, S. Kapur, E. Akça, M. Serdem, and A. Kyzylarslanoglu, 2005. Pottery From the East Mound. In *Changing Materialities at Çatalhöyük: Reports from the 1995–1999 Seasons*, edited by Ian Hodder, pp. 101–138. McDonald Institute for Archaeological Research, London; British Institute for Archaeology at Ankara, Cambridge, UK.

Latour, Bruno, 2005. *Reassembling the Social: An Introduction to Actor-Network-Theory*. Oxford University Press, Oxford, UK; New York.

Liu, L., and Chen, X., 2012. *The Archaeology of China*. Cambridge University Press, Cambridge, UK.

Mellaart, J., 1967. *Çatal Hüyük: A Neolithic Town in Anatolia*. Thames and Hudson, London.

Moore, A. M. T., 1995. The Inception of Potting in Western Asia and Its Impact on Economy and Society. In *The Emergence of Pottery: Technology and Innovation in Ancient Societies*, edited by W. K. Barnett and J. W. Hoopes, pp. 39–53. Smithsonian Institution Press, Washington, D.C.

Özbaşaran, Mihriban, and Güneş Duru, 2011. Akarçay Tepe, A PPNB and PN Settlement in Middle Euphrates—Urfa. In *The Neolithic in Turkey: New Excavations & New Research,* Vol. 2, edited by Nezih Başgelen, Mehmet Özdoğan, and Peter I. Kuniholm, pp. 165–202. Archaeology and Art Publications, Galatasaray, İstanbul, Turkey.

Özdoğan, Mehmet, 2011. Mezraa—Teleilat. In *The Neolithic in Turkey: New Excavations & New Research*, Vol. 2, edited by Nezih Başgelen, Mehmet

Özdoğan, and Peter I. Kuniholm, pp. 203–260. Archaeology and Art Publications, Galatasaray, İstanbul, Turkey.

Özkaya, Vecihi, and Aytaç Coşkun, 2011. Körtik Tepe. In *The Neolithic in Turkey: New Excavations & New Research,* Vol. 1, edited by Nezih Başgelen, Mehmet Özdoğan, and Peter I. Kuniholm, pp. 89–127. Archaeology and Art Publications, Galatasaray, İstanbul, Turkey.

Pigliucci, M., and J. Kaplan, 2006. *Making Sense of Evolution.* University of Chicago Press, Chicago, IL.

Pitter, S., Yalman, N., and Evershed, R., 2013. Absorbed Lipid Residues in the Çatalhöyük Pottery. In *Substantive Technologies at Çatalhöyük: Reports from the 2000–2008* Seasons, edited by Ian Hodder, pp. 193–200. Cotsen Institute of Archaeology, Los Angeles, CA.

Regan, R., and Taylor, J., 2013. The Sequence of Buildings 75, 65, 56, 69, 44 and 10 and External Spaces 119, 129, 130, 144, 299, 314, 319, 329, 333, 339, 367, 372 and 427. In *Çatalhöyük Excavations: the 2000–2008 Seasons*, edited by Ian Hodder, pp. 131–190. Cotsen Institute of Archaeology, Los Angeles, CA.

Rosenberg, Michael, 2011. Hallan Çemi. In *The Neolithic in Turkey: New Excavations & New Research,* Vol. 1, edited by Nezih Başgelen, Mehmet Özdoğan, and Peter I. Kuniholm, pp. 61–78. Archaeology and Art Publications, Galatasaray, İstanbul, Turkey.

Schoop, U. D., 1998. Anadolu'da Kalkolitic Çağda süt ürünleri üretimi. *Arkeologi ve Sanat* 87:26–32.

Skibo, J. M., M. B. Schiffer, and K. C. Reid, 1989. Organic-Tempered Pottery: An Experimental Study. *American Antiquity* 54:122–146.

Smith, J. M., 1993. *The Theory of Evolution.* Cambridge University Press, Cambridge, UK.

Smith, P. E., 1976. Reflections on Four Seasons of Excavations at Tapeh Ganj Dareh. In *Proceedings of the Fourth Annual Symposium on Archaeological Research in Iran*, edited by F. Bagherzadeh, pp. 11–22. Iranian Centre for Archaeological Research, Tehran.

Thomas, Nicholas, 1991. *Entangled Objects: Exchange, Material Culture, and Colonialism in the Pacific.* Harvard University Press, Cambridge, MA.

Vandiver, P. B., 1987. Sequential Slab Construction: A Conservative Southwest Asiatic Ceramic Tradition, ca. 7000–3000 BC. *Paléorient* 13:9–35.

Wendrich, W., 2005. Çatalhöyük Basketry. In *Changing Materialities at Çatalhöyük: Reports from the 1995–1999 Seasons*, edited by Ian Hodder, pp. 333–338. McDonald Institute for Archaeological Research, London; British Institute for Archaeology at Ankara, Cambridge, UK.

Yalman, N., D. Tarkan Özbudak, and H. Gültekin, 2013. The Neolithic Pottery of Çatalhöyük: Recent Studies. In *Substantive Technologies at Çatalhöyük: Reports from the 2000–2008* Seasons, edited by Ian Hodder, pp. 147–180. Cotsen Institute of Archaeology, Los Angeles, CA.

Zeder, M. A., 2009. The Neolithic Macro-(r)evolution: Macroevolutionary Theory and the Study of Culture Change. *Journal of Archaeological Research* 17(1):1–63.

Index

About the Authors

Editors

Lindsay Der is a PhD candidate in the Department of Anthropology at Stanford University and a researcher with the Çatalhöyük Research Project, where she works with the figurines team. Her own research investigates changing human-animal relationships through time and their role in the social organization and maintenance of Çatalhöyük as a Neolithic mega-site. Her research interests include archaeology and ethics, geographic information systems (GIS), public archaeology, religion and ritual, and archaeological survey. She is a recipient of the Stanford Humanities Center's Geballe Dissertation Prize Fellowship at Stanford University and won the Stanford Anthropology and Archaeology Writing in the Major Teaching Award in 2012. She received an MA in anthropology from Stanford University and her BA in anthropology with a minor in Latin at the University of British Columbia.

Francesca Fernandini received her *licenciatura* in archaeology from Pontificia Universidad Católica del Perú and has a doctoral degree in anthropology from Stanford University. Her research focuses on the politics behind imperial formations, particularly on the indirect expressions that followed the Wari expansion in the Andes. Currently she is directing an archaeological research project at Cerro de Oro, a large archaeological site in the Peruvian south coast, in collaboration with the Ministry of Culture of Perú.

Contributors

Willy Yépez Álvarez is a licensed archaeologist and graduate of the Universidad Católica Santa María in Arequipa, Peru. He has directed and participated in numerous projects in southern Peru over the last 25 years and is the co-editor of *Wari en Arequipa? Análisis de los contextos funerarios de La Real* (Museo Arqueológico José María Morante, 2012) and *Tenahaha and the Wari State: A View of the Middle Horizon from the Cotahuasi Valley* (The University of Alabama Press, 2015).

Dorian Q. Fuller is a professor of archaeobotany at the Institute of Archaeology, University College London. He received his PhD from

Cambridge University (2000) on the origins of agriculture in Southern India. Since then, he has expanded his studies in domestication to include all India, China, Sudan, Ethiopia, West Africa, and the Near East. He jointly edits the journal *Archaeological and Anthropological Sciences*, and has recently renewed excavations at the site of Jarmo, Iraqi Kurdistan. He is co-author (with Eleni Asouti) of *Trees and Woodlands of South India* (Left Coast Press, Inc., 2008).

Michelle Hegmon is a professor of anthropology in the School of Human Evolution and Social Change at Arizona State University. Her research has long involved the application of social theory to the archaeology of the American Southwest. She headed the transdisciplinary project "Change is Hard: The Challenges of Path Dependence," which explored issues of path dependence in the Phoenix area through time, including the prehispanic era and recent history.

Ian Hodder is Dunlevie Family Professor of Anthropology at Stanford University. His excavation project, since 1993, has been at Çatalhöyük, Turkey. He was awarded the Oscar Montelius Medal by the Swedish Society of Antiquaries and the Huxley Memorial Medal by the Royal Anthropological Institute. His books include *Reading the Past* (Cambridge University Press, 1986), *The Leopard's Tale: Revealing the Mysteries of Çatalhöyük* (Thames & Hudson, 2006), and *Entangled: An Archaeology of the Relationships Between Humans and Things* (Wiley-Blackwell, 2012).

Jerry B. Howard is the curator of anthropology at the Arizona Museum of Natural History and an adjunct faculty member at Mesa Community College. His research focuses on the large irrigation systems constructed by the Hohokam in the Salt River Valley. This includes research on both the physical operation of the systems and the social and political organization they required.

Justin Jennings is curator of New World archaeology at the Royal Ontario Museum and associate professor of anthropology at the University of Toronto. He is the author or editor of nine books, the most recent of which, *Killing Civilization: A Reassessment of Early Urbanism and its Consequences*, was published in 2016 (University of New Mexico Press, Albuquerque).

Paul J. Lane is professor of global archaeology at Uppsala University, Sweden. He specializes in the later Holocene archaeology of sub-Saharan Africa, with particular focus on the landscape historical ecology, memory and memorialization, the archaeology of space and time, and the transition to food production in eastern Africa. His recent publications include the *Oxford Handbook* *of African Archaeology* (Oxford University Press, 2013) co-edited with Peter Mitchell, and *Slavery in Africa: Archaeology and Memory* (Oxford University Press, 2011), co-edited with Kevin MacDonald.

Leilani Lucas is a postdoctoral research associate at the Institute of Archaeology, University College London. She currently works on the Comparative Pathways towards Agriculture Project. She completed her PhD at the Institute of Archaeology, University College London, on the origins, spread, and development of agriculture in prehistoric Cyprus, and since has worked on material from Kurdistan, Turkey, Comoros Islands, Ethiopia, and the American Southwest.

Stephen A. Mrozowski is a professor of anthropology at the University of Massachusetts Boston and director of the Andrew Fiske Memorial Center for Archaeological Research. He has conducted research throughout New England and the Chesapeake as well as northern Alaska and Britain. His research interests include colonialism, urbanization, and environmental archaeology.

Charlene A. Murphy is a postdoctoral research associate at the Institute of Archaeology, University College London (UCL). She is currently working in South Asia on the Comparative Pathways towards Agriculture Project. She completed her PhD at UCL on Mediterranean archaeobotany, focusing on the city of Pompeii. She has conducted fieldwork in Italy, Turkey, Iraq, the United Kingdom, Canada, India, Bangladesh, and Sri Lanka.

F. Michael O'Hara, III is a consulting archaeologist and ethnographer for Cornerstone Environmental and Ecoplan Associates. He has worked in many parts of the American Southwest. His primary research is on the archaeology of the Flagstaff region with a focus on communal ritual, political organization, intergroup conflict, mortuary practices, and responses to environmental change. O'Hara received his PhD from Arizona State University.

Matthew A. Peeples is a preservation archaeologist at Archaeology Southwest, a nonprofit research and preservation organization in Tucson, Arizona. He received his BA (2003) in anthropology from the University of Texas at Austin and MA (2006) and PhD (2011) degrees at Arizona State University. His research interests are largely comparative and regional in scope, focusing on issues of social identity, social movements, and periods of rapid social change across the American Southwest.

Ling Qin is an associate professor of neolithic archaeology and archaeobotany at the School of Archaeology and Museology, Peking University, Beijing. She completed her PhD on Neolithic social complex in the lower Yangtze River area. She has worked extensively on Neolithic excavations and material cultures in China, jointly directing fieldwork in Zhejiang, Shandong, Henan, and Shaanxi. She is co-editor with Peter Ucko and Jane Hubert of the book *From Concepts of the Past to Practical Strategies: The Teaching of Archaeological Field Techniques* (Saffron Books, 2007).

Stephen W. Silliman is a professor of anthropology and director of the Historical Archaeology Graduate Program at the University of Massachusetts Boston. Using North America as a primary geographical focus, his research and publications focus on historical archaeology, colonialism, postcolonialism, community-engaged archaeology, social identity, practice, and the politics of heritage. He has published recently in *American Antiquity*, *Journal of Social Archaeology*, and several edited volumes.

Chris J. Stevens is a postdoctoral research associate at the Institute of Archaeology, University College London. He currently works on the Comparative Pathways towards Agriculture Project. He completed his PhD at Cambridge University on Iron Age and Romano-British agriculture and since has worked in Italy, Amarna, Egypt, China, and Kurdistan. He is co-editor of *The Archaeology of African Plant Use* (2014, Left Coast Press, Inc.) and co-author of *Environmental Archaeology: Approaches, Techniques & Applications* (Tempus, 2003).

Noa Corcoran-Tadd received an MA in anthropology at Stanford University and is currently a PhD candidate in anthropology at Harvard University. His research centers on the central Andes between the fifteenth and nineteenth centuries, including the emergence of market economies, the transforming roles of imperial infrastructure, and the archaeology of Inka and colonial *tambos*.